Keith Johnstone

Keith Johnstone

A Critical Biography

THERESA ROBBINS DUDECK

Theresa R. Dudeck

B L O O M S B U R Y
LONDON • NEW DELHI • NEW YORK • SYDNEY

Bloomsbury Methuen Drama

An imprint of Bloomsbury Publishing Plc

50 Bedford Square   1385 Broadway
London   New York
WC1B 3DP   NY 10018
UK   USA

www.bloomsbury.com

Bloomsbury is a registered trade mark of Bloomsbury Publishing Plc

First published 2013

© Theresa Robbins Dudeck, 2013

British Library Cataloguing-in-Publication Data
A catalogue record for this book is available from the British Library.

ISBN: PB: 978-1-4081-8327-4
HB: 978-1-4081-8552-0
ePub: 978-1-4081-8401-1
ePDF: 978-1-4081-8471-4

Library of Congress Cataloging-in-Publication Data
A catalog record for this book is available from the Library of Congress.

Typeset by Deanta Global Publishing Services, Chennai, India
Printed and bound in Great Britain

For Dale

CONTENTS

ACKNOWLEDGMENTS

First and foremost, I must thank Keith Johnstone for giving me so much of his time, for allowing me to probe into every aspect of his life, for connecting me to key resources, for sharing his personal archive, for his encouragement and wisdom, and, above all, for his friendship.

I would like to thank the University of Oregon's Department of Theatre Arts for funding several initial research trips. In particular, I want to thank four extraordinary professors for their guidance: Sara Freeman, Theresa J. May, Jennifer Schlueter, and Ann Tedards.

To the folks I interviewed, I am so grateful for the stories and thoughts you shared with me. And thank you to the following individuals and institutions for donating their time, skills, and/or other types of support during this journey: Doug Wong; Frank and Corinna Totino; Brian Cook; Christophe and Isabel Felzines; Ian Parizot; Guri Skeie Gundersen; Maureen and Denny Robeson; David LaRose; Bay Area Theatresports; the University of Calgary Library; and the V&A Theatre and Performance Archive at Blythe House.

Thank you to everyone at Methuen Drama and Bloomsbury Publishing, especially to my enthusiastic publisher Jenny Ridout and delightful assistant editor John O'Donovan.

Finally, to my loving family—Dale Dudeck, Mary Lynne and Thomas Robbins, Alicia Robbins, Tommy Robbins, Jr., and Barbara and John Dudeck—and to my dearest friends, thank you for your unwavering belief in me.

CHAPTER ONE

Introducing Keith Johnstone and his Impro System

Keith Johnstone is a groundbreaking teacher, theorist, and creator of contemporary theatre practices used worldwide. His contribution to pedagogy, to performers and performance technique, to writers, and to theatrical entrepreneurial models is significant. Partly in response to his personal search to rediscover his imaginative potential, Keith has spent over five decades developing and teaching improvisational theatre methods for the classroom and for performance. For him, theatre is an informal classroom where life experiences can be fleshed out collaboratively in order to re-create genuine behavior, relationships, and imaginative stories spontaneously and in dialogue with the public. This first critical biography of Keith Johnstone uses the concept of the classroom as its structural and theoretical frame. Each chapter journeys not only through the corporeal spaces that have served as Keith's transformative "classrooms" but also into the conceptual spaces which inform his pedagogy. It is a journey that continues today.

Keith is still very much alive and teaching all over the world. I have attended and observed his workshops in San Francisco (2006, 2009), London (2010), Stockholm (2010), and Calgary (2008, 2011, 2012). In every location, Keith draws in an enthusiastic group of students who want to learn from the master teacher. In July of 2011, for instance, 14 of the 20 students in Keith's 10-day Calgary workshop hailed from Brazil and other Latin American countries where his improvisational methods are influencing the next generation of theatre makers. This study concludes with a look at Keith's present classroom and at Johnstonian-inspired classrooms developing in various fields and corners of the world.

The Impro System (i.e., my term for denoting Keith's theories, pedagogy, techniques, exercises, games, and terminology) is Keith's most important contribution to theatre practice worldwide. The Impro System is an approach to actor training and theatre practice that encourages spontaneous, collaborative creation using the intuitive, uncensored imaginative responses of the participants. Since 2005, I have been referring to Keith's process as a "system" because, like other complex systems—the solar system, transportation systems, the nervous system—optimal functionality depends on all components working harmoniously. General System Theory is a scientific discipline postulated by Austrian biologist Ludwig von Bertalanffy in the 1950s. In very basic terms, Bertalanffy's theory dictates that all parts of the system interact with each other directly or indirectly but privileges the wholeness of the system over its parts. In this sense, the Impro System is a system because it cannot be reduced down to its parts without decreasing its efficacy. When students apply the theatre games without understanding the theory or when teachers teach the exercises without understanding Keith's pedagogy, the process is compromised. Theatresports, a format Keith created, serves as an example of what can happen when a system goes global and people begin to privilege the parts over the whole.

Theatresports was the vehicle that catapulted Keith's Impro System onto the world stage. After moving from London to Canada, Keith developed this format with a handful of drama students at the University of Calgary (UofC) who were also members of his Loose Moose Theatre Company. Keith cofounded this company to showcase his plays, his improvisational methods, and Theatresports. Inspired by the British pro-wrestling matches, Theatresports pits one team of improvisers against another team for points and audience approval. By the early 1980s, Theatresports leagues were appearing everywhere. Today Theatresports and two other competitive forms created by Keith—Gorilla Theatre and Maestro Impro—are licensed to leagues all over the world.[1] In 1999, Keith published *Impro for Storytellers*, a sourcebook of his formats and games. While assuring his popularity, the Theatresports franchise has amassed a reputation that often makes it difficult to articulate why Keith matters in other contexts like actor training, playwriting, and pedagogy and perhaps accounts for the lack of recognition in serious academic studies of twentieth-century theatre practice. Furthermore, Theatresports has taken on a life of its own, outside of the classroom so to speak, and often departs from Keith's original intentions.

My personal introduction to Keith Johnstone and his Impro System was not through Theatresports or *Impro for Storytellers*. In the early 1990s, I was trained in and became a strong proponent of improvisational theatre techniques primarily through the work of Viola Spolin. Spolin became well-known in America in the early 1960s following the publication of her foundational text, *Improvisation for the Theatre*, and through the work of her son Paul Sills, cofounder of the Compass Players and Chicago's

---

[1] The Theatresports-inspired television program, *Whose Line Is It Anyway?* (United Kingdom and America), was so popular that almost 20 countries have launched their own television shows based on this concept.

Second City. Avery Schreiber, an original Second City member, was my improvisational teacher in Los Angeles, and he taught in the Spolin tradition. Then, in 2001, my friend and colleague, Amy Langer Schwartz, handed me a copy of *Impro: Improvisation and the Theatre* (*Impro*) and said, "You must read this." Published in 1979, *Impro* illuminates the work developed by Keith when he directed and taught classes for the Royal Court Theatre Studio (RCT Studio) in London from 1963 to 1966. Until he moved to Canada, Keith tested his ideas on audiences around the world with his group The Theatre Machine, Britain's first pure improvisational troupe. But the work Keith began developing almost 50 years ago resonates with immediateness today. As I delved into *Impro*, I felt as if Keith was in direct dialogue with me. It was the first time a teacher encouraged me to take risks and to fail good-naturedly; to accept my first spontaneous impulses in lieu of clever or intellectual ideas; to acknowledge my imagination, not my socially-constructed "personality," as my true self; and to be more obvious, since trying to be original only concealed the real me.

Impro is a loosely structured practical guide for psychologically and physically unblocking human beings, thus enabling them to generate good stories with three-dimensional characters through spontaneous collaboration. In the foreword to the book, critic and historian Irving Wardle called it a "guide to imaginative survival." In the foreword to the Swedish translation, Suzanne Osten, film director and artistic director of Stockholm's Unga Klara, an influential theatre company championing children's issues, wrote that *Impro* comprised "alla idéer till ett teaterspråk vi sökte" ("all the ideas for a theatre language we were looking for"; trans. Bagdade). The popularity of Theatresports has indisputably added to sales, but *Impro's* appeal is widespread. Drama training programs, directors, writers, animators, educators, psychotherapists, and an ever-growing number of organizational scholars and business consultants have exploited various tools contained in this text. Keith's second book, *Impro for Storytellers,* organizes the exercises and techniques found in *Impro* into categories and offers additional games and terminology created for or during the evolution of Theatresports. It is a useful resource and does build on and extend his earlier work; even so, it targets Theatresports audiences and this limits its accessibility.

Keith's wit, intelligence, and personality jump off the page in all of his writings (e.g., in his plays; his short stories; *Impro for Storytellers*; *Don't Be Prepared: Theatresports for Teachers*; and *Keith Johnstone's Theatresports and Life-Game Newsletters*). *Impro*, though, seems to capture Keith in the midst of discovery and his writing enables him to integrate the variables into a whole system as if for the first time. Perhaps this explains why *Impro* has been translated into numerous languages and is in its eighth printing. Even though Keith continues to rework, revise, and refine his theories and techniques, *Impro* still illuminates the heart of the Impro System in a way that attracts generation upon generation. In the following introduction to the Impro System, *Impro* serves as the primary source of

information; however, other writings by Keith are occasionally utilized to
reinforce a specific theory, technique, or term.

So what is Keith Johnstone's Impro System and how does it intersect with,
shatter, and/or radically depart from other improvisational processes? First of
all, "impro" and "improv" are abbreviations for improvisation. In standard
British pronunciation, the first and fourth syllables of "improvisation" are
given more stress, and the "o" in "pro" has a partially open "ə" sound as in
"the" (ˌɪm-prə-vī-ˈzā-shən) which is closer to the ō in "imprō." Whereas in
standard American pronunciation, the second and fourth syllables receive
more stress and the "o" has a very open "a" sound as in "father" (im-ˌprä-və-
ˈzā-shən). Therefore, the preferred use of the abbreviation "impro" in Britain
and "improv" (-präv) in America originally stems from phonetics. Largely
due to the title of Keith's book—*Impro: Improvisation and the Theatre*—
"impro" is mistakenly interpreted to mean British-style improvisation, but
actually "impro" and "improv" are synonymous.[2]

Anthony Frost and Ralph Yarrow, professors and historians at the
University of East Anglia (United Kingdom), coauthored *Improvisation in
Drama* (1990, 2007). In both their first and second editions, they define
improvisation as:

[T]he skill of using bodies, space, all human resources, to generate a coher-
ent physical expression of an idea, a situation, a character (even, perhaps,
a text); to do this spontaneously, in response to the immediate stimuli of
one's environment, and to do it *à l'improviste*: as though taken by surprise,
without preconceptions.(4)

Prior to Keith's work with the RCT Studio, improvisation as defined above
was not a new concept in European actor training and developmental
processes. Konstantin Stanislavsky, Jacques Copeau, Michel Saint-Denis,
Jacques Lecoq, Joan Littlewood, and Michael Chekhov all relied on
improvisational theory and technique to develop truthful moments in text-
based performance, to flesh-out characters (masked and unmasked), and to
explore the nature of acting. Improvisations were also used to liberate the
actor's body and imagination, to generate new material, to achieve authentic
ensemble interaction, and to incorporate "play" into the theatrical process.
The Impro System is useful in all of these ways and Keith owes much to his
predecessors and contemporaries; however, several factors render *Impro* and
the Impro System unique. One is its emphasis on "pure" improvisation, that is,
improvisation as a performance in and of itself. In Chicago in the 1950s and
1960s, Paul Sills was presenting performances improvised around scenarios
in the tradition of the *commedia dell'arte* and later using the structure of
Spolin's theatre games. But in Europe, Keith was the first to advocate and

---

[2] I use "impro" and "improvisation" interchangeably and *Impro* in italics to reference Keith's
text, *Impro: Improvisation and the Theatre*.

first to present purely improvised performances without scenarios. He put his improvisers on stage with nothing prepared and with no idea what was going to happen. "It was the ultimate risk," says Keith, "and partly from a mistake. Cause in those days, when I didn't know so much, I thought the *commedia* did that. Actually, they didn't, but it worked."[3] Training in the Impro System also meant training in Keith's clown work, very physical work which required little or no dialogue, so Keith's improvisers had success performing for non-English-speaking audiences.[4] Another factor that renders *Impro* and the Impro System distinctive is its accessibility and this has everything to do with *how* Keith situates himself in his writing and in his process. In order to better understand how Keith processes, imagines, teaches, and creates, one should be acquainted with the Impro System.

Impro is divided into five chapters: "Notes on Myself," "Status," "Spontaneity," "Narrative Skills," and "Masks and Trance." A short chapter on Theatresports was to be included but, after the publishers told Johnstone that the book was too long, he took out what he thought was the least interesting material. In retrospect, Keith feels leaving that chapter out was a disastrous decision. That chapter on Theatresports included vital material for those early Theatresports groups who had to learn the game by copying other groups. "You had groups who had no idea what the basic principles were," says Keith. "It was the least interesting material to me, but it would've been the most interesting thing to Theatresports players."

Keith opens the first chapter of *Impro* with: "As I grew up, everything started getting grey and dull" (13). He concludes the first section with an assertion that serves as the impetus behind the creation of the Impro System: "The dullness was not an inevitable consequence of age, but of education" (14). Going forward, it is clear Keith developed the Impro System not just for unblocking and releasing the talents of the actors at the RCT Studio but for rediscovering the imaginative potential of individuals, like himself, who had been oppressed by their education.

Keith's schooling had conditioned him to favor intellect over imagination: "I learned never to act on impulse, and that whatever came into my mind first should be rejected in favor of better ideas" (82). For a time, he had forgotten that inspiration wasn't intellectual and that failure was part of the learning process. In order to reverse or undo what had been done, Keith began to embrace and teach spontaneity. Although he developed most of the exercises, techniques, and terminology in *Impro* teaching at the RCT Studio in the early 1960s, the theories underpinning his inventions (i.e., solutions to problems) had been germinating since childhood and continued to consolidate until his manuscript was published in 1979. It is important to

---

[3] Unless otherwise cited, quotes by Keith and other biographical information are primarily from the personal conversations/correspondence I had with Keith dating from August 2009 to January 2013.

[4] See section on Theatre Machine in Chapter 3.

remember that Keith had no interest or formal training in the theatre before he saw Peter Hall's production of Samuel Beckett's *Waiting for Godot* in 1955 at the Criterion Theatre in London. His theories, therefore, are not based solely on theatre research, observation, or practice but on a broad range of sources and experiences.

Keith was moved by great silent films before he had any interest in the theatre, and he credits a 4-minute sequence in Dovzhenko's *Earth* (1930) as having an epiphanic impact on his way of judging himself and others. Vassily, a young, Ukrainian farmer, walks home alone in the twilight after a long day of reaping corn with a new tractor purchased collectively by the poor community. The tractor symbolizes a sense of unity and this agitates the well-to-do landowners. The audience senses imminent danger but Vassily heroically continues down the country road. Keith wrote: "The fact that he walks for so long, and that the image is so beautiful, linked with my own experience of being alone in the twilight—the gap between the worlds." Then Vassily dances ecstatically just moments before he is shot and killed. Keith continued:

> The dust swirls around his feet, so that he's like an Indian god, like Siva— and with the man dancing along in the clouds of dust something unlocked in me. In one moment I knew that the valuing of man by their intelligence is crazy, that the peasants watching the night sky might feel more than I feel, that the man who dances might be superior to myself—word-bound and unable to dance. (*Impro* 18)

In *Impro*, Keith does not advocate a complete shutdown of the intellect but rather closing the gap that divides rhetoric from actions. Keith is an intellectual, whether he likes it or not. He is thought of by many as a genius and, over the years, has been invited to attend international think tanks. He aptly uses his intellect to illuminate a moment, an experience, or a process supporting his theories. But the driving force of the Impro System evolves from Keith's desire to dance, that is, to defy his intellect in order to enter the world as an imaginative, physically liberated human being.

After completing his secondary school education, Keith attended a teacher's training college in Exeter. "I had a brilliant art teacher called Anthony Stirling, and then all my work stemmed from his example. It wasn't so much what he taught, as what he *did*" (18). Stirling's teaching methodology was inspired by Lao Tzu's concept of the invisible or unseen leader—a leader who facilitates in such a way, that when the work is accomplished, the followers think they did it all by themselves (Lau 73). Stirling also believed in the artist within and that it was the teacher's job to bring the artist out of the child, not through demonstration or by imposing values of "good and bad" or "right and wrong," but by skillfully setting up experiences in which the student could succeed (*Impro* 20). Keith's first primary school teaching assignment was an opportunity to put Stirling's ideas to the test. Keith succeeded in excavating the "art" from these students who had been written off by others as "ineducable"; and, instead of treating children like "immature adults," he began to regard adults as "atrophied children" (25, 78).

In the early 1960s, behavioral therapist Joseph Wolpe, M.D., published his studies on systematic desensitization of phobias, and Keith immediately saw connections to Stirling's ideas and to his own development of these ideas with the RCT Studio's professional artists. Systematic desensitization is a method of inhibiting neurotic anxiety-response habits in patients. First, the patient is put into a state of relaxation and then, by degrees, exposed to his anxiety-evoking stimuli. Wolpe progresses from the least disturbing stimuli on the patient's "anxiety hierarchy" to the most disturbing until all stimuli are deprived of their ability to evoke fear and anxiety (Wolpe 66). If, however, the patient experiences a setback, Wolpe returns to the bottom of the hierarchy and starts again. Keith immediately incorporated this idea into his work at the RCT Studio and into his Impro System. With students who remained in a constant state of "stage fright," Keith would return to the basics. Instead of writing these students off as "untalented" or as "failures," he saw them as "phobic" (*Impro* 31). Because Keith openly acknowledges that he is also a work in progress, still searching for ways to overcome his own phobias, he establishes an egalitarian classroom space.

Keith's pedagogy is integral to the efficacy of his Impro System as he himself noted: "If you want to apply the methods I'm describing in this book, you may have to teach the way I teach" (29). The ideas he set down in *Impro* represent only the beginning of an ongoing battle against what Paulo Freire called the "banking" concept of education. Freire, renowned theorist of critical pedagogy, used this term to describe an educational system that views students as empty accounts into which teachers deposit information. I see Keith as a Freirean educator who strongly advocates dismantling the "totalitarian teacher" versus "passive student" relationship and creating a partnership in its place. Freire branded this critical and reflective way of transmitting knowledge as "the problem-posing method." This method promotes the idea that "the teacher is no longer merely the-one-who-teaches, but one who is himself taught in dialogue with the students, who in turn while being taught also teach" (Freire 80). Keith never spends too much time explaining the rules of a game or exercise because, he wrote, "If [students] misunderstand me they may invent a much better game" (*Storytellers* 60).[5]

---

[5] Keith doesn't necessarily believe students will invent a better game, but he tells them this so they will laugh and relax. "It's an example of latent manipulation like telling Japanese students I'm deaf and they have to speak up even though they are speaking in Japanese. And it works, it works." In March of 2012, 29 Japanese students from Toho Gakuen College of Drama and Music in Toyko had come to Calgary's Loose Moose Theatre to study with Keith. They spoke no English and were assisted by two translators. I witnessed Keith doing what he said in the quote above and the students did indeed begin to speak louder.

Keith's belief that process cannot be static and that every human being, including himself, is in the process of becoming is crucial to his problem-posing methodology. It is why the Impro System is flexible and has evolved from classroom to classroom.

A few key pedagogical principles should preside over any process utilizing the Impro System. From the start, the teacher teaching the Impro System must adopt a pedagogy that alters the students' attitude to failure. "In a normal education, the student had been very competitive and they're judging the end reward rather than the process," Keith says. "So [the students] have to be happy when they fail and they have to understand that they cannot learn anything unless they fail." Teachers also need to encourage collaboration, not competition, value actions over thoughts, and the authoritarian teacher versus student relationship must be dissolved through the teacher's conduct and transparency. To create a safe space where students do not have to play it safe, the teacher must give students permission to tap into forbidden areas of the mind. "Imagination is as effortless as perception, unless we think it might be 'wrong', which is what our education encourages us to believe," Keith wrote (*Impro* 80). Further reassurance comes from the teacher presenting himself as "living proof that the monsters are not real, and that the imagination will not destroy you" (84).

Most of the improvisational exercises in the Impro System encourage collaboration because they combine the imagination of two or more people and rely on the principle of "give and take" to move the story forward and to create relationships. One improviser will make an "offer" (i.e., any physical or verbal input) and the other improviser will "accept" or "give" credibility to that offer and then "offer" something else, "taking" the initiative, without cancelling any previous offers. Chapter 3 of *Impro* includes offer/block/accept exercises that train students to develop action. "A block is anything that prevents the action from developing, or that wipes out your partner's premise. If it develops the action, it isn't a block" (97). Saying "no" to an offer, therefore, doesn't indicate a block if this response moves the action forward. Exercises in which students "block" actions make it quite clear that accepting (i.e., collaboration) is more rewarding. "In life, most of us are skilled at suppressing action," wrote Keith. "All the improvisation teacher has to do is to reverse this skill and he creates very 'gifted' improvisers" (95).[6] Gifted does not signify an improviser who comes up with clever or better ideas. Any idea is a good one *if* it moves the action forward and solves problems. Many beginning students have difficulty accepting this because, like Keith, they were taught at an early age to "search" for original ideas.

---

[6] We are skilled at suppressing action, Keith reminds me, because as adults we don't want to be altered or out of control. We want our lives to be predictable, planned, and manageable.

Again, Keith reverses this habit by telling students to "be average" or "more obvious" or to "accept your first thoughts."[7] He reminds students that they are one-of-a-kind and "Striving after originality takes you far away from your true self, and makes your work mediocre" (88). An improviser who effortlessly develops action, solves problems, and accepts offers will seem gifted (and benevolent) to audiences.

Developing action is important to writers, too. Like everything else, Keith's theories and techniques on playwriting evolved through personal observation and practical experience, not via a formal education. The legendary Writers' Group (1958) at the Royal Court implemented Keith's "no-discussion" policy, and the playwrights would improvise scenarios as a way of developing relationships and moments in their scripted and nonscripted performances. Also, as a Royal Court play reader and head of the script department, Keith read up to 50 play submissions a week. The plays that interested Keith had characters that altered each other—"If the characters are not altered, you just got a writer, a novelist or something, but I [was] trying to find playwrights." In *Storytellers*, Keith defines "dramatic action" as: "the product of 'interaction'" and he defines "interaction" as "a shift in the balance between two people" (77). So, even if a plot has one action sequence after another, if characters are not altered, if the balance does not shift, the action is useless.

Chapter 4 in *Impro*, "Narrative Skills," includes on-your-feet exercises which develop skills in collaborative structuring of narratives that advance primarily through dramatic action resulting from interaction. Keith doesn't want students to concern themselves with the content (i.e., the underlying meaning) of what they are doing until they master structure. Students must be able to get out of their own way, to let go of their fear and self-consciousness, and allow their imagination some space before they try to assess what it all means psychologically. But "the best improvisers, at some level, know what their work is about," wrote Keith (142). What's important is to return to content only when the student improviser is strong enough to accept responsibility for whatever they unearth from their unconscious. Writers find these narrative techniques appealing and adaptable to their own process. For example, Mark Ravenhill, a contemporary British playwright, credits Keith for turning him into a writer. More specifically, he praises Keith's concept of "reincorporation." Ravenhill's simple paradigm of reincorporation is: "If there's a gun in the first act, have someone fire it in the third. That's pure Chekhov" (Ravenhill). In other words, offers previously introduced should be reincorporated at a later stage in order

---

[7] Keith says getting beginning improvisers to accept their first thoughts is important. But advanced improvisers, who are no longer working from a state of fear, should be aware of the process, aware of what is happening to them and to the story that is unfolding. They should have the ability to choose from a variety of ideas to move the story forward.

to give the story a sense of cohesion for the audience who remembers what happened, perhaps subconsciously, and expects shelved offers to be reintroduced. While many writers and improvisers "reincorporate" instinctively, for the multitudes that don't, Keith turned this concept into something concrete and practical by naming it and creating exercises to develop it. "I made Mark look back instead of forward," says Keith. "He was obviously searching ahead trying to find good stuff. But *Impro* made him suddenly realize that he should look back to see if there was stuff he could reincorporate because that would give him structure."

Keith's "circle of probability" is another concept for structuring narrative and engaging audiences. He did not begin using this term until the early 1990s, but the circle of probability factors into every component of the Impro System.[8] It is another example of how Keith decodes and gives a name to what is obvious to proficient storytellers—writers, improvisers, and directors. Keith has always been rather awkward on the stage proper. He is more comfortable situating himself among and in alliance with the audience, insisting that theatre should be engaging to each and every spectator. If a performance fails to entertain, Keith wants improvisers to ask themselves if trying to be "original," "clever," or, even worse, "funny," interrupted the flow of the narrative or took it outside of the audience's "circle of probability." The circle contains an amalgamation of shadow stories anticipated by each spectator as the plot develops onstage. When the plot parallels and/or is compliant with the imagined shadow story, the spectator is more likely to be dynamically engaged in the journey. Staying within the circle of probability does not mean pandering to the spectator's own ordinary, everyday logic, but rather moving the story forward according to the logic of the imaginary, extraordinary world that has been established in the theatre.

During a rehearsal with actors at the Moscow Art Theatre in the 1920s, Stanislavsky expressed his understanding of what constitutes the circle of probability when he asserted: "The audience that watches a play has its own ideas of how the plot will develop, but it cannot be sure until the end" (Gorchakov, *Stanislavsky* 105). In *Impro*, Keith put it like this: "An audience will remain interested if the story is advancing in some sort of organised manner, but they want to see *routines* interrupted and the action continuing *between* the actors" (141). In *Storytellers*, Keith uses the term "tilt" to define a surprising event that interrupts or "tilts" an everyday routine into the chaotic future. The "platform" is the everyday routine, the "stability that precedes the chaos" (89–92). A strong tilt should alter the characters, throw them off-balance, and if the tilt lands just outside of the audience's circle

---

[8] Keith also uses the term "circle of expectation."

of probability, a justification is needed. In other words, an improviser or playwright can do something illogical and unexpected as long as she can justify her action and integrate it somehow back into the audience's circle of probability.

Not unlike the film hero Vassily walking and dancing into imminent danger, Keith believes: "The improviser has to be like a man walking backwards. He sees where he has been, but he pays no attention to the future" (*Impro* 116). Keith reminds his students that audiences want to see actors get into trouble, to go on adventures, and to accept offers normal people would block when survival instincts tell them to play it safe. Brave improvisers must be willing to accept the role of "hero" which means taking great risks and suffering in the pursuit of a worthwhile goal (*Storytellers* 78). Only in his later writings does Keith articulate this concept in this way, but it is imperative to the Impro System's theories on structuring narratives and on overcoming fear. In his *Theatresports and Life-Game Newsletter One* (1987), he wrote:

> [A] story establishes a hero and then torments him, physically or psychologically (I think that covers most of the world's literature). . . .
>
> Dramatists have an unspoken agreement with us. They present us with a hero, and then guarantee that something unpleasant will happen to him. Everyone understands this, at least at an unconscious level. If the film opens with the hero (or heroine) standing at a bus stop, we won't be in the least surprised if a car screeches around the corner and machine-guns the queue. If nothing untoward occurs, and the hero gets on the bus, then we classify the line-up as 'introduction', and we presume that something will happen on the journey. (3–4)

But even if a beginning improviser understands this, once he steps onstage, "fear" often stops him from entering the dark forest and encountering the monsters.

Keith observed time and again improvisers protecting themselves from "imaginary dangers" as if the dangers were really happening (*Storytellers* 130). Similar to Wolpe's technique of getting patients into a state of relaxation before exposing them to their anxiety-evoking stimuli, Keith establishes a safe theatre classroom space where students can confront their own personal creative blocks without fearing actual harm. When improvisers trust the "safety net," they are more likely to "jump" and ignore their protective instincts for fun and for the enjoyment of the spectators. Getting beginning improvisers to "jump," to be in the moment, and to abolish self-consciousness requires some manipulation. Split-attention games and techniques are meant to engage the conscious mind so the intuitive, creative part of the mind can take over. They require total involvement. Trying to steal someone's hat while playing a scene, or asking insane questions to "jerk" spontaneous answers from a fellow player, or two players creating a story alternating one-word-at-a-time are some of the Impro System's split-attention techniques.

As mentioned earlier, the teacher/student hierarchy needs to be dissolved by means of the teacher's conduct and transparency in order to create an ideal environment for learning the Impro System. Teaching and using "status" is how Keith accomplishes this. Chapter 2 of *Impro* names, decodes, and offers ways to reconstruct "status" behavior, that is, social behavior that can be achieved voluntarily. This chapter alone has had a profound effect on drama training worldwide and is probably the most important component of the Impro System.[9] In Eva Mekler's *Masters of the Stage: British Acting Teachers Talk About Their Craft* (1989), acting teachers from The Drama Studio (London), The Guildford School of Acting and Dance, and The Royal Scottish Academy of Music and Drama professed to be using Keith's status theory and exercises with their students.

Status, according to Keith, is not what a person *is* but what he *plays*. It is learned physical and verbal behavior which determines placement on the social pecking-order. Status operates on what Keith calls the "see-saw" principle, or what Frost and Yarrow define as "a dynamic interactive process of continual adjustment" (115). At the RCT Studio, Keith noticed this continual and automatic adjustment to other bodies, objects, and to the space among his students having casual conversations and he called it "the kinetic dance," that is, the dance of movement (*Storytellers* 232). Both comedy and tragedy work on the "see-saw" principle. "A comedian is someone paid to lower his own or other people's status" and a tragic plot usually involves "the ousting of a high-status animal [character] from the pack" (*Impro* 39–40).

Many of Keith's status and pecking-order games were adapted from naturalist Konrad Lorenz's documented observations of a jackdaw colony in Alterberg, Germany. In his most popular book, *King Solomon's Ring: New Light on Animal Ways* (1952), Lorenz noted that these socially inclined birds maintained a "pecking-order" analogous to human beings. "In the jackdaw colony, those of the higher orders, particularly the despot himself, are not aggressive towards the birds that stand far beneath them," observed Lorenz. "[I]t is only in their relations towards their immediate inferiors that they are constantly irritable; this applies especially to the despot and the pretender to the throne – Number One and Number Two" (148). Keith's status exercises start with simple scenes in which students keep their status slightly above/below their partners or play status to the space using both

[9] In his review of *Impro* for *Theatre Journal* in 1984, Albert Pertalion wrote: "The section on Status, which explains the shifting power in relationships, is worth the price of the book alone" (441).

physical and verbal adjustments. Increasingly, the exercises and games become physically challenging and absurd (e.g., master-servant games, pecking-order clown games, *commedia dell'arte* scenarios, and maximum status gap scenes).

Keith has a hard time understanding why colleges do not teach status skills to teachers. He himself is a status expert in the classroom and raises or lowers his status as needed in order to keep discipline and, simultaneously, to create a safe space for students to step out of their "preferred" status roles. According to Keith, bad drama schools exploit the habituated status of their students, casting them into "types" instead of widening their range (*Impro* 55–6). Frost and Yarrow expressed that Keith's status work releases actors and "actors as people" from habitual modes of behavior and "produces an extension of the range of existential choice, which is the most serious and far-reaching effect of the play element in culture" (154). They also wrote that status exercises are invaluable to writers and suggested that writers think of "status" as a verb (213). Human beings, like other social animals, constantly work to maintain or adjust their level of dominance. Once students recognize this, then it is possible not only to challenge and disrupt their own socially constructed positioning but to re-create truthful—which does not imply natural—behavior on the stage. In the end, status work renders conduct in the classroom, of the teacher, and in everyday life transparent.

Chapter 5, "Masks and Trance," was inspired by the mask classes taught by Keith and William Gaskill at the RCT Studio. It was the Royal Court's artistic director George Devine who introduced both men to the basic mask techniques that his teacher, Michel Saint-Denis, inherited from Jacques Copeau, the uncle of Saint-Denis. Chapter 5 is the longest and most dense in *Impro* and Keith relies largely on secondary sources to flesh out his ideas on mask work and trance states, whereas the previous chapters ("Status," "Spontaneity," and "Narrative Skills") rely mostly on primary sources or personal experiences. It is Keith's least favorite chapter and the one that has continued to trouble him for over 30 years. In fact, he spent the last few years writing a new, longer mask treatise called *The Thing in the Mirror*. In this new essay especially, it is clear Keith's understanding of the mask is informed by his own search for self and from his experience of feeling "other" in an Anglo-centered world that tends to universalize rather than particularize. Unable to elude his whiteness or his British heritage likely intensifies the problematic aspects of writing about something as precolonial and primitive as masks, and he struggles to work through any unintentional biases in all of his writings.

The "Masks and Trance" chapter in *Impro* is divided into 15 subsections: an opening section on Devine and the half-mask or "character mask" classes at the Court; examples of mask work by Stanislavsky, Vakhtangov, and Chaplin; a short explanation of why masks were driven out of our Western culture; facial expressions as masks; entering trance states; possession cults (e.g., Haitian voodoo); an 11-page introduction to teaching beginning mask work; a closer look at particular masks Keith uses frequently in his own plays (e.g., the Waif and the Executioner); beginning mask exercises; a section on tragic masks; and a concluding section confronting the "unfounded" fears people have in regard to the "dangers" of mask work.

Teachers, including Keith, often teach the Impro System without using any exercise, technique, or theory from the "Masks and Trance" chapter, so this component often gets ignored and/or detached from the rest of the work. I myself have had difficulty filtering through this chapter and have only recently realized how connected and integral it is to the whole system. Keith believes western education is not only responsible for suppressing the imagination but also the Mask because of our anti-trance culture; and a Mask, wrote Keith, "is a device for driving the personality out of the body and allowing a spirit to take possession of it" (148). Keith is an atheist and doesn't believe in spirits, so this is his poetic way of saying a mask is a tool for getting out of the way of the socially constructed self and giving freedom to the instinctive, uncensored self. For Keith, it is simply a matter of the brain. "We find the Mask strange because we don't understand how irrational our responses to the face are anyway," wrote Keith, "and we don't realise that much of our lives is spent in some form of trance, i.e. absorbed" (148–50).

Often we call moments of trance something else like "in the zone" or "daydreaming" or "inspiration." Inspired artists, athletes, and even children are often in the moment, allowing a "spirit of play" or that "something other than" their intellect to take control. For Keith, mask work is another, quite powerful improvisatory technique for getting at the imaginative, artistic, childlike part of the mind. And like any spontaneous activity, mask work has the potential to "be therapeutic because of the intense abreactions involved" (200). Psychologists use the term "abreaction" to mean "a release or discharge of emotional energy following the recollection of a painful memory that has been repressed. It can occur spontaneously or during psychotherapy, especially under hypnosis, and may lead to catharsis" (Colman 2). Keith uses the term abreaction to mean a catharsis that happens when an individual finally unshackles their primal impulses. This is chiefly why, Keith reminds us once more in the second to last paragraph of *Impro*: "[T]he teacher's job is to keep the student *safe*, and to protect him so that he can regress" (200). Regress, that is, not to a deteriorated state, but to a more corporeal, intuitive one.

For over 30 years, *Impro: Improvisation and the Theatre* has dramatically influenced creative processes all over the world. If, after its publication in 1979, Keith had retired from teaching, writing, and the theatre, I believe *Impro* would still be considered an important achievement in and of itself and would continue to be rediscovered by ensuing generations of theatre artists. Nevertheless, I proffer *Impro's* attraction to an ever-growing heterogeneous audience has much to do with *how* Keith transmits his knowledge in various classrooms around the world. Keith still teaches at the age of eighty, because, he humbly admits, "I don't know how to do it yet." For almost five decades, thousands of students have had the opportunity to see Keith Johnstone—the master teacher—at work. No matter he is frequently referred to as a "genius," a "guru," or as "the Pope of Impro," Keith engages students with an unassuming charisma. He renders himself accessible and, through his teaching, embodies the Impro System's pedagogical theory.

As articulated earlier, Keith wants improvisers to be like the "man walking backwards," who has "seen where he has been, but pays no attention to the future." Paying no attention to the future does not imply shutting off the intellectual mind from imagining the possibilities the future may hold based on previous patterns. It simply means one must take in the historic landscape and remain open to surprises not anticipated. As a historian writing about a unique, enduring subject like Keith Johnstone, I progressed in a comparable way. I arrived at each archive, interview, location, and chapter of writing with a meticulously prepared plan but with a readiness to abandon that plan when the surprising occurred. The most thrilling surprise I encountered was Keith's dedication to this project.

Over the last 4 years, Keith has granted me hours of interviews, responded to dozens of e-mails, gave me full access to his personal archive, welcomed me as an observer/assistant in his international workshops, and proofread my chapters offering input but never asking me to take a less critical stance. My friendship with Keith has enriched this study, and it has also forced me to deliberately distance myself at times—to strive to step away from my personal views and desires—in order to include contrasting perspectives. Although it was not always easy for me to critically analyze the man who has been my mentor for so many years, these other perspectives have allowed me to illuminate Keith as a multifaceted and imperfect human being. Moreover, in writing this first analytic study on Keith, I endeavored to be as accurate and comprehensive as possible. I owed that to my readers, to Keith, and to everyone who personally contributed to this project. Finally, Keith is not a fan of tedious jargon, so while my goal was to deliver a piece of critical scholarship, I tried to write in an accessible way because that is how Keith wants his life story sent into the world.

The subsequent chapters in this book chart Keith's life and career and, concurrently, trace the evolution, motivating factors, and content of his various "classrooms" and his Impro System. Chapter 2, "The formative years," documents most of Keith's early life in Britain from his birth in 1933 through the first 7 years of his tenure at the Royal Court Theatre (RCT, Court). This chapter reveals a complex young man, highly intelligent yet struggling to stay afloat in the British school system and possessing an avid curiosity that transports him in unexpected directions, most notably to RCT in 1956. The Court was Keith's university classroom where he would try his hand at many things, working collaboratively and imaginatively with some of the greatest theatre makers of the twentieth century.

Chapter 3, "All the world is a classroom," begins with Keith's 3-year tenure as a teacher and director of the RCT Studio. During this relatively short period, Keith developed his impro theories and techniques and created a system for training actors, directors, and playwrights (i.e., The Impro System). He left the Court in 1966 recognized as an innovative teacher and director of impro. From 1966 to 1972, Keith applied his skills as a teacher at the Royal Academy of Dramatic Art (RADA). During this same period, he refined his skills as a teacher and director with his impro troupe, The Theatre Machine, as they demonstrated their work in classrooms and on stages all over the United Kingdom and Western Europe. Eugenio Barba discovered Keith's work through Theatre Machine and this third chapter documents their two encounters. An invitation to teach at the Statens Teaterskole in Copenhagen, Denmark, came soon thereafter. It is here Keith wrote and directed his controversial play, *The Last Bird*, for the student's senior project. In 1972, Keith decided to leave RADA, Theatre Machine, and the United Kingdom for a variety of reasons, but primarily because Canada offered this internationally recognized teacher of impro a steady paycheck.

Chapter 4, "The master teacher in the university classroom," covers Keith's 23-year career as a professor of acting at the University of Calgary (UofC). Chronologically, this chapter overlaps with Chapter 5, "From classroom to world stage: The Loose Moose Theatre Company"; however, a few years after Loose Moose's inception, Keith detached the work of his company from the university, although his pedagogy continued to intersect. Therefore, Chapter 4 will take a comprehensive look at Keith's unconventional pedagogy within a conventional university structure and the consequences of that. This fourth chapter will also cover Keith's limited production work at UofC and explore how his rehearsals essentially became an extension of the classroom.

Chapter 5, "From classroom to world stage: The Loose Moose Theatre Company," offers a compressed history of Keith's company under his artistic direction (1977 to 1998). Unable to document in one chapter every project this avant-garde theatre company took on, the focus is on Keith's leadership, his production work, and his pedagogy, and how all three played into the formation and perpetuation of Loose Moose. As Theatresports took the Impro System and *Impro* beyond Calgary, international workshops often whisked Keith away from his company at crucial times. The Swedish and Danish theatre communities, for instance, summoned him and this fifth chapter documents several of Keith's forays teaching and directing in Sweden and Denmark.

Even before Keith stepped down as artistic director of Loose Moose, he had started to distance himself from his company and the competitive formats he had created. His center of attention had shifted to teaching his Impro System to a new generation of international students. Chapter 6,

"What now? What comes next? What classrooms still remain?" will examine this shift. Now at an age when most would be enjoying retirement, Keith spends several months out of each year teaching improvisational workshops in Sweden, Denmark, Norway, the United Kingdom, Germany, the United States, and Canada. Famous and not-so-famous students of all ages, types, and from various professions travel great distances to study with the "guru of improvisation," a title he acquired in the 1990s. In this final chapter, his guru identity and the structure of his current and possibly final classroom environment are unpacked.

The Impro System continues to influence thousands, but a few notable teachers, individual performers, and companies are dedicated to taking his work forward in a way that honors Keith's ideal theatre-as-classroom environment. The last part of this concluding chapter pays tribute to these practitioners, all of whom are former students of Keith's. For instance, London's ingenious Improbable theatre company, the group that took Keith's Life Game all over the United Kingdom and to America, is mentioned here. For Improbable, reviving Life Game every few years is akin to returning to the classroom and, in this final chapter, co-artistic director Lee Simpson explains why. Also, some of the most popular improvisers from Brazil, where impro is enjoying a renaissance, share their success stories and their hopes for impro's future classrooms. Lastly, in the section on applied improvisation, celebrity actor Peter Coyote tells us how he uses the Impro System in training Zen Buddhist priests, a classroom beyond any I had anticipated discovering when first embarking on this journey.

"What Comes Next?" is not only a narrative development game invented by Keith but the forward-looking question that concludes this book: What comes next? What classrooms still remain? That is, what other academic and artistic disciplines and/or organizational structures might profit from a system that inspires creativity and innovation through collaboration and assists in the development of interpersonal and leadership skills? Several visionary improvisational artists and teachers from around the world will join me in imagining the possibilities, bearing in mind that the greatest inspirations are unanticipated and often arrive at the precise moment they are needed.

CHAPTER TWO

The formative years

I was a misfit.

KEITH JOHNSTONE

*Some see Nature all ridicule and deformity . . . and some
scarce see Nature at all.
But to the eyes of the man of the imagination,
Nature is Imagination itself.
As a man is, so he sees.*

WILLIAM BLAKE[1]

Keith Johnstone was 18 years old when he discovered the poetry of William Blake, and from that moment forward, Keith would freely declare what he had always felt to be true—the real man is the imagination. This chapter documents the first 30 years of Keith's life in Britain, from 1933 to 1963. During this time, Keith was a student of many types of "classrooms." In some of Keith's earliest classrooms, his imagination was not valued; but after he entered a teacher-training college at the age of 18, he began to see that his imagination did have worth. Then he discovered Samuel Beckett and, shortly thereafter, stumbled into the Royal Court Theatre where his imagination was unleashed. Not eligible for entrance into a university, the professional theatre world offered Keith an education like no other. In 1963, when the Royal Court Theatre Studio opened, Keith was ready

---

[1] From Blake's letter to the Reverend John Trusler, 13 August 1799.

to "graduate" and accept the challenges of teaching; however, over the preceding 7 years, he had drifted through the classroom spaces of the Royal Court like an undergraduate student who had not yet declared his major. Interestingly, Keith never wanted to be a teacher. His British schooling nearly destroyed his belief in formal education. Paradoxically, working to undo the damage inflicted mostly by his secondary school education is how Keith evolved into a teacher, but he did not intentionally pursue a career in teaching. The teaching profession pursued him. This chapter takes us to that moment of initial pursuit.

The London Blitz began on 7 September, 1940. This 8-month bombing campaign of London by the Germans killed thousands of people, left over a million homeless, and, obviously, disrupted theatre as usual. Consequently, theatre dispersed to the British provinces. A 7-year-old Keith was not directly affected by the vibrant provincial theatre scene during World War II. He recalls only one "enthusiastic" amateur theatre group coming to his small town. The circus, on the other hand, came through once a year and Keith attempted to run away with them. The world of itinerant clowns, jugglers, tightrope walkers, acrobats, musicians, and trained animals intrigued Keith. It seemed to be a sanctuary for talented, left-handed misfits, like him, who did not conform to British social norms. But the circus folk chased him away. "They didn't show the slightest interest in kidnapping small children" (Interview with W. Hall).

Donald Keith Johnstone was born on 21 February 1933, in Brixham, a poor fishing town in the county of Devon, in southwest England. "Keith" was an unusual name at that time but everyone in the family—except for mum—liked it, so Keith went by his middle name even though he would've preferred something more along the lines of Hopalong Cassidy.[2] The Johnstones were a lower middle-class family. Richard Donald Johnstone, Keith's father, was a pharmacist and the son of a regimental sergeant major. His mother, Linda Georgina Carter, was a housewife who also helped out with her husband's chemist shop. According to Keith, she resented her life's situation and often took it out on him and his little sister Rita, 6 years his junior.[3] Keith also had an older half-sister, Jean, from his father's first marriage. The Johnstones lived in a three-story row house with an attic on the edge of Brixham Harbour. "Johnstone Chemist" occupied the first floor at street level and the family's living quarters occupied the other three. Keith played around the harbor but his parents did not allow him to play with the fishermen's children.

---

[2] Keith liked to watch cowboy films in his youth.
[3] Keith and Rita discovered, years after the fact, that their mum had told each of them separately that they were "wretched and useless" but that the other one was "brilliant and wonderful."

The Johnstones—Keith (left), *Linda, Jean, Richard.*
Photo Credit: From Keith Johnstone's personal collection.

Keith, around age eight, with Rita at Shoalstone Beach, Brixham.
Photo Credit: From Keith Johnstone's personal collection.

"My parents said no to everything and they had a very tedious, terribly boring life" (Interview with W. Hall).[4]

Keith did not respond to "no" very well. He was exceptionally bright. He read fluently at a very early age, in part, so he could settle into a corner and linger unnoticed by his mum. At the age of 3, his parents enrolled him in Miss Veysey's School, a new private school with only nine students. One afternoon, Miss Veysey came into the chemist shop and asked Keith's parents how they taught their son to read. His parents replied, "Oh, he doesn't read. He just memorizes things." Miss Veysey then had Keith read an excerpt from a newspaper and his parents were amazed. "They didn't know how it happened," recalls Keith. He had taught himself to read the comic books he loved like *The Dandy* featuring the Wild West character Desperate Dan. He also played piano and read music by the age of 6, but he could never memorize a piece by heart.[5] Memorizing dates, names, or numbers has always been problematic for Keith and he had trouble on exams which required this type of regurgitation.

Around this age, Keith's curious nature drew him further and further away from the harbor. In a few years, he would make it all the way to the solid limestone cliffs just outside of town. These cliffs provided a playground for Keith. It was also a place of sadness for the families of the children and tourists who fell from the cliffs each year. There was a time when Keith fell but his "good angel" suddenly took over. "It switched the universe into slow motion, and turned my ten-year-old self into a detached observer," wrote Keith in *The Thing in the Mirror*. "A scraggly branch floated up to me at about an inch a second . . . . I observed my fingers curl around it as if they had all the time in the world" (4). The branch reduced his speed and Keith survived the 25-foot drop. This incident gave him an early lesson in the power of noninterference, that is, getting out of the way of the reasoning intellect so that the instinctive part of the brain can function.

Keith's aptitude for visual art also surfaced at a young age. His parents showed a customer some of their son's drawings and this customer happened to be Stephen Southwold, a famous British writer who published under the pen name Neil Bell. Bell saw potential in this young man's drawings and every Sunday morning for several years he would give Keith art lessons. "I liked him but he was really odd," says Keith. "He didn't really understand the local culture. He suggested my mum should strip naked and I could draw her. That's about as likely as my mum flying to the moon. I realized he came from a quite different point of view." Still,

---

[4]   Brixham fisherman's joke Keith told the audience during an interview: "Brixham fisherman dies and goes to heaven and meets St. Peter, the patron saint of fishermen who asks him, "What did you do on earth?" The fisherman replies, "I was a Brixham fisherman." St. Peter says, "Come on in! You've had your hell" (Interview with W. Hall).

[5]   Keith is an accomplished pianist, but he still finds it difficult to memorize an entire piece. He usually plays with sheet music.

Keith found Bell's lifestyle quite appealing. As a writer, Bell did not have to leave his nice little home "Sea Mist" on Berry Head Road to go to work. The fisherman Keith ran into daily toiled at the docks and other grown-ups would complain about their work or say, "The school days are the happiest days of your life." This statement often preceded a question Keith found quite annoying: "What are you going to be when you grow up?" Reflecting on Bell's routine, Keith began answering, "I wanna be a writer." This answer seemed suitable. Keith, after all, did like writing. Moreover, this response typically confused the grown-ups and stopped the conversation then and there.[6]

As the war intensified, Keith was evacuated to his grandparent's home in Glastonbury, a town 85 miles northeast of Brixham. He was enrolled in St. John's Church School for the next 2 years. Keith describes this school as a "ghastly" place where children got caned. Keith kept a low profile, laid his body across four chairs in the back of the classroom, and found refuge in books. Not comic books, though. Comic books—which typically had an anti-school stance—were banned. Keith remembers seeing his teacher drag a boy out of the room for reading a comic book and thinking, "That's how I learned to read. There's something wrong here." Keith observed the world in a different way, figuratively and literally, and right around the age of nine, he adopted a contrarian attitude to everything: "I decided never to believe anything because it was *convenient*. I began reversing every statement to see if the opposite was also true" (*Impro* 14). Six years later, an accident would leave Keith almost blind in one eye. A kid first jabbed him in the buttocks with a Torquay United Supporter's badge and then Keith proceeded to chase the kid. When Keith caught up, the kid held his hand in the air and accidentally pushed the pin through Keith's left eye, tearing his iris. It is because of his contrariness that Keith is able to turn negative experiences like this one into positive experiences or to reframe them as "offers." An "offer" is an impro term which means a contribution, either physical or verbal, that a player makes to an improvised scenario. An offer can also denote a gift or a constructive teaching moment. Losing half his sight was a nuisance, but Keith used this opportunity to become an expert assessor of eye movements, a skill he finds useful especially when teaching acting.[7]

Keith returned to Miss Veysey's School in Brixham just before the Education Act of 1944 was enacted. This Act introduced the Tripartite System of secondary education into England and Wales and made secondary

---

[6] Correspondence between Keith and Neil Bell continued for years. In Keith's personal archive, letters from Bell dating from the early to late 1950s indicate that Keith continued to solicit advice from Bell, not only on painting, but also on writing.

[7] Over the years, Keith has exercised his left eye by placing a patch over the right eye. Although his left eye still has a tendency to look askew, his vision has vastly improved.

education free to all children. The 11-plus exam, based on the IQ test, was given to students during their last year of primary school, around the age of 11, to determine what type of school the student should be placed into. Keith not only took the 11-plus but a similar exam during a 2-year prep school program run by Totnes Grammar School. He did surprisingly well on both exams and was accepted into Totnes, welcomed by the Headmaster, and put into the A-ability (advanced level) stream as a "future scholar," but soon everything changed. By the end of his first year, Keith had slipped to the bottom of the class. He was then held back a year and placed in the "B-stream" for less intelligent children. But Keith managed to do well enough so that the Headmaster could not transfer him to another school, which he tried to do. "I don't think I realized then that my memory was worse than other people, but it obviously was," says Keith. "I just think there was a sudden decline in memory. Why that happened I don't know. Quite possibly a concussion. I certainly smashed my head a few times. I'm sorry my headmaster took it personally. He should've just accepted it as a fact of nature."[8] It is no wonder Keith remembers the 11-mile bus trip to Totnes from Brixham with a detour through Paignton as a very long ride.

Keith became increasingly self-conscious and uncomfortable in his own body. His speech defects intensified, his posture worsened, and the harder he tried to succeed, the less he could imaginatively respond. "The eagle never lost so much time, as when he submitted to learn of the crow," wrote William Blake in *The Marriage of Heaven and Hell* (xix). Keith tenders this phrase as relevant to his experience in grammar school. Instead of wasting time on subjects that did not interest him, Keith withdrew even further into literature of his own choosing. By the age of 12, he had read *The Bhagavad-Gita*, *The Epic of Gilgamesh*, and other cheap paperbacks sold in the local Tobacconist shop. He read most of the books about Freud, books on Greek mythology, and the 30 or more nonfiction books in the Brixham Library. Keith devoured anything that caught his eye including editorials and labels on cereal boxes.

In 1946, the war was over but 13-year-old Keith was fighting his own intellectual battles. One day an English teacher told the class that Theosophists were idiots. Although Keith is an atheist and grew up in a home where religion was more of a formality than a requirement, he felt morally obligated to investigate what seemed to be unfair criticism.[9]

---

[8] At age 40, Keith took a German language class at the University of Calgary and, although he worked very hard, he was the worst student. At that point he realized he had not been "lazy" in grammar school. He was simply hopeless at memorizing and regurgitating information just for the sake of acquiring knowledge. Einstein said, "Never memorize something you can look up." Keith would agree. When learning is crucial to solving a problem or fulfilling a need, however, Keith has less difficulty remembering.

[9] Keith was sent to Sunday school at the local Methodist church because, he suspects, his parents thought it would be good for business. He called it "a very tedious experience."

Keith around age fourteen.
Photo Credit: From Keith Johnstone's personal collection.

Keith attended a Theosophist group meeting on a Sunday in Torquay in a space, he was surprised to discover, right across from the shop where he had always purchased his piano music. Fifteen women and a few of their husbands were in attendance. "No hymns were sung. No animals were sacrificed," wrote Keith. "There was just a fifty-minute lecture by a plump lady who kept insisting that we were all Gods. She invited questions, but I was too shy to ask, 'so why do I have a toothache?'" (*Thing* 9). Every Sunday for several months, Keith would visit the Theosophists in Torquay, avoid most of the meetings, but take advantage of the free cake and tea, and check out a book from their private collection of writings and scripture on eastern and western religious philosophy and mysticism (e.g., Dr. Paul Brunton's *A Search in Secret India* and novels by Rabindranath Tagore).[10] "Without those books, and without Freud's insistence that we are ignorant of our own motives," contended Keith, "I might have accepted the 'voice in my head' as the 'real me'" (*Thing* 9).

As I skimmed through two issues of *The Totnesian*—the Totnes Grammar School magazine—I found Keith's name throughout. In the 1950 Summer Term issue, Keith submitted the "Chess Club Report" as Secretary of the club. He also wrote the "Music Club" report and apparently impressed the audience

---

[10] Keith remembers being the only one who passed the divinity exam at age 16 because he had such a deep interest in theology, that is, in the absurdity of it all.

at a fund-raising concert for the school orchestra: "Of the instrumentalists, D. K. Johnstone (L. VI.) gave very mature renderings of Beethoven's "Marche Funebre" and "Clair de Lune" (Debussy) on the piano and was worthily encored" (11). In addition, Keith's short story, "The Man Who Desired Immortality," about a Greek scholar who burns down a sacred Egyptian temple to attain immortality, was published in this issue. Evidently, Keith was valued when the editors of the school magazine needed material. "Yes," says Keith, "but there were no other writers." In the end, the boys rewarded for academic excellence and accepted into major universities were the clever ones who used their intellect over their imagination. Keith's imagination was not required in a "banking concept" educational structure, but his initiative to self-educate would be rewarded as he traversed forward into adulthood.

First forays in teaching

On the university entrance exams, Keith passed in geography and art but failed in English and therefore wasn't academically qualified to enter a major university. So in 1951, at the age of 18, Keith entered a 2-year teacher training course at St. Luke's College in Exeter.

Keith at Brixham Harbour, 1951.
Photo Credit: From Keith Johnstone's personal collection.

Although he never really wanted to be a teacher and the Headmaster at Totnes had told him he wasn't "the right type" to teach, Keith hoped that 2 years of teacher training would improve his interactive skills (*Thing*, 89). Moreover, the country was desperately trying to replace teachers who had died in the war, so teaching jobs were virtually guaranteed. In the beginning, Keith specialized in art and music but switched to art and economics after a year. He passed his art class, effortlessly. This young man who "felt crippled, and unfit for life" had been released by a great teacher, Anthony Stirling.

As I said in the introductory chapter, Stirling was a process-oriented teacher who believed in setting up experiences where the student could succeed. His methodology was inspired by Lao Tzu's philosophy of the unseen leader, a leader who motivates others to accomplish tasks on their own. Although Stirling never mentioned Lao Tzu in class, he did recommend that Keith read the *Tao Te Ching* and Thomas Urquhart's seventeeth-century translation of Mikhail Bakhtin's *Rebelais and His World*. Keith says he never understood or liked Bakhtin's book: "It's full of weird jokes like debates on what is the best thing to wipe your ass with and then they agree that a live goose is the thing. Not quite my humor. But Lao Tzu was amazing. A very good suggestion." After studying with Stirling, Keith was convinced that his previous education had been destructive, that trying harder or trying to get it right is useless when it comes to inspired creativity, and that a teacher's job is to initiate a process that disrupts the judgmental voice in the head. Stirling's pedagogy, the *Tao Te Ching*, and everything Keith had read and experienced before and going forward would inform and inspire his own pedagogy.

Keith actually failed the 2-year teacher training course because he did not pass economics; however, the instructors really wanted Keith to teach because he got an excellent evaluation from the Headmaster at the local primary school where he did his 3 weeks of supervised student teaching. Assigned to a class of 8- and 9-year-old art students, Keith decided to take them to the harbor to create paintings of the boats. Then he had the students submit flower paintings to a local gardening society art competition and they won many prizes. He poured plaster into cardboard boxes so they could create statues. And he made use of the old, disused blackboards allowing students to stand on chairs and ladders and draw all over them. This Headmaster was impressed and said as much; so the instructors at St. Luke's College invited Keith to take English instead of economics (and by correspondence) and made sure he passed the second time.

Keith's first full-time teaching assignment was in Battersea, situated on the south side of the River Thames in the London Borough of Wandsworth. Today, Battersea is considered a trendy, up-and-coming hotspot to live, work, and dine; but in 1953, it was an industrial, working-class area. Most new teachers recoiled from this area but Keith, who had previously worked as a Christmas postman there, loved it. The all-boys school was named after the street it was located on—Wix's Lane. During Keith's 2-year tenure, the board of education changed the name to Wix J.B. School. "They didn't like the Dickensian sound," says Keith. "Wix's Lane is much nicer." Walking by the well-preserved but ominous-looking Victorian school built in 1902, surrounded by high security gates, one can imagine Dickens himself might have had this structure in mind for a story set in an oppressive boarding school. Looks, however, can be deceiving. In 2006, Wix Primary School was the first state school to open a bilingual stream in conjunction with the French Lycée and now serves as a successful model for other language conversion schools around the world. Teachers at the school are respected, but this was not the case when Keith was teaching. In the 1950s, teachers at Wix's Lane were disliked by the locals who perceived education as something the middle-class imposed on their working-class culture. Keith thought his colleagues perpetuated that conception by adopting a "colonist's attitude" toward the children. "[T]hey referred to them as 'poor stock', and they disliked exactly those children I found most inventive," wrote Keith (*Impro* 20).

Keith was assigned to a class of 46 boys who were labeled as "average 8-year-olds" and "ineducable 10-year-olds." Right away, he put Stirling's idea of "non-interference" to the test. Instead of depositing information into the students, Keith tried to create process-oriented tasks for every subject. He encouraged the children to solve problems through game-playing so that the "pressure to get things right was coming from the children, not the teacher" (22). Although Keith spent only 2 years at Wix's Lane followed by a year of supply teaching, his observations of and discoveries made with these young children would influence the rest of his career. Children labeled as "dull" were often bored and uninspired by a banking concept of education, the kind of education Keith had been subjected to until he met Stirling. He recognized himself in these children who did not fit into a conventional system of education, and he would continually fight against any doctrinaire, one-size-fits-all approach. Keith took this attitude with him into the world of professional theatre, a world he knew nothing about and had no interest in until the summer of 1955.

Waiting for Godot

On 21 February 1954, Keith's short story "The Monastery" had its first of two readings on the BBC's *Third Programme*, a leading cultural and intellectual radio broadcast—quite an achievement for an unknown writer from Brixham.[11] Still, by the end of the year, Keith decided he wanted to pursue a career as a painter and he began palling around with a group of young, roke, bohemian-like painters he met in an art class at the Battersea Men's Institute. Peter Lloyd Jones was one of those fellows. In his 2011 book, *Come Back That Boy! An Evacuee's Tale*, Jones describes Keith as "a tall, gangling fellow with a mop of dark hair that constantly dropped over his face, an irritation which he corrected with frequent backward flicks

---

[11] Pat Fardell, an Australian working in London, heard the broadcast and wrote a fan letter to Keith. They met up shortly thereafter and began an affair. Pat is the mother of Keith's first son, Dan. Although Keith has maintained a relationship with Dan, it is Pat who raised him in Sydney, Australia.

of the head." On Keith's paintings, Jones remembers them as "in-yer-face," "polemical outbursts," "stirring stuff" for the 1950s, and in the same spirit as Franz Kafka's short story *Metamorphosis*.[12]

Toward the end of the summer of 1955, Jones and the others invited Keith to go with them to see Peter Hall's English-language premier production of *Waiting for Godot* at the Criterion Theatre in the West End of London. Keith doubted theatre could ever be as profound as a Kurosawa or Keaton film, but he reluctantly agreed (*Impro* 24). Keith wanted to leave after the first act. He was sure the author didn't need a second act because the first act was perfect, "a complete statement," but his group of friends convinced him to stay ("Meeting Beckett" 2). "I was so pleased. It was the same act again but everything's worse. The character's situation had become worse!" Keith went back and saw Hall's production seven more times. Samuel Beckett's play immediately changed Keith's mind about theatre, about its distinctive ability to engage audiences like no other medium.

How could a 3-hour play about two men out of work who do nothing on a practically empty stage captivate a young man who previously found sanctuary in comic books, myths, music, silent cinema, and cowboy films? "Godot returned theatre to its metaphorical roots," wrote Peter Hall. "The stage was an image of life passing – in hope, despair, companionship, and loneliness. To our times, the images on the cinema screen are real, though they are only made of flickering light. Since Godot, the stage is the place of fantasy. Film is simile, lifelike; theatre is metaphor, about life itself." Keith, like so many, experienced his own life, his own ruminations as he watched *Waiting for Godot*. The action in the play made perfect sense to Keith: "Lucky carries a bag of sand 'cause his work is pointless. Pozzo is going blind 'cause as you go on in life, everything gets worse." Estragon and Vladimir remain hopeful under hopeless circumstances because they have no choice. To Keith, their situation was no different than that of friends and relatives in Brixham, poor fisherman and shopkeepers drudging through daily life not knowing why they existed but having no other alternative but to exist and to make the best of it. "There's nothing difficult to understand about *Godot* unless you don't want to hear the message," says Keith.

Waiting for Godot connected to Keith on another level, too. He had been waiting for 11 years, half of his life, to outgrow his awkwardness and to figure out what he was waiting for. Like Estragon and Vladimir, he waited with hope, curiosity, and good-nature. Moreover, he was part of a generation who grew up during World War II but never fought; a generation who were promised (but didn't get) a future with no slums, no social problems, "The Wellsian world of the future," Keith calls it; a generation whose own creative

---

[12] Jones describes Keith's painting "Myxamatosis" as a "large Surrealist allegory . . . expressing his outrage at the death of so many rabbits from a mysterious virus disease." Myxamatosis is a disease that killed almost 99 per cent of the rabbit population in Britain between 1953 and 1955, and newspapers had been reporting stories of estate owners and farmers deliberately spreading the disease.

impulses, needs, and desires seemed somewhat insignificant during the war years and anticlimactic in the decade following. Then, Beckett revealed that even a common man's mundane daily routine—waiting, watching, doubting, hoping, conversing, eating, and drinking—could be interesting to a theatre audience *if* the audience is having a comparable experience and *if* the routine is unexpectedly interrupted.

In most theatre prior to Beckett, audiences were usually a step ahead of the characters in the play. Traditional plotting hinted at things to come and so the audience could anticipate the conflict, the climatic event, and the denouement to some extent. But with *Waiting for Godot*, the audience waits with the characters. They anticipate what the characters anticipate. They are surprised at the exact moment the characters are surprised, and they hope, alongside Vladimir and Estragon, that Godot will arrive. Furthermore, the character's comical repartee and physical interplay, reminiscent of the comedy teams of vaudeville and music hall, depend on audience reaction. If Beckett's rhythms are delivered organically and the audience response is incorporated into those rhythms each night, the performances should seem spontaneous, almost improvisational.

After the war, the vibrant provincial theatre did not transfer back to London.[13] For the most part, theatre in London's West End, because of reduction in available properties and exorbitant rental costs, had become very commercial, safe, conservative, and dependent upon celebrities and spectacle. *Waiting for Godot* was none of those things, and for Keith, it was an epiphany. Theatre could actually be a medium for engaging audiences with his own experiences and imaginings without distressing over grammar, spelling, or conventional structures; a place where the suffering he had experienced in his youth could be expressed through metaphor and humor. Little did Keith know, within a year, he would not only be commissioned to write a play for the hottest new theatre in London, but he would meet and establish a personal and professional relationship with Beckett himself.

The Royal Court Theatre—A "school" for playwrights

[T]his place is a sort of school, after all.

GEORGE DEVINE (Rebellato 84)

---

[13] During the war, the provinces rallied to keep theatre alive when London shut down. Non-traditional venues were used (e.g., factories, bomb sites, and tube shelters) and nontraditional audiences were treated to nontraditional and older forms of theatre (e.g., Living Newspaper, variety theatre, and music hall). Unfortunately, when the war ended, the exciting efforts made by professional and amateur theatre groups touring the provinces did not transfer back to London with a few exceptions (e.g., Unity Theatre and Littlewood's Theatre Workshop) (Davies 125–59).

"Sound the trumpets! Beat the drum! There is great news for the English theatre. In London, last week, there was launched a pioneering enterprise which is devoted—believe it or not—to staging serious plays by living authors." Richard Findlater, reporting for *The Tribune* in April of 1956, was calling attention to the arrival of the English Stage Company at the old Royal Court Theatre (RCT, Court) in Sloane Square.[14] George Devine, an established director, actor, and teacher in London, was the first artistic director and Tony Richardson, a young television producer at the time, his associate director. Of course, what started out as a dream to build a European art theatre with a permanent company producing new plays in repertory was abandoned within a year to keep the theatre afloat. Mixing new works by new playwrights with works by established playwrights, producing the occasional star vehicle and classic revival, plus transferring productions to the West End and Broadway became the survival strategy. Still, the theatre remained a writer's theatre and launched the careers of many celebrated playwrights of the twentieth century.

Devine believed in nurturing the talent of writers, directors, designers, and actors, and, during his tenure as artistic director of the Court, implemented educational policies and opportunities which created a "theatre-as-classroom" atmosphere. Critic and historian Irving Wardle said Devine's legacy was his conviction that "it was always necessary for those with the skills and background and the professional knowledge to keep on investing in those who haven't got there yet . . ." (Doty 37–8). Many of Devine's principles and training ideas came out of his experiences working with and alongside his master teacher, Michel Saint-Denis.

Saint-Denis, nephew of Jacques Copeau, developed and disseminated his uncle's ideas through his celebrated *Compagnie des Quinze*. From 1930 to 1935, Saint-Denis and Devine ran the London Theatre Studio, and after the war, they established the Old Vic Theatre School (1947) with a third partner, Glen Byam Shaw. Although both schools were short-lived, the impact on a generation of theatre practitioners was considerable. Britain was introduced to a new approach to actor training. Saint-Denis believed the actor should be a flexible instrument and training should integrate mime, movement, masks, song, dance, and classes for developing the imagination. Like Copeau, Saint-Denis proposed using improvisational techniques for developing the actor's imagination and his ability to create spontaneously. He used improvisation in rehearsals before working on texts, for devising new texts, and as a way to integrate all aspects of the actor's training to bring a preexisting text to life (Gordon 148–52). Devine took these ideas with him to the Court and, departing from Saint-Denis' strictness in regard to directing a production,

---

[14] The Royal Court Theatre in Sloane Square was built in 1888. It had once been home to Harley Granville-Barker and J.E. Vedrenne's company (1904–07) which produced notable premiers of several plays by George Bernard Shaw. The theatre was damaged during the Blitz, closed for over a decade, reconstructed and reopened in 1952.

he gave his creative teams more freedom to develop their work according to their individual instincts (Roberts, *RCT Modern* 43).

Meanwhile, a supply teacher/painter from Battersea with a new appreciation for the theatre unofficially collaborated on a film script with Lorenza Mazzetti which never got made. Mazzetti was a waitress in a coffee bar that Keith frequented and they discovered their mutual love for Kafka, Chaplin, and silent films. One afternoon, after going to see the last short Chaplin had made for Essanay Films, Mazzetti took Keith to a very tall building in Soho Square. They went up and up an ever-narrowing staircase and into a garret room filled with 35-millimeter film strips. Sitting in the middle of it all was Mazzetti's film editor, Lindsay Anderson. Keith says he looked like a gnome. Anderson was editing the film, *Together*, which Mazzetti directed.[15]

Keith had just won a prize for a short story he submitted to an *Observer Newspaper* competition and Anderson convinced his friend Richardson to take a risk and commission a play from this unknown writer for RCT. Keith refused the commission at first but, when his teaching money ran out, he went back to the Court to see if the offer still stood. Like other penniless writers who had the ability, he was brought into the Court and offered a job as a play reader. In any given week, he would read up to 50 scripts at 5 shillings a script. Within a short amount of time, Keith was placed in charge of the entire script department.

The third play of the first RCT season, John Osborne's *Look Back in Anger*, opened on May 8 under the direction of Richardson. This play was selected from 750 scripts submitted to the RCT's call for new scripts advertised in *The Stage* 3 months prior. Osborne, an unknown playwright from the lower middle class, had had his play rejected by dozens of agents and managers before he submitted it to Court. Richard "Dicky" Buckle, a well-known ballet critic for the *Observer*, read and liked the play but warned against doing it since it might "insult" the audience. Phillip Roberts, author of *The Royal Court Theatre and the Modern Stage* (1999), expressed that Buckle's response revealed audience expectations of the time: "It is a remark about theatre as confirmatory of the audience's *status quo*. The notion that theatre should be in any way disturbing, let alone bad mannered, was inconceivable" (48). Even members of the RCT Council were divided in their opinion of Osborne's play.

Today, the opening of *Look Back in Anger* is considered a watershed moment in the history of British theatre and a cornerstone of the "Angry

---

[15] This 49-minute film explores the lives of two deaf-mute dockworkers in East London. It received its premier in the first Free Cinema film festival organized by Anderson in 1956. Anderson's own documentary film was part of the festival and Tony Richardson also contributed a film. Manzetti is probably best known for her novel *Il Cielo Cade* ("The Sky Falls") based on her tragic childhood in Italy during World War II. In 2000, her novel was made into a film starring Isabella Rossellini.

Young Man" movement within the writing community. "It was the first British play that openly dramatized bruising emotion, and it was the first to give the alienated lower classes and youth of England a weapon," wrote John Heilpern, drama critic for the *New York Observer*. In truth, ticket sales did not pick up until an 18-minute clip of the production was aired on Grenada TV on October 16. Then the RCT filled up with enthusiastic, younger audiences, the television generation who had limited or no connection to the well-made drawing room plays of the West End (Roberts, *RCT Modern* 48–9). The play also caught the mood of a country shaken by the humiliating Suez Canal crisis in Egypt. Forced by the United States and USSR to end their military invasion on November 6, Britain lost their reputation as a global power and was propelled into a period of imperial decline.

Keith was not influenced by Osborne's writing style and believes the critics magnified the sociopolitical issues within the play; nevertheless, for a second time, he was exposed to theatre that created an immediate communion between actor and spectator. This may not have interested Keith at the time, but it opened the gate for writer/directors, like him, who believed theatre should tap into the mythos of working and lower-class audiences.[16] Furthermore, profits from transfers and the sale of film rights of Osborne's work insured the Court's survival and, consequently, Keith's career in the theatre.[17]

Samuel Beckett—An arranged meeting

On 3 April 1957, Roger Blin's production of Beckett's *Fin de Partie* (*Endgame*) and *Acte Sans Parole* (*Act Without Words*) premiered at RCT for a 1-week run. Devine invited Blin and his company of French actors to the Court after learning they had lost their theatre space in Paris (Roberts, *RCT Modern* 58). During the short run, Devine had an intimate gathering at his home. Devine, Beckett, Blin, Jean Marais (an actor in *Endgame*), Osborne, writer Colin Wilson, and Keith were in attendance. The house was full of tobacco smoke and Keith got sick. At the time, he thought he was allergic to the alcohol but later realized it was the smoke intensified by the lack of ventilation. "Beckett sat by me and said hardly anything all night . . . like the door mouse in *Alice in Wonderland*," Keith recalls. As

---

[16] For Keith, theatre that taps into the mythos of its audience also means theatre that stays within an audience's circle of probability.

[17] *Look Back in Anger* transferred to the West End in November and to Broadway the following year. Osborne's *The Entertainer* directed by Richardson and written as a star vehicle for Laurence Olivier opened at the RCT in April of 1957 and transferred to the West End in September. Both *Look Back in Anger* and *The Entertainer* were made into films directed by Richardson.

Keith was leaving, Beckett followed him into the hallway and asked him to have lunch with him the next day. "I'm sure it's because it had been recommended by George Devine. I don't see why else he would have done it." Looking back, Ann Jellicoe, another young writer commissioned by the Court in 1957, said Beckett, like Devine and Richardson and many others, reacted to Keith's "intelligence, his teeming ideas, his innocence, his idealism" (*World*). Whatever his initial response, Beckett did take an interest in this young man, 27 years his junior, and a unique type of friendship was formed. Not a casual, palling around kind of friendship – "I never teased Beckett and he never teased me," says Keith – but a friendship based on mutual respect.

In a handwritten letter dated 4 April 1957, Beckett told Keith he liked a short story Keith had sent to him "very much" and he took it upon himself to send it on to the editor of *The Paris Review* with the advice to publish it.

Letter to Keith from Samuel Beckett, 4 April 1957. (At the top of the letter, Beckett's address in dark black ink was written by Keith)

Photo Credit: From Keith Johnstone's personal collection.

Keith remembers sending the short story "The Return" to Beckett. "The Return" is about Keith's most discernible memories of his dad and his family in the months leading up to his dad's death from cerebral arteriosclerosis. But Keith's dad died on 4 January 1958, in Glastonbury, and Beckett's letter was written in 1957, so Keith must have sent Beckett a different short story. In any case, *The Paris Review* did not publish Keith's short story. In 1962, however, Beckett's London publisher John Calder did publish "The Return" upon Beckett's request in *New Writers 2*, the second of a series of books that featured up-and-coming European writers. Here is an excerpt from the end of "The Return," after the funeral service, after the coffin had been lowered into the gravesite, and after everyone had left except for Keith, who chose to walk home:

> I wondered if I could go back to see the grave filled in—I would have liked to watch, it would have been so slow and final. But it might have been a breach of etiquette.
>
> I walked back across the flooded moors and the road was dark against the reflected sky. There were bristly trees and marooned cows. Tomorrow I would be in London again: today I was glad of a half hour of silence.
>
> Dad had done everything they'd told him—but for what return? I wasn't grieving because my father had died, that would be selfish. I grieved because he'd never lived, not properly. (92–3)

Over the next 10 years, Beckett often invited Keith to lunch with him in London. They usually sat opposite one another and had monosyllabic conversations or ate in silence. As Beckett got more comfortable as a director, many artists would observe his rehearsals. In the beginning, however, Keith was the first to be personally invited by Beckett into his rehearsal space, so he attended as many Beckett rehearsals as possible. They served as master classes in what to do and what not to do as a director.[18] Keith admired Beckett, his kindness, and his brilliant mind but he did not like his tendency at times to be inflexible. In 1964, for example, Beckett's one-act *Play*, directed by Devine, was presented on double-bill at Olivier's National Theatre with Keith's adaptation of *Philoctetes* by Sophocles.[19] Even with Devine in the director's chair, Keith recalls Beckett giving the three actors—Billie Whitelaw, Robert Stephens, and Rosemary Harris—the exact inflection and pacing of every line. Furthermore, Beckett insisted the actors, placed in funeral urns with only their heads protruding, deliver

---

[18] In Keith's personal collection of papers, I found 36 pages of notes Keith had taken at one of Beckett's rehearsals of *Endgame* at the Court (1958). He also watched Beckett at work at the Court during rehearsals of *Krapp's Last Tape* (1958) and *Happy Days* (1962).

[19] *Philoctetes* was directed by Gaskill and starred Colin Blakely in the title role.

the text as rapidly as possible. "None of us could hear a bloody word. Might as well have been gibberish," asserts Keith. Martin Esslin in his review for *Plays and Players* agreed that the "original" and "unusual" *Play* was not instantly comprehensible but, he added, it was "a dizzy feat of sheer technical virtuosity" that, like great music, required more than one hearing to appreciate its "full glory." Keith may not have been impressed with Beckett's "technical" direction, but he was deeply influenced by Beckett's writing and most certainly by the personal advice Beckett gave to him in another letter dated 7 March 1958: "A theatre stage is an area of maximum verbal presence and maximum corporeal presence. Any dimming of the one or the other, or of the one by the other, is anti-theatrical" (1). Written on a wall in the RCT office for many years, all of Keith's consequent theatre endeavors have aspired toward this aesthetic.[20]

Sunday Night productions without décor

In 1957, Devine implemented "Sunday Night productions without décor," a plan that would allow the company to present new, often riskier plays being considered for the main season. Devine openly declared RCT writers had the "right to fail," a term first used by Richardson, and Sunday Night productions created a space where playwrights could fail (or succeed) without massive financial repercussions. "Without décor" meant rehearsed up to dress rehearsal point but presented with a minimum of scenery and costumes and at a fraction of the cost of a full-scale production. Billed as private club performances to evade the Lord Chamberlain, Sunday Nights enabled promising writers to see and hear their work uncensored and offered new directors an opportunity to show Devine what they could do. Writers like John Arden, N. F. "Wally" Simpson, Doris Lessing, Wole Soyinka, and Keith had their first plays produced as a Sunday Night production. Directors like John Dexter, Lindsay Anderson, William Gaskill, and Anthony Page got their feet wet on Sunday Nights. Often the most experimental, immediate, and exciting new work took place on Sunday Nights.[21] For Keith, Sunday Nights were performance classes presented in front of audiences who, for the most part, understood the

---

[20] Keith's essay, "Meeting Beckett," offers a more thorough account of his personal and professional relationship with Beckett. It can be found in *Wie Meine Frau Dem Wahnsinn Verfiel* ("My Wife's Madness"), a collection of Keith's short stories and plays published in German in 2009. An updated version of this essay in English is in *The Last Bird: Stories and Plays* by Keith Johnstone published in 2012. Both collections are published by Alexander Verlag Berlin.

[21] The Theatre Upstairs opened in February of 1969 and replaced Sunday Night productions without décor. Before 1969, however, all Sunday Night productions were performed on the main Royal Court stage.

nature of the process. Keith directed and/or wrote approximately thirteen Sunday Night productions from 1958 to 1963.

Gaskill directed Keith's first commissioned play, *Brixham Regatta*, as a Sunday Night production without décor and as part of the Aldeburgh Festival on 22 June 1958. Gaskill met Keith the year before and described him as "a large earnest man who chewed huge cooking apples and carried scripts around in carrier bags" (*Sense* 25). Brought into the Court by Richardson, Gaskill had already directed three plays for the main season by the summer of 1958, but that did not stop him from taking advantage of Sunday Night opportunities.[22]

Keith around age twenty-five.
Photo Credit: Roger Mayne.

Brixham Regatta was presented on a double-bill with another one-act by Keith called *For Children* directed by Ann Jellicoe, whose own first play, *The Sport of My Mad Mother*, premiered 4 months earlier under her own direction.[23] *For Children* revolves around a boy and a girl who discover a

---

[22] Gaskill had directed two plays by N. F. Simpson (*A Resounding Tinkle* and *The Hole*) and one by Osborne and Anthony Creighton (*Epitaph for George Dillon*) for the RCT's 1958 main stage season.

[23] *Sport* had tied for third place with N.F. Simpson's *A Resounding Tinkle* in an *Observer* play competition (1956). According to Jellicoe, Devine is listed as a co-director for *Sport* only as a protective and supportive measure (Doty 36). Gaskill confirmed: "[T]hough George oversaw the staging it was in every important aspect directed by Ann" (*Sense* 32).

skeleton in the forest. Through their conversation, the audience learns the children have just escaped from a fire in which their home was destroyed and their parents killed. Patrick Gibbs of the *Daily Telegraph* called this play, "A delicate illustration of the way children think, and of their peculiar attitude towards death . . ." ("Human"). *Brixham Regatta* is influenced by the writing style of Beckett and Keith did send the play to Beckett for feedback earlier in the year. Beckett's response, typed up in a two-page letter, is "an example of a great writer giving advice to an unknown writer (me) in such as way as not to discourage him," wrote Keith ("Meeting Beckett"). This is the same letter in which Beckett expressed his view of what a theatre stage should be. Only recently did I happen to exhume this letter from a large box, stacked in Keith's basement, loaded with miscellaneous papers. Keith was thrilled. He hadn't seen this letter for decades. It is an important letter for Keith—even though he never revised *Brixham Regatta* to incorporate Beckett's suggestions—and it reveals much about Beckett, about his unassuming, kind nature (see entire letter on pages 39–40).

The title *Brixham Regatta* suggests boating or sailing races, but Keith's "regatta" is a circus sideshow where a hard-working showman displays large animals (Beckett called them "monsters"), getting progressively more dangerous, alongside three human exhibits—his zombie-like son Alexander, a crippled man, and a tortured man. Alexander, the star attraction, is blind, deaf, dumb, and paralyzed in the beginning, but, through his sister's maternal and sensual love, he emerges from his stupor. Their sexual intercourse also induces the animals to break loose from their cages. In the end, the father and haggish mother are left alone and bitter. Keith deliberately used information from Melanie Klein (1882–1960), a child psychoanalyst inspired by Freud, for developing the young characters.

A handful of critics blasted *Brixham Regatta* with words like "horrifying," "mystifying," and "baffling." In reference to both *For Children* and *Brixham Regatta*, a critic for the *Sunday Times* declared, "Of these horrors I can hardly trust myself to speak. They showed a preoccupation with mortality, disease and what I thought to be a peculiarly revolting manifestation of sadism" (Rev. of *Brixham*).[24] Other critics, however, were impressed. Gibbs called the play "a grotesque menagerie . . . where the human beings who run the show as a spectacle hardly differ from the strange animals – and

---

[24] This response by critics was not unlike the fierce response Sara Kane's play *Blasted* received after it opened at the Court's Theatre Upstairs in 1995. Kane was a playwright associated with the 1990s "In-Yer-Face Theatre" movement in Britain. Mark Ravenhill is another key playwright associated with this movement and, as mentioned in Chapter 1, was and still is largely influenced by Keith's narrative techniques. *Brixham Regatta*, like *Blasted*, was a metaphorical statement about the sociopolitical culture in Britain and the psychological and physical violence born from that culture. Keith's play was a precursor of things to come.

March 7th 1958   6 Rue des Favorites
                                  Paris 15me

Dear Keith Johnstone

    I apologize for not having written to you before now about
your play. Obligations, attempts to write, interruptions, tiredness -
the usual mess.

    Assessment of writing is not my affair. There is no advice I wish
to give anyone in this domain - or in any other. The more I go the
less I know about the whole dreary business. I quiver a little juster
to my own thorns, that's the only progress. And perhaps it's
imagination.

    The thought is hateful to me of the distress and harm I may cause
a young man like you by my arbitrariness and expression of personal
warp. Do not for God's sake take too much to heart what follows.

    The idea of your play is strong, a great deal of the writing re-
markably fine and theatre, and yet the play doesn't come off - for
me.

    Up to the arrival of the invisible monsters I was quite absorbed.
At that point I drifted out and never really got back in again.

    The invisible audience of The Chairs is acceptable (though to
me unsatisfactory) because proceeding from and illuminative of
a human situation. In your case the invisibility seems to be above
all a technical necessity. Visible listeners in The Chairs would
kill the play, visible monsters in yours would improve it. Here
then you fall out of your vehicle. Not because xxxxxxx we don't see
the brutes, but because you bring them on and don't show them. Only
what is off stage is legitimate matter for evocation. What is on
stage never. What is on stage is to be seen, with the greatest xxxxxx
possible acuity. (Even your family on the floor is not sufficiently
visible, you should indicate a raised place.) A theatre stage is an
area of maximum verbal presence and maximum ~~corporeal~~
presence. Any dimming of the one or the other, or of the one by
the other, is anti-theatrical. (I can hear you from here say you
want to be anti-theatrical. By all means. But not suicide.) Your
play then breaks down for me the moment you invite me to look and
deny me vision. The true theatre-goer's eyes are a ravenous organ.
Words for the hidden (heart and next door), but not in lieu and
place of what is there and patent for your players, when there is no
or insufficient psychological xxxxxxx ground for the discrimination.
Conclusion, your monsters will be much more present, and oppressive,
if you don't bring them on (as much roaring off as you like), and
not only that, but the writing whereby they are communicated will
tend towards a much higher level.

    If you can't bear to banish them altogether, at least reduce
them. You say you are looking for a way of shortening the thing.
This would certainly be the most satisfactory.

Letter to Keith from Samuel Beckett, 7 March 1958.
Photo Credit: From Keith Johnstone's personal collection.

human beings – which they exhibit," and he compared it to Beckett's *Fin
de partie*. *The Times* critic called it "a bracing play" that persuades the
audience through dialogue and, under Gaskill's direction, revealed a "light
within the characters . . . [that] shone out against the darkness as though on
some canvas by a Spanish painter of the golden age" ("Double").

```
                        are excellent,
      The flags, on the contrary,/because they extend the visible.
Here is a perfect example, it seems to me, of dramatic expressive-
ness.

      What interests me most in your play is the children relation-
ship, the parents relationship, the children- parents relation-
ship, in of course your climate of monstrosity and cruelty. With
Molloy and Co out of the way these could be stated more fully and
the extraordinary progress of Alexander made more acceptable.

      The dialogue is excellentxvery often very good idea. Pages 9-11
impressed me particularly.

      This is only a small part of what I would try and say, with your
help, over a glass of wine. This one-sided business revolts me. So
I'll leave it at that. The main point is made, if it is one.

      You tell me you haven't the courage to rewrite it. Without that
courage - apart altogether from your agreeing or disagreeing with
me in the present instance - I'm afraid you can't hope to get very
far.

      Forgive me if I have irritated you and if what I have said
seems to you entirely irrelevant. I should like nothing better than
to be able to help you. But this is not the way writers help one
another. Our conversation in London gave me the impression that you
were not very interested in writing. That is very understandable.
But if it did come to matter more to you I am pretty sure, from the
little you have shown me, that the results would be considerable.

                        Kind regards to Pat.
                        Yours ever
```

Letter to Keith from Samuel Beckett, 7 March 1958 (continued).
Photo Credit: From Keith Johnstone's personal collection.

A sharp divide in critical response for new plays at the Court was not unusual in 1958. But critical failures galvanized the young playwrights and their directors who were keen on doing the work they wanted to do rather than kowtowing to the demands of traditional British audiences. "Very good to be a playwright then," says Keith. "You were all in the same boat. You'd get your play put on and they [critics] would savage it. But we liked each other's plays." And they really liked one another. Jellicoe remembers audiences walking out of the theatre during Keith's play. "It was awful," she says. "Keith couldn't bare it so he went to the Festival pub next door. When the play was over, we couldn't find him. Then we realized he was on the beach and, at that moment, an enormous thunderstorm broke out!" So Keith walked through the storm toward Jellicoe and Gaskill and the others and they all embraced each other in a long hug. Next, they were off to the pub for a drink and a rather wild night in Aldeburgh. "We had a lot of fun in those days," muses Jellicoe. "Very badly behaved!" (P.I.).[25]

Lastly, a young playwright named Harold Pinter liked *Brixham Regatta* and sent Keith a fan letter, the only fan letter he ever received from another playwright. A month earlier, Pinter's first full-length play, *The Birthday Party*, had been slaughtered by the critics the day after it opened at the Lyric Hammersmith in London.[26] Although never an official Court playwright, Pinter knew Gaskill, Simpson, Jellicoe, and Keith, and he held a RCT writer's pass which allowed him to attend rehearsals and performances for free. Gaskill and Keith appropriately gave Pinter, distraught and destitute after his play's failure in London, the cameo role of the tortured man in *Brixham Regatta*. For 20 pounds, Pinter was carried on the stage, stood motionless, and was carried off again. After the performance, Gaskill told Keith that Pinter wasn't very good in the part.

The Writers' Group

The RCT playwrights' commitment to each other and to each other's work was, in part, due to the relationship they had developed in the Writers' Group. What started out as a discussion group would evolve into an intimate classroom for a handful of Court playwrights and directors to explore the nature of theatre collectively and in practical ways. The first meeting took place in January of 1958 at an old paint shop in Flood Street, Chelsea. "It was romantic but dirty," wrote Jellicoe. "We sat on boxes, creaking chairs, anything to hand, in a strict circle surrounded by debris and droughts" (Findlater, *At the Royal* 52). Devine, Saint-Denis, and about 13 directors and writers, including Keith, were in attendance. It was Devine's initial idea to create such a group but he soon withdrew and put Gaskill in charge, although all members of the group participated as directors, teachers, and students. The weekly meetings eventually moved to Anne Piper's Hammersmith home overlooking the water and only two doors down from Devine's. Gaskill remembered the "large room on the first floor which always had a blazing fire" with "fresh coffee and bread and cheese for the hungry writers" (*Sense* 36). Although Devine gave classes and others who were invited would drop in on occasion, the devotees of the

---

[25] Photographer Roger Mayne, Jellicoe's future husband, was with the group on this night.

[26] Pinter's play had a successful pre-London tour at the Cambridge Arts Theatre but did not fare well with the critics in London and closed after eight performances. Harold Hobson, critic for the *Sunday Times*, loved the play but his review came out too late to save it from closing. He wrote: "Pinter, on the evidence of his work, possesses the most original, disturbing and arresting talent in theatrical London" ("The Screw"). Hobson's review had a residual effect. Today, *The Birthday Party* is considered a classic.

group were Gaskill, Johnstone, Jellicoe, Arnold Wesker, John Arden, Wole Soyinka, and Edward Bond.[27]

Prompted by Keith, a no-discussion policy was put into effect after Gaskill took over from Devine.[28] "He [Keith] believed that things should be shown happening in the theatre, not analysed and talked about," wrote Jellicoe. "It is hard now to remember how fresh this idea was in 1958, but it chimed in with my own thinking and had great influence in the way the group began to operate" (Findlater, *At the Royal* 54). The moment anyone in the group began discussing something, Gaskill, Keith, or another writer would say, "Go and show us." And that is how improvisation became their primary tool of exploration. Over the next 2 years, this group of seven would become very close and collaboratively develop moments for performance through improvisational means.

Gaskill had studied mime with Etienne Decroux and the first improvisatory exercise the group tried was from Decroux. A single chair was placed in the center of the room and one-by-one the writers would launch an improvised scene, sitting in or using the chair. Gaskill thought this exercise influenced the last scene in Bond's infamous play *Saved*, produced at the Court in 1965 (*Sense* 36). The group explored Stanislavsky's improvisations on objectives and often they improvised around themes or spontaneous ideas. Jellicoe recalled "boring scenes at bus stops" which were made more interesting by increasing the difficulty of the conditions (Findlater, *At the Royal* 56).[29] Living Newspaper techniques, mock interviews, and sometimes impersonations of each other were endeavored. Soyinka, for example, generated a funny imitation of a very "wooden" Keith on the stage. Occasionally, a writer would get stuck and the group would help the writer work through the block. An improvisation in one workshop around an old bed directly contributed to a memorable moment in Jellicoe's play *The Knack*, which she was in the process of writing. Jellicoe set up a scene between a group of customers and an old man in a junkyard. When the

---

[27] Others were invited and did not attend or dropped out early. They included: Osborne, who despised the Writers' Group and never attended a meeting; Pinter and Simpson, who were both invited but didn't like groups in general; Donald Howarth, a playwright who wasn't good at improvisation; and director John Dexter, who dropped out about the same time as Devine (Findlater, *At the Royal* 22, 53–5; Doty 87).

[28] Bertolt Brecht had a no-discussion policy in rehearsals (Schneider 85). But this wasn't known to the Writers' Group at the time. Brecht, however, did have a brief relationship with the Court in 1956. As the Berliner Ensemble was preparing for its first visit to London and just before Brecht's death on August 17, Brecht gave Devine permission to direct *The Good Woman of Setzuan* (trans. by Eric Bentley) with Peggy Ashcroft in the title role. The production opened at RCT on October 31. A Brechtian aesthetic persisted at RCT. In a 1958 article for *Theatre Arts*, Devine said: "I believe the future [of RCT] lies somewhere in a triangle between Brecht, Beckett and Ionesco" (Roberts, *RCT Modern* 64).

[29] "That was because people at bus stops interested me," says Keith. It was in the pursuit of the natural kinetic dance demonstrated by people at bus stops that Keith discovered and developed his work on status years later.

old man refused to sell his bed, the customers began to tease him. Gaskill, who was in the improvisation, suddenly yelled, "It's not a bed, it's a piano!" Devine's daughter, Harriet, insisted, "It's a bed!" (Gaskill, *Sense* 37). The improvisation took off from there and Jellicoe found a way to end Act I of *The Knack*.

One unforgettable Wednesday evening, Devine gave the Writers' Group a class in comic mask technique in the tradition of Saint-Denis and Copeau.[30] He brought in a box of 40 or so dusty half-masks (also called character masks) that he had used with students at the Old Vic Theatre School and before that at the London Theatre Studio. After a tedious 40-minute lecture, Devine gave a demonstration. He put on a half-mask, looked at his reflection in a mirror, and then turned to the group. "We saw a 'toad-god' who laughed and laughed as if we were funny and despicable," wrote Johnstone in the "Masks and Trance" chapter of *Impro*. "I don't know how long the 'scene' lasted, it was timeless" (142). Gaskill said it only lasted a minute or less, "but it shook us" (*Sense* 43). Devine told Keith the mask class had been a failure because no one in the group had been inhabited by a mask "spirit." On the contrary, for Gaskill and Keith, Devine's demonstration revealed an alternative, nonintellectual approach to acting, wherein an actor "empties his mind to receive the influence, the identity, of another being" (*Sense* 43). They used Devine's masks and applied his techniques in the RCT Studio classes beginning in 1963.[31] Furthermore, Arden wrote his play, *The Happy Haven*, especially for masked characters and Gaskill directed it at the Court in 1960. As revealed in the previous chapter, Keith believes mask work can be a potent tool for getting at the imaginative, childlike part of the mind; for freeing student actors physically and psychologically from their socially constructed, restrictive personalities; and for allowing students to explore other "selves." From this point on, Keith would use half-mask techniques in the Devine/Saint-Denis/Copeau-tradition in most of his own plays and in the classroom.

At the beginning of 1958, Keith had found a group of student-like artists he could relate to, create with, and support. Wesker and Arden, like Keith, had not been influenced by the theatre growing up. In college, Arden studied architecture. Wesker, although accepted into RADA, failed to get a grant and ended up working numerous jobs and worked as a trained pastry cook in London and Paris. Pinter, who wasn't a part of the Writer's Group, but assumed to be, did not see or read plays in his youth and did

---

[30] On another night, Devine talked to the group about comic style. When he mentioned Shaw and Congreve, Keith, who detested Shaw, began to constantly interrupt and "destroyed the evening," wrote Jellicoe. "It was interesting that George was depressed rather than angry" (Findlater, *At the Royal* 56).

[31] In *The Thing in the Mirror* (2011), Keith wrote: "George's masks gave us an advantage over anyone starting from scratch, because they'd been tested on generations of students and the less effective ones had been discarded" (40).

not get accepted into a university because he had no Latin (Marowitz 99). Bond, who dropped out of school at 15, was a part of the group because Johnstone invited him in after reading *Klaxon at Atreus Place*, the first play Bond submitted to the Court. Keith didn't like the play, but he knew Bond was a playwright because his characters altered one another.[32] Gaskill, although formally educated at Oxford, was as eager as Keith to discover new approaches to the theatre. And in Jellicoe, Keith found a friend for life, an artistic collaborator, and a lover. For the next 2 years, Jellicoe and Keith were inseparable. They had a lot in common including poor eyesight and large eyeglasses. (Gaskill, *Sense* 26)[33] Keith, who had always felt like a misfit, finally found himself in a creative learning environment that honored the unique talents and processes of each individual. He reminisces, "At the Royal Court, you had a lot of freedom. You could say anything you liked, however crazy, without upsetting people."

Jellicoe's first play, *The Sport of My Mad Mother*, went into rehearsals at around the same time the first Writers' Group meeting took place. At a dress rehearsal, Jellicoe, Jocelyn Herbert (set designer), Gaskill, Devine, Keith, and several others agreed that—in Gaskill's words—"the set looked too pure, too clinical" (*Sense* 32). So Keith drove to Battersea, put a group of children he knew who were out playing in the street into a taxi, and brought them back to the theatre where they proceeded to decorate the set with colored chalk. "Actually, when I think about it now, I really shouldn't do that kind of thing," Keith muses. "I'm kidnapping the kids, I'm not asking their parents. But it made Jocelyn and Ann a bit happier."

The Sport of My Mad Mother was considered the first real unconventional play on the Court's main stage. *Look Back in Anger* was gritty and shocking but still realistic and conventional in structure. *The Sport of My Mad Mother*, on the other hand, combines realism with nonrealism, prose with verse, or what Mark Taylor in *Plays and Players* described as "halting, repetitive word jazz for seven characters." Everyone at the Court, most of all Keith, wanted Jellicoe's play to be understood. Unfortunately, the reviews were poor and the show closed after only 14 performances. But every night a group of writers and directors would stand at the back of the virtually empty house and cheer. "It was the beginning of the embattled community which provided the creative core of the work over the next two years," stated Gaskill (*Sense* 33). Jellicoe's *Sport*, Pinter's *The Birthday Party*, Keith's *Brixham Regatta*, and finally Arden's *Live Like Pigs* were

---

[32] Bond's first two plays, *Klaxon at Atreus Place* and *The Fiery Tree*, were never published or staged at the Court. The first play of Bond's to be staged at the Court was *The Pope's Wedding*. Directed by Keith, it was given a Sunday Night performance on 9 December 1962 (Findlater, *At the Royal* 54).

[33] Gaskill wrote: "For a time they (Johnstone and Jellicoe) were very influenced by Aldous Huxley's *The Art of Seeing* and went round wearing eye patches on alternate eyes" (*Sense* 26).

bashed by the majority of critics in 1958. Keith was enraged but not one to publically raise his voice, so he expressed himself through his writing.

Six writers of the Court wrote short plays for a group of young actors studying Meisner techniques under new associate director Anthony Page to perform as a Sunday Night production on 19 October 1958 ("Rehearsal Group"). Jellicoe directed the last play of the evening, *The Nigger Hunt*, a 20-minute piece by Keith that attacked the critics and brought the audience to their feet. *The Nigger Hunt* characterizes the "critics" as a horrifying giant hunting a black writer. The giant's weapon is a handful of reviews, not a club. The black writer escapes by painting his face white. "[A]n idea Wole Soyinka was to use in his play *The Invention*," wrote Gaskill (*Sense* 40). The critics hated the play but the audience shouted "bravo" and "author." Keith, who Arden referred to as the "unpaid conscience of the Royal Court," gave a small moment of triumph to the writers who had been bruised by the press over the past 8 months (Gaskill, *Sense* 25).

Nine days later, Beckett's *Endgame* with Devine in the role of Hamm opened at the Court on a double bill with *Krapp's Last Tape*. By this time, Keith was known as the Court's expert on Beckett. For the publicity brochure, an essay written by Keith titled "An Approach to End-Game" was included. Examining reviews of Beckett's French-language premier of *Endgame* (*Fin de Partie*) produced at the Court a year earlier and judgments publicly made regarding Beckett's persona, Keith works to resolve "the apparent paradox between Beckett the man and Beckett the writer" (1):

> Beckett doesn't approve of his characters' actions; if he does the play becomes nonsense. The play assumes the humanity of its audience, and outrages it systematically, but Beckett shares the outrage. It is this which produces the compassion and the tragic irony of Beckett's "End-Game". The real paradox of the play is that by stating an absolute pessimism it projects its opposite. It is an enormous protest against the sad conditions of this world. Beckett's irony demands compassion from his audience. (3)

Endgame was originally scheduled to open after *The Sport of My Mad Mother*, but the Lord Chamberlain refused a license for public performance even though he had licensed the play previously in its French version. For 6 months, the Court and Beckett fought the Lord Chamberlain over Hamm's reference to God which cast doubt on Christ's parentage: "The bastard! He doesn't exist!" (Findlater, *At the Royal* 47). Like so many, Keith was bewildered by the ludicrous actions of the censor and he refers to this moment in time as "the death of censorship" because "the whole thing was crumbling." Even so, it would take another 10 years for the Theatres Act of 1968 to eradicate stage censorship completely. Meanwhile, fighting with the Lord Chamberlain, with the critics, and actively taking part in sociopolitical events became daily occurrences in 1959 and into the tumultuous 1960s for the writers and directors of the Court. As Gaskill said, "We were an embattled theatre" (Doty 58).

Eleven Men Dead at Hola Camp—*An improvised dramatic protest*

On 3 March 1959, 11 detainees were beaten to death at Hola Camp, a colonial prison camp established in Hola, Kenya, during the Mau Mau anticolonial guerilla campaign. On 19 July 1959, Gaskill and Keith staged a devised, largely improvised Sunday Night production based on this event. It was a risky undertaking on several fronts. The Lord Chamberlain did not allow unscripted, improvised public performances in England. Furthermore, restrictions on the reporting of current events that had not yet been debated in Parliament prompted the RCT Council to insist on contacting Sir Gerald Gardiner, a leading member of the Queen's Counsel. So Gaskill and Keith went to see him. "He had really nice old furniture," remembers Keith, "and one ancient chair I sat on collapsed under me. He was quite nice about it." Gardiner essentially told Gaskill and Keith that, if they were sued, they would have no defense even if they were telling the truth, because all potential witnesses were held up in a jail in Kenya. Despite Gardiner's advice, the RCT Council allowed the show to go on but disassociated itself entirely. During the performance, founding Secretary Greville Poke was sent by Neville Blond—chairman of the board of directors—around to the side of the dress circle and clapped for silence. He announced to the audience that the board of directors would have nothing to do with what was happening on the stage. "We had never done anything as positively political as this before, nor had the Court, and the Council were shit-scared," wrote Gaskill (*Sense* 37). Soon after Poke's statement, an actor yelled out something bordering on, "If you think we worked hard on this for two weeks just for some aesthetic reason, if you think this was not a political statement, you're out of your mind!" Then the play was abandoned and it became a wild, heated discussion between the audience and the black actors. "It raged," says Keith. "That's when the audience really started becoming a volcano. I got called Bwana Johnstone by Christopher Logue after that." After listening to the taped recording of the entire evening, Devine told Keith it was the first time he heard an audience so vociferous in the theatre.

Eleven Men Dead at Hola Camp evolved in part because of the improvisational processes being explored in the Writers' Group. They had been improvising scenes for over a year and, therefore, an improvised/devised performance in front of a live audience seemed like a plausible next step. A press release called the upcoming event "an experiment in a new form of theatre." A short outline of what to expect from the performance followed: "There is no script but there will be a man in charge of the facts to say what actually happened, and the improvisations will be linked by dramatised excerpts from the Inquiry and songs by Royal Court writers written for the occasion" (English Stage).[34] Ten black actors including Soyinka and Bloke Modisane, a celebrated South African actor/writer/journalist who had just fled to England, made up most of the ensemble. A young Nigel Davenport served as the "man in charge" reading actual excerpts from the House of Commons debates (i.e., Hansard).

Gaskill remembered the performance itself as "a strange mixture of inadequate improvisation, political passion, beautiful songs by Wole Soyinka, and tremendous audience response. It was way ahead of its time and came out of our group commitment" (*Sense* 38). Keith describes it as a "bizarre disaster" that was "remarkable for the attempt" and he clearly remembers the volcanic audience who was "so sympathetic they pushed everything towards comedy." Critics, for the most part, were also sympathetic although many did not know what to make of this new form of "documentary-dramatic improvisation," as Cecil Wilson of the *Daily Mail* branded it. A language had not been invented to describe devised performances based on political events.[35] And some were not so keen on accepting improvisation, which had been used primarily in training up to this point, as a viable performance mode in and of itself. "Actors are actors, not dramatists. Words don't, apparently, come easily to them," wrote A. Alvarez, a critic for *The New Statesmen*. Alvarez characterized all of the black actors, except for Soyinka, as "self-conscious, subdued, overguarded in their reactions and prone to the giggles." That Soyinka's improvised performance stood out is a testament to his 1-year experience with the Writers' Group.

In concurrence with Alvarez, about half of the press used definitive phrases and words like "tended toward monotony," "unendurable boredom," "an embarrassment," and "fallacious" to describe the evening. The other half, however, found the evening meaningful. Wilson wrote: "The whole performance proved that, given a strong ready-made theme, any cast of born actors (which all coloured actors seem to be) can manage very well without a playwright." Writing for the *News Chronicle*, Alan Dent thought the actors performed "as easily as children in a game of make-believe." Notwithstanding the colonialistic connotations, these critical responses indicated that something wonderful had taken place—a mostly improvised performance engaged an RCT audience for three hours. "The only time the evening sagged," declared Wilson, "was when the two

[34] The announcement ended with an apology for sending a different type of notice due to a printing strike.
[35] Although Joan Littlewood and her Theatre Workshop's *Oh! What a Lovely War* (1963) and Peter Brook's *US* at RSC (1966) would soon bring this kind of devised political theatre to the fore in London.

white producers [Johnstone and Gaskill] broke into the action with fussy marginal comments." Elizabeth Young, writing for *The Tribune*, did not depict the performance as "successful" but did not consider it a waste of time either. The concluding sentence of her review expressed a desire undoubtedly shared by the directors and cast members: "I hope the E.S.S. [English Stage Society] will carry on experimenting with this awkward but potentially very effective form."

In his essay "Improvisation and All That Jazz" published in *Plays and Players* in 1965, Keith wrote: "The main lesson of the Hola fiasco was that improvisation is a highly specialised skill, only to be attempted by a group who have practised together, and have a common technique." A common technique and this type of group would eventually emerge out of the work of the RCT Studio (1963–66) and it was this so-called "fiasco" that had planted the seed. With *Hola Camp*, Keith had witnessed an audience engaged like never before in a theatrical event devised in less than 2 weeks. He had discovered the value of a no-discussion policy, of putting an idea on its feet, and of spontaneous creation. Most notably, *Hola Camp* had an impact because the subject matter was timely for that particular audience. "Audience participation is an essential part of the structure. Without it the evening would not have been complete," wrote Gaskill and Keith in their follow-up report. Moving into the 1960s, a time when more and more theatre artists began to experiment with forms they found interesting in spite of audiences, Keith made his decisions based on his uncompromising belief: the real knowledge is in the audience.

Johnstone as a Royal Court Theatre director

In 1960, the Writers' Group met less regularly and then stopped meeting altogether. "There were attempts to revive it," wrote Jellicoe, "but they never took. The need had passed" (Findlater, *At the Royal* 56). The idea that education was important to the development of the theatre, however, was not forgotten by Devine and, in his 1960 Memorandum to the Council, he proposed a studio for training playwrights, actors, directors, designers, and composers (Roberts, *RCT 1965* 9). Meanwhile, Keith continued to run the script department and worked primarily as a director, not a writer, of the Court. Indeed, he did not write another play until 1965. Perhaps because Keith started out as a playwright, as a director he was never partnered with one particular playwright as was customary at the Court (e.g., Richardson with Osborne, Gaskill with N. F. Simpson, Dexter with Wesker). From 1960 to 1965, Keith directed nine plays by eight different authors, two by Kon Fraser and one by each of the following: Bartho Smit, J.A. Cuddon, Jellicoe, Frank Hilton, Edward Bond, Leonard Kingston, and Simpson. Out of the nine plays, only three were produced as part of the main stage season: Ann Jellicoe's *The Knack* in 1962, Frank Hilton's *Day of the Prince* in 1963, and

Simpson's *The Cresta Run* in 1965. The other six were given only Sunday Night productions without décor.[36]

A Johnstone-Bond pairing would have been plausible. After all, it was Keith who first spotted Bond's plays coming into the script department, and it was Keith who invited Bond to join the Writers' Group. Irving Wardle called Bond a "pupil" of Keith's in the introduction to *Impro*. Keith reluctantly admits he may have had some influence on Bond but, he says, "I think Edward would have been Edward anyway." Keith's direction of Bond's first play, *The Pope's Wedding*, produced at RCT in 1962, did garner critical attention, good and bad, even though it only received a Sunday Night production. In 1965, Keith was slated to direct Bond's *Saved*, now famed as the play instrumental in bringing theatre censorship laws to an end, but he passed on this opportunity. He calls the infamous stoning-of-the-baby scene by a group of 18-year-olds on welfare, "crap." Apparently, Bond had based this scene on a real incident involving a group of 10-year-olds, not 18-year-olds, and Keith found Bond's alteration of the events deceptive. Ultimately, Gaskill, who had been slated to direct Simpson's *The Cresta Run*, took *Saved* and Keith took the Simpson play (Roberts, *RCT Modern* 109). "*Saved* is much better," Keith says, "but I didn't believe in the stoning scene." Gaskill was able to accept Bond's artistic license but not Keith. "The Royal Court was never a commercial theatre, but it had to make compromises and Keith was essentially a non-compromising person," said Gaskill (*World*). Keith's dedication was and is to integrity, not to what is marketable, cultural, or even controversial. It is a quality that makes him a brilliant teacher but also one that casts him as a misfit or as a lone wolf lurking just outside of the mainstream. Thus, the Johnstone-Bond pairing was not to be.

Court politics

Wesker's *The Kitchen* and Osborne's *Luther* (starring Albert Finney) were the two biggest box-office successes at the Court in July and August of 1961. Both playwrights were also members of the Committee of 100, an antiwar and nuclear armament resistance group. While planning a sit-down protest, Wesker and half of the Committee members were arrested. In response, Keith and almost all of the RCT artists joined the "Ban the Bomb" demonstration in Trafalgar Square on September 17. Hundreds were arrested and jailed overnight including Osborne, Gaskill, Anderson, and

---

[36] Fraser's *Eleven Plus* (1960); Smit's *The Maimed* (1960); Cuddon's *The Triple Alliance* (1961); Fraser's *Sacred Cow* (1962); Hilton's *Day of the Prince* (1962); Bond's *The Pope's Wedding* (1962); Kingston's *Edgware Road Blues* (1963) which transferred as *Travelling Light* to Prince of Wales Theatre in 1964 where 22-year-old Michael Crawford joined the cast (Findlater, *At the Royal* "Appendix I").

Page (Gaskill, *Sense* 39). The close bond shared by those within the Writers' Group extended to all members of the RCT community when individual freedoms were compromised in any shape or form.[37]

On the political home front, Devine was finding it difficult to execute the goals he had set for his company (i.e., to establish a training center, a permanent ensemble, to reach a wider audience, and to acquire additional theatre space). In order to secure a larger space, a scheme to merge the Old Vic with the English Stage Company for 3 years under Devine's artistic direction was proposed. Unfortunately, due to financial strain on both sides and to the developing plans for a National Theatre which would involve the Old Vic, the scheme was abandoned. To reach a wider audience, a joint venture between the Court and a regional repertory company based at Cambridge Arts Theatre was initiated, but it lasted only 2 months.

To make matters worse, two of Devine's competitors were having success with exactly those goals he had proposed. The Shakespeare Memorial Theatre in Stratford-upon-Avon became the Royal Shakespeare Company in 1961, and artistic director Peter Hall invited Saint-Denis and Peter Brook to form a directorate for the newly permanent ensemble of actors. Hall had leased the Aldwych Theatre in London a few years prior and was now looking to hire RCT talent for both Stratford and London productions.[38] Furthermore, Joan Littlewood's eclectic company Theatre Workshop founded the East 15 Acting School to provide versatile, physical, and improvisational training to actors. Training that was in direct opposition to what Littlewood called "the tennis club, cup-and-saucer, French-window stuff" taught at RADA (Holdsworth 45). In spite of the RCT's successes in 1961, none of Devine's goals were realized. Conceivably as a consequence, he had a nervous breakdown in the fall and took a 3-month leave of absence. Devine's health would continue to decline over the next 4 years which meant major changes for everyone at the Court.

The Knack

One is born with an intuition as to how to get women.
But this feeling can be developed with experience and confidence,
in certain people, Colin, to some degree. A man can develop the knack.

TOLEN (48)

---

[37] Wesker said in a 1966 interview: "We were all of us somehow absorbing the same kind of atmosphere, the war had been a formative part of our lives, followed by the hope of 1945, and the general decline from then on. So that we were the generation at the end of that decline, desperately wanting to find something, being tired of the pessimism and the mediocrity, and all the energy that was spent on being anti-Soviet and anti-Communist" (Marowitz 83).

[38] E.g., Gaskill directed and Jocelyn Herbert designed *Richard III* in May starring Christopher Plummer and Dame Edith Evans.

The "knack" is sexual magnetism or the "trick" of getting a girl. Tolen, an arrogant, well-sculpted, Casanova-type musician, apparently has the knack.[39] Colin, an insecure, ineffectual, and inept teacher, desperately wants it. And Tom, a self-assured, garrulous but lucid thinker and artist, is content with or without it. When Nancy, a naive 17-year-old girl from the North Country looking for the YWCA, wanders into the shabby London house shared by these men, the game is on. Tolen is determined to show Colin the art of seduction but is constantly frustrated by Tom who also wants Colin to get the girl but with integrity. *The Knack*, a three-act comedy about sex and domination, takes place in Tom's mostly unfurnished room on the ground floor.

In October of 1961, Jellicoe's *The Knack*, directed by Keith, had its successful premier at the Cambridge Arts Theatre and then opened on the Court's main stage in March of 1962 and ran for 23 performances.[40] One afternoon, the Court's stage manager delivered a message to Keith's place and was stunned to find his room to be an exact replica of Tom's room. "She kind of had a semi-nervous breakdown because suddenly reality wasn't reality anymore," remembers Keith. For about 2 years, Keith had been renting a room in photographer Roger Mayne's home on Addison Avenue in Holland Park. Around 1958, famed editor Diana Athill from André Deutsch Publishing had introduced the two men in hopes they would collaborate on a project about children in primary school (Mayne). Mayne ended up photographing Jellicoe's production of *The Sport of My Mad Mother* and the three of them—Mayne, Jellicoe, and Keith—have remained friends ever since. Jellicoe was also living in Mayne's Holland Park home when Keith was there because she and Mayne were dating. They would marry the following year and are still married today. Jellicoe wrote most of *The Knack*, however, during her 2-year affair with Keith and the character of Tom is essentially him.

During the writing phase, Keith recalls that Jellicoe, on occasion, asked questions like, "What would Tom say in this bit?" and then she'd jot down Keith's responses. Tom's weird jokes, his eccentricities, and almost all of his anecdotes are Keith-like. In the first act, for example, Tom recommends a piano game—like one Keith invented for a small group of boys at a school in North Kensington—to Colin, who is having trouble teaching young students about music.[41]

---

[39] According to Keith, Jellicoe modeled the character of Tolen after a weight lifter who took dance lessons at Arthur Murray Studios, was a friend of Dali, and would never sit in a "low-status" chair (S.F. Wksp 2009).

[40] Johnstone and Jellicoe are listed as codirectors for the main stage production even though Johnstone is listed as the sole director for the premier tour which opened at Cambridge Arts Center, then went to the Theatre Royal Bath, and finally to the New Theatre in Cardiff.

[41] Keith was hired by this primary school in North Kensington to teach a film class 2 days a week to 8-year-olds. Keith had no budget so he purchased cheap white leader film, soaked it

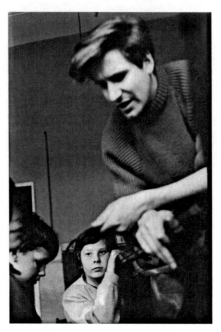

Keith playing his piano game with school children in North Kensington, London.
Photo Credit: Roger Mayne.

Assuming a Johnstonian pedagogy, Tom proceeds:

> TOM. You get the piano and you get the kids and you say it's a game
> see? "Right," you say, "You've not to look at the keys, 'cos that's
> cheating."
> COLIN. Not look –
> TOM. If they look at each other playing, they'll just copy each other.
> Now, don't put your own brain between them and the direct
> experience. Don't intellectualize. Let them come right up against it.
> And don't talk about music, talk about noise.
> COLIN. Noi –
> TOM. What else is music but an arrangement of noises? I'm serious.
> "Now," you say, "one of you come out here and make noises on the

---

in water (which softened the emulsion), and had the students use compass points to scratch
dots, then circles, into each frame. Then he'd run the film through the projector to show the
kids how the dot or circle could move across the screen and back. Then the dots and circles
became fishes and different colors of paint were rubbed into the notches. Eventually, using
this layered technique, the students created a film about a school of fish swimming to and
fro, being eaten by bigger fish, and so forth, and the British Film Institute awarded this film
with a special prize.

piano." And finally one of them will come out and sort of hit the keys, bang, bang. "Right," you say, "now someone come out and make the same noise."

COLIN. Eh?

TOM. The same noise. That's the first step. They'll have to *listen* to see they hit in the same place – and they can do it more or less 'cos they can sort of – you know – clout it in the middle bit. So next you get them all going round the piano in a circle, all making the same noise, and they'll love that. When they get a bit cheesed, you develop it. "OK," you say, "let's have another noise."

COLIN. I don't see the point, I mean—

TOM. Now listen, this way they'll find out for themselves, give them a direct experience and they'll discover for themselves—all the basic principles of music and they won't shy away—they won't think of it as culture, it'll be pop to them. Listen! You, goon, moron, you don't like Bartok, do you?

COLIN. No.

TOM. Don't be so pleased with yourself. You don't understand it, your ear's full of Bach, it stops at Mahler. But after a few lessons like this, you play those kids Schoenberg, you play them Bartok. They'll know what he's doing. I bet they will! It'll be rock'n roll to them. My God, I ought to be a teacher! My God, I'm a genius! (43–4)

"Don't intellectualize. Don't get too pleased with yourself. Experience it. Don't call it culture"—these are statements Keith still uses regularly in his international workshops. Furthermore, Keith, like Tom, was a fan of Hungarian composer Béla Bartók, whose driving rhythms and unique tonal and polytonal melodies, inspired by European folk music, often twist in unanticipated directions assuming an improvisational feel (Machlis 188–91).

Harold Hobson, drama critic for the *Sunday Times*, thought the character of Tom was "as near to a portrait of a good man as you are likely to get in modern drama," and he found his "repeated fluking" to be "one of the play's most legitimate satisfactions." Tom, in fact, provides most of the comic relief in the play. R.B. Marriott, critic for *The Stage*, found the play lacking in conviction but comically effective when Tom, "the best realized and most naturally-drawn character," skips about, perches on a ladder, "and delivers speeches that are a blend of youthful psychology, philosophy, and biology." If Tom's banter is funny and engaging then perhaps we can assume Keith was funny and engaging as well. In any case, the response to the character of Tom was gratifying for Keith.

Overall, the reviews for the London production on the Court's main stage were positive. To describe the directing, critics used expressions like "effectively restless," "a cunning, breezy job," and staged "with a persuasively lilting rhythm." Hobson thought the performances by Rita Tushingham, Julian Glover, James Bolan, and Philip Locke were "unexaggerated and exact."[42] Felix Barker, of the *Evening News*, described the performances as "perfectly judged." T.C. Worsley, in his review for the *Financial Times*, summed up the entire experience as "a rum evening— odd, interesting, bawdy, tantalizing and exasperating."

Wolsey's last word, "exasperating," likely referred to the third act. W.A. Darlington, of the *Daily Telegraph*, called this act "feeble" and one that "doesn't amount to anything but a rough-and-tumble, at the end of which Colin seems to be going to get his taste of experience, if anybody cares." About halfway into the third act, Nancy, who has just recovered from a fainting spell, threatens the three men with rape unless one of them actually agrees to rape her. She proceeds to shout and chant "rape" as the scene spirals out of control. Keith admits this act was/is problematic. "When we went into rehearsals, we did change things. I took the end of the third act and put it at the beginning and told Ann to write the rest of the third act which she did. But it was still weak." Jellicoe began writing the third act when her 2-year affair with Keith broke up, and her raw emotional desperation can be seen through the character of Nancy. But not everyone disliked the third act. "Miss Tushingham's yelping taunts in the third act, and her enraptured faint in the second bite into the senses. Nobody should miss them, provided his senses are the right senses," concluded Hobson.

Likely influenced by Keith's directorial process and from her experience with the Writers' Group, Jellicoe suggests using an improvisational approach in several places in the published script. For example, immediately following the playing-the-bed-as-a-piano scene, a scene which came directly from a Writers' Group improvisation, Jellicoe wrote: "All of the above could be arranged or improvised to suit different actors and different productions provided the sequence of events is clear" (54). Mark Taylor, in his review for *Plays and Players*, found this piano bed scene, in particular, to be "one of the funniest as well as one of the most moving on the London stage." Clearly, the application of improvisation to playwriting worked. In addition, James Bolan, who played Tom, had his own improvisational moment of genius when part of the set collapsed on him during a performance. Directly to the audience Bolan cried, "What a household!" and while the audience laughed, the set was repaired (Johnstone, *Newsletter Five* 2).

The Knack enjoyed further success after its run at the Court. In 1964, Mike Nichols directed the play off-Broadway as the opening production of the New Theatre in New York City.[43] In 1965, the film version, directed by Richard Lester, premiered in a music video-style similar to Lester's other popular films—*A Hard Day's Night* (1964) and *Help!* (1965). The film

---

[42] Tushingham was the only member of the London cast that was also in the Cambridge cast. She played Nancy again in the 1965 film version, *The Knack . . . and How to Get It*. While working on *The Knack* at RCT, her debut film performance in Shelagh Delaney's *A Taste of Honey* (1961), directed by Tony Richardson, was garnering accolades.

[43] George Segal, Brian Bedford, and Roddy Maude-Roxby were in this production.

"Piano bed" scene from The Knack *with James Bolam* (left),
Philip Locke, and Rita Tushingham.

Photo Credit: Photo by Roger Mayne © V&A Images/Victoria and Albert Museum.

starred Tushingham and Michael Crawford as Colin and won the *Palme d'Or* at the Cannes Film Festival. When *The Knack* was revived at the Court in February of 1966, Jellicoe wanted someone like Keith to direct, but Gaskill wanted a fresh eye and hired Desmond O'Donovan.[44] "It was a dreadful production," wrote Jellicoe. "*The Knack* is very easy to mistime" (*The Knack* 16). Keith had an instinctive sense of comedic timing but, until *The Knack*, he had only directed tragicomedies as Sunday Night productions without décor. After *The Knack*, though, Keith would have the opportunity to explore and develop his instincts at the RCT Studio.

---

[44] O'Donovan was Gaskill's lover at the time and Gaskill replaced Keith and Iain Cuthbertson, his associate directors, with O'Donovan at the end of the 1966 season. Gaskill calls his decision a mistake because of their emotional ties, but O'Donovan did have previous successes at the Court and at the National Theatre (*Sense* 75).

CHAPTER THREE

All the world is a classroom

If you can find the door, go through it, everything will become effortless.
For me, I have to be shoved through.

KEITH JOHNSTONE

Once Keith is shoved through the door, he does not retreat. He pushes aside the inner critic, steps into the unknown terror, and allows the imagination to go to work. Discussed in this chapter are two of Keith's most successful plays—*Moby Dick: A Sir and Perkins Story* and *The Last Bird*. Out of necessity, both were written in less than a week. When Keith needs to write something or structure a performance in a limited amount of time, and when he cares passionately about the people involved or for the topic, he often does his best work. The urgency prohibits the inner censor, that thing that turns Keith into "a pillar of salt over and over again," from looking back (London Wksp). Instead of constantly rechecking and revising his work, deadlines force Keith to trust his spontaneous instincts. Knowing this, he deliberately places himself into time-sensitive creative circumstances, but he did not place himself into a teaching position at the RCT Studio. Devine shoved him through that door, and Keith had no time to look back or forward from 1963 to 1966. He only had time to find solutions in the moment and, accordingly, developed his own system. Keith may have begun his tenure at the Studio as the greenest teacher, but he emerged as a celebrated teacher, director, and innovator of impro.

This third chapter begins with the Studio years which are also the last 3 years of Keith's tenure at RCT. Once Keith surrendered to the profession that had pursued him, he had to move on because teachers were no longer needed at the Court. But he took with him four exceptional improvisers who become known as The Theatre Machine. Next, this chapter navigates from Keith's first semester teaching at RADA in the fall of 1966 to the summer of 1971 when he leaves RADA, the Theatre Machine, and the United Kingdom for more secure employment in Canada. Touring with Theatre Machine during this period introduced Keith to classrooms and audiences beyond Britain and, consequently, he was invited to teach in British Columbia, Denmark, and for theatre pioneer, Eugenio Barba. Above all, as the artistic director of Theatre Machine, Keith learned to take charge under difficult and diverse circumstances and to trust his instincts. Anne Bogart, the celebrated theatre director and founder of SITI Company, wrote in her 1995 essay titled "Terror, Disorientation and Difficulty":

> Directing is about feeling, about being in the room with other people . . . about having a feel for time and space, about breathing and responding fully to the situation at hand, being able to plunge and encourage a plunge into the unknown at the right moment. (9)

By the summer of 1971, Keith had taken the plunge thousands of times as a director and a teacher and was ready to respond to whatever Canada had to offer.

The Royal Court Theatre Studio

Open to all members of the profession.

("THREE LESSONS")

Devine's dream of establishing a training studio for professional theatre artists was about to come true. Jocelyn Herbert, a designer at the Court (and Devine's longtime lover), discovered that the Jeanetta Cochrane Theatre in Kingsway, which had just been built by the Central School of Arts and Crafts, was available to the Court for free.[1] So in the winter of 1963, the first 8-week term of the RCT Studio commenced (Browne 46). About 30 professional theatre artists, mostly actors, from several major theatres took part and were charged only 2 shillings and a sixpence for the entire course. Unlike training centers attached to specific companies, the RCT Studio was the first professional acting studio in England for all union members. The goals of the first term were to explore and research the nature of comic improvisation and especially the nature of improvising in public (Findlater,

---

[1] According to Keith, the studio space was available because Princess Margaret had a cold! "The day she was to open the theatre, she stayed in bed with a chill or with one of those guardsmen," says Keith. So, until the Princess could reschedule, the theatre could not be officially opened.

At the Royal 72). Gaskill served as director for the first term and taught comic improvisation, comic mask, and "the epic narrative," a class using Brechtian techniques. Claude Chagrin taught mime. Devine taught "comic tricks" which included things like pratfalls and double-takes (Browne 46).[2] Finally, Keith, who didn't know a thing about training professional actors, decided to teach a class called "Narrative Skills."

"I started with 'Narrative Skills' because I hoped I knew more about them than the actors did," says Keith. In the beginning, he utilized a few Stanislavski exercises but he did not work from a textbook. "I got to try things out. I had to do it on my own" (Calgary Wksp 2011). Keith may have had no formal theatre training but, for 7 years, he had closely observed actors, directors, and writers in process at the Court. He had not written a play since *Brixham Regatta*, but he had read thousands of scripts as head of the script department. Keith's 2-year stint at Wix's Lane was his only formal, full-time teaching experience, but he had spent his entire life watching and analyzing teachers. Plus he had read books on everything, including Wolpe's recently published findings in the *American Journal of Psychiatry* on "systematic desensitization of phobias," and had been obsessed with silent cinema comedy for years. It is no wonder Keith posted a list of "Things My Teachers Stopped Me From Doing" on the first day of class and used it as a syllabus. Over the next 3 years, Keith combined his life experiences with his imagination and his intellect to create his own improvisational system for training actors, directors, and playwrights. The RCT Studio was, in a sense, Keith's research laboratory where he took the complexity of human behavior, broke it down to its independent variables, and then created simple formulas that would spontaneously re-create human behavior on the stage.

As Keith had done with the Writers' Group, he implemented a no-discussion policy in his "Narrative Skills" class. Then he consulted his "Things My Teachers Stopped Me From Doing" list and began to create exercises, games, and techniques that would allow students to experience exactly those prohibited things. "Making faces" was at the top of the list, so Keith created a series of "making faces" games, mostly involving masters and servants, which trained actors to really "see the other person" and not just "assume" them. His teachers made him concentrate on one thing at a time, thus he developed split-attention games. He shouted "be more obvious" because his teachers always rewarded "originality" (*Storytellers* XI–XII). He used and developed basic clowning exercises, introduced to him by Gaskill, to get students to clown around, to be foolish and immature, instead of intellectual and responsible. In fact, most of the games, techniques, and exercises found in Keith's *Impro* were developed at the RCT Studio.

---

[2] Keith remembers Devine always wanting to write a book called *Angels and Scram* which would catalogue all of the gags in silent film (S.F. Wksp 2009).

On 28 April 1963, the Studio demonstrated mime, clowning, and comic improvisations on a Sunday night and called the performance *First Results*. Keith considered this public demonstration premature. Like *Hola Camp*, "[T]he improvisation suffered from the pressure of the audience," he wrote ("Improvisation and All" 14). Nonetheless, the dramatic critic for *The Times* described the event as "visual" and found the comic mask work, directed by Gaskill, most entertaining: "What emerged in the end [of the mask session] was a collection of characters who seemed to have escaped from the Beatrix Potter books" ("Three Lessons"). The work of this first experimental term garnered attention, and the RCT Studio was awarded a 3-year yearly grant of £2500 from the Calouste Gulbenkian Trust, which meant teachers could be paid. It was also decided that the National Theatre would run in conjunction with and contribute a payment to the Studio's operational fund.[3]

During the Studio's first spring term, Keith directed Frank Hilton's modern farce, *Day of the Prince*, for the main stage season.[4] The generally positive reviews indicated he was putting comedic techniques, explored in the Studio, to use. The play is set in the suburban home of the eccentric Pringle family. Mum (Angela Baddeley) is the domineering matriarch. The eldest son, Bert (Bernard Bresslaw), a physically enormous moron and mamma's boy, is building a fall-out shelter under the kitchen. Seventeen-year-old Virginia (Pauline Boty), the beautiful blond virgin, is just waiting for her prince to arrive. A browbeaten Dad, a genius younger son, and an older spinster daughter complete this oddball family of characters.[5] When Virginia's black, educated Jamaican Prince arrives to take her away, the Pringle family senses there is something wrong with him but cannot put their finger on it. They subject the Prince to a trial and disqualify him as a potential suitor not because of his skin color (which is never mentioned), but because he bites his fingernails.

"The piece is perfectly cast and acted under Keith Johnstone's direction with all the high seriousness that farce demands," wrote T. C. Worsley. "It is–NUTS," claimed Arthur Thirkell for the *Daily Mirror*. R. B. Marriot found Keith's direction imaginative and subtle, and W. A. Darlington found the slapstick sequence in the final moments of the play "fun" although

---

[3] This partnership proved unrealistic. The inflexible schedules of the actors in the National's permanent repertory company made it difficult for them to attend classes on a regular basis (Browne 47).

[4] Keith also directed *Day of the Prince* as a Sunday Night production on 16 September 1962.

[5] Baddeley played Mrs. Bridges in *Upstairs, Downstairs*. Bresslaw was a regular in the *Carry On* series of British comedy films. Boty was a notable painter in/founder of the British pop art movement.

Hilton's writing unoriginal and stylistically incongruous. Denis Blewett of the *Daily Telegraph* tendered, "[I]t must be a long time since the rafters in this earnest auditorium rattled to such a gust of lowdown laughter." Lastly, Mr Julian Hall, a patron of the Court, wrote a thank you letter to the cast and crew for an enjoyable evening:

> It [the performance] made me feel that I was not merely a 'customer', being 'served' by the cast as a matter of routine, as I have felt on my most recent visits to theatres in the West End. Last night at the Royal Court, the play seemed to be being done for my pleasure and for that of the audience generally, by a cast for whom it was a pleasure to do this play. I came away refreshed, and convinced that there is an alternative to the boredom which most theatre-going has afforded lately. (Shaw)

Keith obviously directed his actors to include the audience and, most importantly, to have a good time—two integral components of what was developing into Johnstone's Impro System.

In the fall of 1963, the RCT Studio reopened under Keith's direction. Even before the Studio's first term, Gaskill had been summoned to join Laurence Olivier and John Dexter in starting the National Theatre at the Old Vic.[6] Gaskill eventually accepted Olivier's offer but continued to teach at the Studio on occasion. During the 1963/1964 season, Keith supervised and planned four 8-week terms at the Studio and continued to teach. He also took over Gaskill's mask classes using Devine's cherished collection of half-masks.

Devine, who viewed masks primarily as a device for training, would use full-length mirrors for the students to study their newly masked selves. Keith, on the other hand, wanted the masked characters to be able to improvise in public, so he began to adapt the technique accordingly. For example, he began using handheld mirrors which allowed the masks to "turn themselves on" from any part of the stage. When Devine found out Keith was changing the "sacred" technique, he took over the mask classes and gave his comedy classes to Keith. After a few weeks, however, Devine discovered that the students who had worked with masks under Gaskill and Keith were having more success than the others, so Devine handed back the torch. "From then on I taught the half-Mask classes, and the comedy classes," wrote Keith (*Thing* 46–8).

By the fall of 1964, Keith had added several notable teachers to his staff: Swedish dancer/mime Yat Malmgren, a leading authority on stage

---

[6]   Olivier's first choice was Devine but Devine did not want to be second in command (Gaskill, *Sense* 54).

movement; Doreen Cannon, a Stanislavsky-technique practitioner who trained under Uta Hagen in New York City and created and ran the acting department at the Drama Centre, London; and Marc Wilkinson, composer and Director of Music at the National. Also, Keith put into place a student selection process. He told Frank Cox in an interview for *Plays and Players* December 1964 issue:

> I just can't hope to keep a staff such as this if the students themselves aren't keen. So conditions here are arduous, hell sometimes, to weed out the people who won't want to work. We invite prospective students to come and watch what we're doing, and then I grill them at an interview, and if they still want to join after that [. . .]! (9)

Once students made the cut, Keith advised them to "come and go according to their own needs" (9).

The Studio's work was chiefly concerned with acting techniques that relied on spontaneity and imagination. It was an anti-literary approach. "We're trying to give them [the students] freedom, to make them childish, to play games, to do strange, weird things—like working with the masks . . . it can be alarming," said Keith (9). His "Narrative Skills" classes were now divided into two classes, "Spontaneity" and "Status." He had been trying for some time to find ways of re-creating casual behavior and conversation spontaneously on the stage. Behavior he had observed among people at bus stops and between students taking a coffee break. He tried using various scenarios but nothing seemed to work. Then, in May of 1964, he attended the Moscow Art Theatre's production of *The Cherry Orchard*, presented at the Aldwych Theatre as part of the first World Theatre Season annual festival of foreign plays, and something clicked. "Everyone on stage seemed to have chosen the *strongest* possible motives for each action . . . ," wrote Keith in his chapter on status in *Impro*. "The effect was 'theatrical' but not like life as I knew it. I asked myself for the first time what were the *weakest* possible motives . . . .When I returned to the studio I set the first of my status exercises" (33).

Keith began by getting the students to attain a status position just a fraction above or below their partners. "The actors seemed to know exactly what I meant and the work was transformed" (33).[7] Going forward, he developed a range of status techniques, exercises, and games. As pointed out in Chapter 1, Keith's work on status has had a profound effect on

---

[7] When the students began to exaggerate the status just to get laughs, Keith ceased all status work for a few months. Then he asked students to "match status," i.e., try to stay at the same status level as their scene partner, and this adjustment allowed students, once again, to see how "status" could be applied to create truthful, subtle acting (S. F. Wksp 2009; Calgary Wksp 2011).

drama training worldwide and is one of the most important components of the Impro System. "Status was everywhere. It's what theatre is all about," says Keith. "Chaplin and Keaton had a very good understanding of it. Shakespeare understood it. Everybody understands it. It's intuitive. I don't know why anyone didn't put it into practice before."

In Keith's comedy classes, comic improvisation and clowning techniques continued to be explored and developed. "Comic improvisation does not necessarily imply an imitation of the old Italian comedy," Keith pointed out in his essay, "Improvisation and All That Jazz." He continued:

> [O]ther examples of comic improvisation as an art rather than an exercise can be found in certain wrestling bouts (wrestling matches providing our only surviving example of a popular improvised theatre), and in the tradition of the silent film. But I can say now that in trying to establish public improvisation one is looking for something very old rather than trying to find something new. One is also inevitably trying to re-establish a *popular* art; improvisation without great audience *rapport* must always be inferior to good and well acted text. (14)

Keith's goal was to take improvisation out of the theatre classroom, into the public classroom, and to make it a popular theatre form. The success of professional wrestling in England, a theatricalized "sport" (that would later inspire Theatresports), indicated that his goal was feasible.[8] The next logical step was to develop skills and techniques that would create "great audience rapport." Needing audiences to improvise with but averse to putting up another premature Sunday night showcase, Keith launched his "public classes."

The public classes gave students the right to fail in front of an audience. Improvised shows were still illegal in London but the censor left Keith's public classes—also called "demonstrations"—alone. "In this relaxed semi-class atmosphere it was possible to do good work in public," Keith alleged ("Improvisation and All" 14). Devine, who stood by his writers and truly gave them the right to fail, had established Sunday Nights without décor for similar purposes—to give playwrights and their directors a chance to show their work without the pressure or costs affiliated with a full-scale production. When Keith said, "I don't think you've got the right to fail unless you care very much about the thing that's failing," he was vocalizing a belief Devine had put into practice (Gaskill, "Three" 11). Keith was carrying forward Devine's legacy in more ways than one.

---

8 Gaskill and Dexter shared Keith's interest in wrestling: "We fantasized about replacing wrestlers with improvisers," Keith wrote in *Impro for Storytellers*. "An 'impossible dream' since every word and gesture on the public stage had to be okayed by the Lord Chamberlain" (1).

For the first public class/demonstration, Keith took more than 20 Studio students to a contemporary theatre appreciation class he was teaching at Morley College in the Waterloo District of London. Keith would start out by saying something like: "We're going to demonstrate the techniques we're using at the Studio." He consciously avoided using the word "comedy" because he wanted audiences to respond organically, and they did, that is, after the student improvisers got over their initial stage fright. When the work got as good as it had been in the safety of the Studio, then audiences "laughed far more than we would've done," says Keith. Encouraged by audiences' responses, he wrote to six London colleges, offered free public class/demonstrations, and the requests began pouring in from everywhere.

Keith eventually reduced the number of actors he would take to four or five and, with support from the Ministry of Education, toured to colleges, youth centers, and educational conferences. In *The Royal Court Theatre 1965-1972*, Philip Roberts documents: "Between September of 1964 and July of 1965, Studio actors worked at five London training colleges and visited Winchester, Dartington Hall and Rolle College, Devon, Oxford, Hatfield, Bath, Cambridge and Henley-on-Thames" (14). These public classes provided financial support to the Studio and essential research opportunities for Keith. From the stage proper, Keith would explain the training methods to the audience, observe their reactions, and side-coach the actors: "If a scene got boring I'd say "Recognize her!" or something to change the relationship. I was very good at saving scenes and telling them what to do without knowing why. I worked out why later."

In January of 1965, Devine announced his retirement from the Court and it was soon decided, as indicated by Devine's wishes, that Gaskill would take over.[9] Gaskill hired two associate directors, Keith and Iain Cuthbertson, a Scottish actor and general manager of the Glasgow Citizens Theatre. Also, 21 actors were selected and, from this group, the directors hoped to finally establish a permanent ensemble. *Plays and Players* interviewed the new RCT triumvirate of directors for their November issue. When asked why the decision was made to divide the artistic direction in three, Gaskill replied: "Three is a very good number. . . . The important thing is to have three people of equal strength in their own right" (Gaskill, "Three" 9). The interview revealed the strengths of each director. Gaskill had the proficiency and experience to deal with the bureaucratic, artistic, and political maneuverings of a large theatre company. Cuthbertson was connected to theatre in the provinces and would augment outreach efforts. Keith could carry forward the work of the Studio and find ways to integrate the Studio's work into the work of the theatre itself and improvisation into a writers' theatre. Actually, plans were already underway to bring

---

[9] About 6 months later, Devine suffered a stroke.

the Studio's work in public improvisation to the main stage and Gaskill seemed most enthusiastic: "This Christmas presentation isn't quite the sort of production that has so far been associated with the Court and I think it will be an opportunity for making more use of improvisation than anything we've done in the past" (10).

Clowning

Keith's public "clowning" demonstrations with four or five actors had been so successful that the Court asked him to put it up as a Christmas presentation for children. Keith asked for and received three test audiences preopening. He wanted to see how children would react to the straight presentation of the clowning exercises with audience participation. "The kids hated it," says Keith and he had only 2 days to fix it. Keith felt the children wanted characters they could identify with and a narrative, so he had Gaskill say "yes" to everything he offered and proceeded to improvise what became the story of *Clowning* (later titled *The Defeat of Giant Big-Nose*). The show begins with a master clown teaching clowns-in-training the tricks of the trade (e.g., mimed master/servant scenes and simple hat and mirror games). Then the clowns drift into the story of Jim and Enid's escape from their cruel master, Big-Nose, and their eventual success as clowns in a circus.

The six cast members and Keith improvised around the structure all weekend long and opened *Clowning* on Monday afternoon, 20 September, to a theatre full of children. At one point, Keith looked through the curtain because the house was so silent only to discover the children sitting there like "hypnotized rabbits." Keith tenders, "It was because the actors were playing narrative, no jokes. They were just telling the story and the children were fascinated." Over the next few weeks, as the actors got more familiar with the structure, the "clowning" found its way back in. The children always reacted with enthusiasm but Keith says the hypnotic power disappeared: "When the actors just played the narrative, the kids were absolutely entranced. I wish they didn't have to do the acting bit and just get on with the story. Brecht would've felt the same."

"A fairly primitive plot," wrote B.A. Young in his review of *Clowning* for the *Financial Times*. "[I]t does nothing to enlarge the children's mental or moral horizon. On the other hand, the children were having the time of their lives." Most critics agreed with Young's assessment. For adults, the plot may have been lacking, but they were treated to mime that was "deft and engaging," according to Geoffrey Moorhouse of *The Guardian*. Moreover, this improvised performance gave young audiences "an enthralling escape-ritual in which a chirpy clown called Nobody-Nose with a huge red hooter steps through the walls with cargoes of rescued prisoners chirruping 'Through the walls'," reminisced a critic for *The Observer*. "In the interval the theatre was crammed with children who were barging into the building yelling the password with their eyes shut" ("For children").[10] The talented cast included Ben Benison, Roddy Maude-Roxby, and Richard Morgan, three of the original four members of what would soon become known as The Theatre Machine. John Muirhead and Lucy Fleming were also in the cast and would frequently be invited to improvise with Theatre Machine over the next decade.

Keith was surprised the Lord Chamberlain allowed *Clowning* to go on. A running order/outline of the show had been sent to the Lord Chamberlain's office, preopening, describing the event as a "lecture" with an introduction, audience participation, and abyss and status exercises for clowns. Keith used to describe his clown work as "the abyss" because the clown must leap over one precipice after another without looking down or else he falls into an abyss. The following reply from the Lord Chamberlain's Assistant Comptroller exposes their fear of leaping without a safety net, that is, their fear of allowing pure impro, and also proves how ludicrous the censorship laws had gotten:

Dear Sir,

I have read Mr. Keith Johnston's [misspelled] quite absorbing lecture on clown and Mask Work, which seems to me to contain the ingredients for an acceptable 'copy' within the meaning of the Theatres Act. As you know, whether we wish to or not, we are precluded from allowing completely unfettered improvisations, since no copy can be submitted beforehand. Such illegal improvisation would be exemplified by the actors working out a situation based on a spontaneous phrase from the audience.

Your 'lecturers' are not in this category and properly presented there is a sufficient framework to constitute a 'copy'. . . .

The Lord Chamberlain wishes to put as little restraint as possible upon what seems to be an admirable entertainment and the one definite prohibition we should legally need to make would be upon working up of unforeseeable situations produced by the audience. I do not know whether "clowns answer questions put to them by the audience" is designed to fall into this category, but if it is it would be the one thing which I fear would have to be disallowed. If on the other hand the questions invited are true questions designed to elucidate some aspect of the lecture, then they would not be a part of the entertainment. (Royal Court. Copy)

In this letter, Keith was also asked to submit an "MS" (manuscript) with the lecturer's actual and intended dialogue and more detailed lists of "tricks" that

---

[10] These mostly positive reviews must have been a relief to Keith considering the disastrous notices received for N. F. Simpson's *The Cresta Run* which he directed in October.

may be used in order to further fulfill the acceptable "copy" requirements. Keith complied and the show went forward. It is possible that the Lord Chamberlain "put as little restraint" on *Clowning* because the *Saved* affair was already drawing too much attention to the antiquated British censorship laws. The Lord Chamberlain refused to grant Bond's *Saved* a license for performance unless major cuts were made including the deletion of two vital scenes and multiple words and phrases (e.g., every single "Christ"). Gaskill, Bond, and RCT Council members decided to defy the censor and put on the play unedited and billed as club performances in November of 1965. Charged with presenting an unlicensed play, the Court soon found itself in the middle of a long legal battle fighting stage censorship which, eventually, they won.[11]

Johnstone's last season at the Royal Court

At the end of 1965, the RCT Studio ceased operations partly due to a lack of financial support. Box office takings for the past year were considerably low and the budget had to be tightened. Additionally, the work in the Studio was not influencing the work seen on the main stage in any significant way and, as Keith had warned, "[I]f it doesn't I don't see how it can survive" (Gaskill, "Three" 9). Without the Studio, a large portion of Keith's job as associate director was eliminated. He could still supervise the script department, direct, and write plays. In box office terms, however, the productions Keith had directed in the past were not considered successful, and he had not written anything since *Brixham Regatta* (which only received a Sunday Night production in 1958). Could Keith write a box office or even a critical success for the Court's main season?

The Performing Giant

On 3 March 1966, Keith's second play, a 1-hour one-act called *The Performing Giant*, opened at the Court as a main stage production on a double-bill with David Cregan's *Transcending*. Gaskill co-directed *The Performing Giant* with Keith and Marc Wilkinson composed the music. Simply, the storyline follows seven potholers, basically clowns in a circus

---

[11] Keith recalls waiting with Gaskill in the Lord Chamberlain's office, eyeing a large stack of official, blank, Lord Chamberlain stationery and imagining the possibilities of possessing that stationery. "We could close every theatre in England and cause a hell of a row," said Keith to Gaskill. Keith also tells me that playwrights would put additional obscenities in their plays for bargaining power. One time, Keith suggested to the Lord Chamberlain to put a referee at the side of the stage who would blow a whistle when something offensive was spoken. I imagine the Lord Chamberlain did not find that amusing.

act, on their journey through the body of a performing giant. In order to gain access to the giant's interior, which they intend to exploit and turn into an amusement park, the potholers bribe the giant with a beautiful girl—Gladys. The giant is attacked, blinded, and subdued by the potholers after he tries to free Gladys from their clutches. Gladys finally summons the strength to fight back and dislodges the potholers from the giant's body. They vanish and the giant and Gladys are left alone and in love. The play purportedly symbolizes adults destroying innocent, adolescent sexual impulses with their mature ideas of conformity and morality. It is about "the sort of problems I experienced," wrote Keith in a letter to a school teacher who planned on bringing his class of sixth-formers to a performance. "[A]nd it is expressed in terms of potholers exploring a giant, which is the image of the sort of power and helplessness one feels at this age" (Letter to G. Gould).

Unfortunately, almost every critic loathed the production. A few critics admired the imagery and clowning, but found the allegorical theme confusing and/or unnecessary. In a personal letter to Pinter, Keith called the reviews "diabolical" and he predicted empty houses for the remainder of the run. He wanted Pinter to see the play for himself on the following Saturday when Bond and Jellicoe would be in attendance and ready to discuss whether or not a protest should be considered (Letter to Harold). The next day Pinter replied in his own handwriting:

> I'm afraid Saturday is quite impossible for me to see the play. I shall certainly do my best to see it though. I noticed the press "treatment" all right. I must say though that generally speaking I've never been happy about "protests", either on my behalf or anyone else's—so I'm not sure I could be of much aid in that direction. Yours, Harold.(Letter to Keith)

The protest never materialized but, obviously, Keith was affected by the harsh critical response. Headings such as "The 'Giant' is Such a Bore," "Fun? Like Having a Tooth Pulled," and "Just Jabber, Jabber, Toil and Drivel" say it all.

Surprisingly, a few positive responses were found buried beneath the wreckage. The *Observer's* drama critic thought Keith's stage pictures were genuine and "simply and beautifully" executed by Gaskill ("Intestinal"). Anthony Seymour of *The Yorkshire Post* hailed the production as "intriguing theatre." And Alan Brien, writing for *The Sunday Telegraph*, claimed that Keith was simply "obeying the impulse which rules all serious artists." That is, "searching for fresh ways in which we can know ourselves." Although Brien felt that Keith ran out of ideas about halfway through, he judged the play's first impact as "powerful and disturbing." Nonetheless, Keith's inability to achieve box office success either as a writer or as a director of the Court likely influenced what happened next. In accordance with

Roddy Maude-Roxby (center) *in Johnstone's* The Performing Giant,
Royal Court, 1966.
Photo Credit: John Haynes.[12]

Gaskill's wishes, at a management committee meeting on 22 April 1966, Keith announced that "he and Iain Cuthbertson would not be continuing at the Royal Court in the future'" (Roberts, *RCT 1965* 47).

Gaskill described the combination of himself, Cuthbertson, and Johnstone as "disastrous" in his memoirs. "Keith was to be the committed, uncompromising voice and Iain was to stand for traditional and popular theatre values. They are both very large, very emotional men and I don't think I have the coolest of heads" (*Sense* 65). He goes on to say Keith "was never really happy as a director and wanted to develop his theories of comedy and improvisational theatre" (65). Keith disagrees with the first part of this claim only. He was happy as a director and according to Jellicoe, "He was a very good director" (P.I.). Nevertheless, Keith never had a box office success. Even *The Knack*, a critical success by all accounts, earned a

---

[12] John Haynes was the official Royal Court Theatre photographer from 1970 to 1994. He is known especially for his portraits of Beckett. The first play he ever photographed was *The Cresta Run* (1965), directed by Keith. Haynes told me it was Keith who encouraged him to take his first pictures in the theatre (Message to author).

Roddy Maude-Roxby (left), *Dennis Waterman, Jack Shepherd,*
William Stewart, and Lucy Fleming (in box) *in Johnstone's*
The Performing Giant, *Royal Court, 1966.*

Photo Credit: John Haynes.

modest 49 per cent in ticket sales (Findlater, *At the Royal* "Appendix 2"). With pressure on Gaskill to tighten the budget, to end the repertory system, and to consolidate positions on the artistic committee, some hard decisions had to be made including hiring directors and producing plays most likely to bring in revenue (Roberts, *RCT 1965* 46–9).

After a decade at the Court, it was time for Keith to move on to other things. He hung around through the summer, though, and used the newly acquired club space at the top of the Court's Sloane Square building to give public impro classes. This space eventually became the Theatre Upstairs. Beginning in January of 1966, Keith directed "classes in" or "demonstrations of improvised comedy," under the title of "Instant Theatre," "Actors at Work," and eventually as *Caught in the Act* when it became a weekly lunchtime show at the Jeanetta Cochrane Theatre. Remember, improvisation is still illegal at this time, but because Keith was essentially giving classes in comic impro through a demonstration of exercises, the censor was "absolutely screwed," avows Keith. "What could they do? You're allowed to teach in public." The regular improvisers in these shows were Ben Benison, Richard Morgan, Lucy Fleming, and Anthony (Tony) Trent. But sessions at the Theatre Upstairs were often open to other RCT company members. Furthermore, after several performances of Thomas Middleton's *A Chaste*

Maid in Cheapside, directed by Gaskill for the Court's main stage, Roddy Maude-Roxby remembers arriving with Keith, Benison, Morgan, and Trent (i.e., the five original Theatre Machine members), inviting audiences to hang around to watch sessions of improvised work and then proceeding to improvise using the *Chaste Maid* set and cast, which included Fleming. Jack Shepherd was also in the cast and became a regular participant in these sessions. He recalled:

> We, the actors, would sit on chairs at the front of the stage, and after being primed by Keith and, sometimes, suggestions from the audience, we would set off on a series of strange improvised journeys. Keith would then retreat into the wings to watch, though he was often given to bounding on stage unexpectedly (like a Demon King in woolly pullover and glasses) to alter the scene, or give us fresh instructions. (Findlater, *At the Royal* 105–6)[13]

These improvised entertainments with clowning, slapstick, masks, and improvised journeys gave Keith the chance to continue his research and to keep his favorite improvisers working together in front of an audience on a weekly basis.[14]

The beginning of 1966 also marked the death of Devine. After suffering a second heart attack, he passed away on January 20 at the age of 55. Five days later, Beckett, Gaskill, and Keith shared a taxi to the funeral. Reflecting back, Gaskill wrote: "Perhaps his [Devine's] greatest ability was his belief in other people, not as valuable properties but in their potential. He once said to me about Keith, 'Oh, we may have to wait five years to see anything at all,' and he was prepared to wait that long" (*Sense* 73). Exactly 10 years after Keith stumbled into the doors of the Royal Court Theatre in Sloane Square, he was about to make his departure as an innovative teacher of improvisation. Although Keith had also been the Court's chief play reader, head of the script department, their expert on Beckett, a bold director, and an influence on writers like Jellicoe and Bond, his reputation as a teacher at the Studio garnered the most attention.[15] He was, in fact, offered and accepted

---

[13] Shepherd is a stage and film actor and played the title role in the British detective series *Wycliffe* from 1994 to 1998. He was also in *The Performing Giant* and invited by Keith, on occasion, to perform with Theatre Machine.

[14] Around this time, Keith also began an informal writers' group for Court playwrights at an upstairs space in the Old Vic Theatre, home of Olivier's National.

[15] The "chief play reader" was not an official position. Keith became the "unofficial" chief play reader because Devine and Richardson relied on his taste and knowledge: "They'd been to university so they knew all about Elizabethan theory of Ben Jonson's Humours but they never heard of Wedekind or Büchner. They hadn't read Strindberg. They hadn't read anything by the Japanese. But I'd read everything," says Keith. "So in a situation where completely new stuff was arriving, it was really useful to have someone like me there."

a teaching job beginning in the fall at the Royal Academy of Dramatic Art (RADA). Devine, who was a good judge of character with a deep passion for and belief in teaching, probably had a notion that Keith would make a fine teacher, but he allowed him to discover this in his own time and in his own way.

The Royal Academy of Dramatic Art

Hugh Cruttwell, the newly appointed director of RADA, wanted to shake up the acting program. Keith had inquired about a possible job at RADA and Cruttwell, who admired Keith's work at the RCT Studio, hired him to teach improvisation in the fall of 1966.[16] Cruttwell told Keith later on he did not like that some students made it through RADA using only technical skills and without feeling or experiencing anything. Keith calls technical acting with no emotion "zombie acting" or "taxidermy on the stage" or sometimes "necrophilia theatre." According to Keith, actors accused of partaking in such theatre have no kinetic dance. "Everything is planned beforehand. . . . Some of the great English actors of the last generation, or before, wanted to be on the stage alone. . . . My emphasis is all on working together" (Kearley 80). Cruttwell knew this and asked Keith to devise methods that would force the students to experience, not just play at, different roles. Meet the Monster, a storytelling game that takes control away from the individual and gives it to the group, was one of Keith's solutions.

Keith first experimented with Meet the Monster at Dartington College of Arts located at Dartington Hall in Devon. Commuting from London, he taught improvisation courses there each week. He had first been invited to Dartington Hall about 6 years prior to teach opera singers at the Summer School of Music directed by William Glock and Hans Keller and, in the fall of 1965, he took the cast of *Clowning* there to prepare for their upcoming production.[17] Keith also taught longer courses which required him to actually live in the residence hall in a room once occupied by Michael Chekhov (Johnstone, *Thing* 89).

Back at the RCT Studio, Keith would blindfold two students and have them play word-at-a-time in order to stop them from trying to control the future. At RADA (and with Theatre Machine), he had students compose letters one-word-at-a-time. Meet the Monster takes these games to the next,

---

[16] Cruttwell was married to famous British actress Geraldine McEwan from 1953 until his death in 2002. Keith admired Cruttwell's propensity to cast against type.
[17] Keith told me Glock and Keller were a bit snobby at first. Then he informed them that Carl Neilsen's *Symphony No. 5* had an improvised part for two sets of side drums intended to drown out the orchestra. Keith recalls they regarded him with suspicion after that.

trance-inducing level. Two students construct a story together but they are blindfolded and protected by guides, that is, the rest of the group. Soon the guides take a more active role in the story adding sounds, becoming characters or offering encounters with animals or monsters. "As the group become more skilled, so the 'visions' of the storytellers become more vivid, and more trance-inducing," wrote Keith. "If the story-tellers mime flying they may be picked up and flown about. If they say that a monster is engulfing them the entire group may embrace them and crush them to the ground" (*Newsletter Five* 4). Eventually, the guides can take over the storytelling altogether and lead the blindfolded duo through the fantasy. At Dartington Hall, Meet the Monster exercises caused some consternation among the drama faculty who felt students should never be "out of control" in a social situation; therefore, it was decided, for some reason, art and music students were no longer allowed to participate. But the drama students at Dartington and RADA continued to Meet the Monster with pleasure.[18]

Keith enjoyed working at RADA for a number of reasons. First, he had absolute freedom to teach whatever and however he wanted. "Nobody ever checked up on me. Nobody ever saw my classes, there were no complaints. I could experiment there" (P.I. 16 July 2011). And he did. He directed Calderón's *Life Is a Dream* in a gloomy, cave-like room with actors illuminating one another with flashlights. Ben Benison, hired by Crutwell upon Keith's recommendation to teach mime, says Keith's direction was "innovative for RADA back then" and remembers Keith's popularity among the students (Message to author).[19] Keith once permitted a class of students to play Group-Yes for six successive lessons nonstop. "They were getting something that they desperately needed but I felt guilty being paid to teach them," wrote Keith in *Impro for Storytellers* (35–6). Or he sent students to eat at restaurants where they could only speak in gibberish, furtively, and with the proviso that they had to leave the customers in a better state then when they arrived. Second, the drama department wasn't in the basement which, in Keith's recollection, was the common placement of Canadian drama departments. "Closer to Hell, I suppose," he said (S. F. Wksp 2009). Third, RADA professors would talk about their students over lunch, a behavior Keith had not witnessed before or since in a university theatre department. These conversations gave Keith the opportunity to hear about his student's progress in voice classes and movement classes, for example, and created an atmosphere of reciprocity. Lastly, over his 5-year tenure at RADA, his schedule remained flexible which allowed him to teach hundreds

---

[18] At one point Keith took Theatre Machine to Dartington Hall for two weeks and they played Meet the Monster and other games with the students.

[19] Benison stayed on the RADA faculty for several decades and became a celebrated teacher of mime. Keith says, "Ben was lovely as a teacher." Benison says that Keith's influence on him as a teacher "was immeasurable."

of workshops at places like Dartington Hall, for groups of advanced drama teachers in programs arranged and funded by the Ministry of Education, and for summer theatre schools such as the one administered by the Royal Shakespeare Company (Johnstone, *Storytellers* XI). Keith also took a 3-month sabbatical in 1968 to be a guest director at the University of Victoria, B.C., and he continued to tour and give public classes with Theatre Machine.

The Theatre Machine

The only way to validate the work was to go onstage with a pride of improviser lions.

KEITH JOHNSTONE (*Storytellers* XII)

The four "lions"—Ben Benison, Roddy Maude-Roxby, Richard Morgan, and Anthony (Tony) Trent—did not start out as Keith's best improvisers. They were the actors who were not getting much work at the Court or elsewhere so they were available. "But they became the best," avows Keith.[20] In 1966 and 1967, they toured with Keith as their director to hundreds of schools and colleges including Oxford, Cambridge, and over 120 schools in Wales doing public classes/demonstrations. Eventually, demonstrations gave way to shows. Once a week, for example, they could be seen at the Cochrane Theatre and they were booked at the Mercury Theatre in Notting Hill Gate for a month.[21] Surprisingly, before the Theatres Act of 1968 was ratified, the censor never interfered, and Keith and his troupe became very popular. They were invited by the Canadian government to perform at the 1967 International and Universal Exposition (Expo 67) in Montreal. It is for this event they officially identified themselves as The Theatre Machine.

The organizers of Expo 67 scheduled Theatre Machine to perform in the Youth Pavilion in 20-minute segments because they did not believe an

---

[20] Benison was a mining surveyor and professional tap/jazz dancer before he found his way to the Court. He studied under the great choreographer Buddy Bradley. Maude-Roxby was a student at the Royal College of Art when he first met Keith, Gaskill, and Jellicoe, who would attend the comic revues he directed at the end of each term. Morgan had worked with Joan Littlewood's Theatre Workshop before making his debut at RCT in John Osborne's *A Patriot for Me*. Trent was a student at the Central School of Arts and Crafts which built the Jeannetta Cochrane Theatre where the RCT Studio operated. He studied at RCT Studio under Keith.

[21] Part of the film *The Red Shoes* (1948) was filmed in The Mercury Theatre. This film had an enormous effect on Keith as a young man not because of the dancing but because it showed a different world from the one he lived in. A world where people could earn a living and travel to interesting places working as artists. When Keith realized he was standing on the same stage, he says, "It was like the completion of a cycle."

improvisation group (or any group) could hold an audience's attention any longer than that in the middle of a fairground. Keith declares, "We did six hours a day, three hours before and three hours after lunch, just to piss off the stupid Canadians." He loved the theatre space provided, though, and they were a hit with audiences. When they returned to London, the British Council sent Keith and his Theatre Machine on a European tour. Over the next 4 years, the stages of Europe (e.g., Germany, Austria, Switzerland, Yugoslavia, Denmark, Croatia, Belgium) would become Keith's primary classroom space where he would discover how to adeptly direct a team of remarkable improvisers, instinctively evaluate a range of audiences, and triumph over his own stage fright by essentially walking over the abyss.

Keith once used the expression "the abyss" to describe the type of clown work he teaches, that is, clowning dependent upon living in the present moment and leaping from one precipice to another without looking down. In his essay "The Abyss" published in *Program 2: Royal Court* covering the Court's season from December 1965 through January 1966, Keith wrote: "A skilled clown has no need to think ahead, he trusts always that ideas will present themselves. . . .When people start to learn clowning they attempt far too much, they won't allow the events to carry them, they think 'I do this' instead of 'this happens'" (27). Simply put, the clown— like the improviser—must not preplan. He must focus on the present and allow ideas to come to him spontaneously. When Keith first began directing Theatre Machine performances from the stage proper, he suffered from a continual state of stress knowing he had to come up with one idea after another. He finally solved this problem by practicing what he preached. He would simply wait until something—the next precipice—presented itself and then do something physical (e.g., move a chair or grab a balloon) or shout something completely random like, "Two people on the stage!" Once the two improvisers were in place, an idea would miraculously surface. Keith trained himself to trust his imaginative instincts and to remain open to ideas not anticipated. Remember his doctrine: "The improviser has to be like a man walking backwards. He sees where he has been, but pays no attention to the future" (*Impro* 116). As director of The Theatre Machine, he followed this doctrine.

Even during public classes/demonstrations, Keith suffered from a mild form of stage fright once he stepped onto the stage. He wasn't a performer and he was relatively shy and awkward in front of any audience. Part of Keith's fear came from not remembering the names of the improvisers on the spot, so he wrote their names on the palm of his hand. Then he imagined the audience as a great big, loving, sexy beast that wanted to take the improvisers home. He treated every audience with benevolence and presented himself as their humble servant and they responded. At Theatre Machine performances in Germany, Keith says a strange rustling noise was heard as each show commenced. One evening, Benison crept into the audience to find out what was making the noise only to discover hundreds of Germans unfolding their arms. They were relaxing because Keith, as the genial emcee, had just welcomed them. Benison says this is true. Maude-Roxby replied: "I think that's right. When we were first going to Germany in the 60s, we were very aware of the posture of the Germans, which tended to be heads down and sort of collapsed, and we would comment on that [in the show]. We'd announce 'We will now see two Germans!' and the improvisers would come on in that way." The German audiences in every city, in every location, loved Theatre Machine. In Hamburg, they were booked for a month-long engagement to packed houses after a successful 10-minute appearance on a popular German television program (c. 1968).[22] Maude-Roxby remembers German spectators saying things like, "This is exquisite silliness, a quality that is very obscure to us," and that they enjoyed witnessing this type of flexibility and freedom.

Once Keith had his fear under control, it was easier to manage the fear of his improvisers. When one or more of his troupe had fallen into their personal abyss and couldn't get out, Keith would sometimes tell them to "fuck about" or "make my life difficult" and everything seemed to improve. Keith gave his improvisers permission to be naughty, to be playful in a nondestructive way and without fear of repercussion (Stockholm Wksp). "[W]e were presenting a continuing skirmish between me and the players," wrote Keith. "[T]hey would start one scene while I was setting up another; I would force them to complete undigested material, and they would retaliate by doing the opposite of whatever I was asking" (Storytellers 18). But that didn't mean Keith wasn't having a good time. Benison and Maude-Roxby both vividly recall Keith rolling with laughter on the side of the stage. Critics abroad often compared Theatre Machine's work to the antics of Charlie Chaplin and Buster Keaton, clowns of the silent film era who certainly knew how to jump from one precipice to the next as they escaped from authority figures.[23] According to film critic Richard Schickel, Chaplin lived out a child's version of paradise on the big screen: "To be a child and yet to be able to escape all the punishments, all the dreary learning experiences, inherent in that condition is to be in a state of regressive bliss" (17). Keith allowed for playing and scuffling on the stage and this put everyone in a state of bliss.

---

[22] The television show was called *Showbühne*. When Theatre Machine arrived at the studio, the director panicked after realizing they were indeed improvisers with no preset plan, so he had no way of directing where and when to point the cameras. Keith solved the problem by giving a number to each Theatre Machine member, including himself, and they proceeded to speak in numerical order during the entire 10-minute segment.

[23] Maude-Roxby says one German critic actually commended Theatre Machine's brilliant political prowess in a scene involving balloons: "We had all sorts of colors of balloons, but towards the end, there were just red and white ones left. And by chance, the last one to survive was a white one. The critic saw it as the survival of hope against Communism."

When asked to describe an archetypal Theatre Machine performance, Keith answers, "Oh God. Variety." He equates consistency to religion because it draws a circle around itself and shuts out all other ideas. For the first ten or so performances, Theatre Machine was consistently using antinarrative "filler" games. Keith justifies this because he regarded the games as "scaffolding used while we were making the building." Once Theatre Machine built their foundation, more and more narrative-based scenes were added. Filler games were not abandoned but instead inserted between longer scenes for contrast. One could say Keith was consistent in his insistence on variety.

Keith used a structure similar to the old Whitehall farces of the 1950s and 1960s for performances which he later outlines as: "1. Establish yourself as 'funny'; 2. Fight the laughter—taking the brakes off just before the interval; 3. Let the audience laugh all they wish for the last fifteen minutes" (*Newsletter Two* 8). But why fight the laughter at all? Because constant laughter, like continuous filler games, is wearisome. An audience needs to breathe, they want to experience a range of emotions and be taken on adventures. Or as Keith put it in a piece of writing I recently dug out of his basement, "People can't laugh for long without getting ill, they collapse on the floor, and cough up bits of lung, and they can even resent laughing." Impro based on storytelling gives audiences what they want and impro based on physical storytelling can overcome language barriers. Theatre Machine was so successful abroad because all four were physical comedians and clowns. Benison was also a brilliant mime, and they had many games like "Making Faces" or scenes using only one word—sometimes using a foreign word given to them by the audience—which did not rely on language. And sometimes, as in Hamburg, they were provided with a translator.

Theatre Machine would be on the stage opening suitcases, hanging clothing on racks, blowing up balloons, and calmly decking the periphery of the stage with props as audiences arrived. To every performance, Keith hauled at least two suitcases full of stuff and, of course, long airship balloons. At the RCT Studio, he began using multicolored, airship balloons, measuring about a yard in length with his student improvisers and mask students. "Balloons invigorate us," wrote Keith in *Impro for Storytellers*. "[T]hey're brightly coloured, they move strangely, they're 'safe' and 'dangerous' at the same time . . ." (254). They are also phallic, spontaneous—exploding or deflating at unexpected moments—and can transform into a range of objects and creatures. Theatre Machine would place hundreds of balloons in boxes at the sides of the stage or, using static electricity, stick them to the walls and on the ceiling. They would even ask audience members to pass partly tied balloons from the back to the front of the house during setup, hoping one would unexpectedly come undone! One of Theatre Machine's regular venues was the intimate cellar of the Freemasons Arms in Hampstead. On Monday nights, on a tiny stage, Theatre Machine would perform for a large crowd crammed into a very intimate space. As the spectators arrived, the atmosphere moistened and the balloons began falling. Keith, directing the show sitting on top of an upright piano holding a beer, could reach up and take a balloon at will because the ceiling was so low or sometimes, as he says, "The balloons would fall into my hands and that looked quite spontaneous."

Keith, as director, would always be the first person to speak to the audience. "Generally, you could count on Keith engaging the audience and speaking brilliantly as he does in his classes now. Very accurately and with minute detail," Maude-Roxby says. Then he would introduce a subject, like status, call on two players to do a scene, then two more, or three or four, and that was the basic format. Keith would always explain to the audience newly introduced techniques and games. He would also prompt the players from the sides with suggestions like, "Tell her the truth, tell her how you lost your eye!" The improvisers could choose to ignore Keith's instructions, that is, to ignore their master, but they did so at their own risk, because the audience also heard the instruction and the idea was now part of their circle of probability.

Each Theatre Machine performance included one or more master/servant scenes. European audiences instinctively understood the dynamics of this type of relationship whether the status transactions were physical or verbal. "We couldn't go around Europe without master/servant scenes," said Keith (London Wksp). Also, you could expect to see at least one hat game. Hat games were developed at the RCT Studio after Gaskill came in

Keith (on right) *watching Ben Benison and Richard Morgan do a hat routine during a Theatre Machine performance.*
Photo Credit: Courtesy of Ben Benison.

one day and shouted, "I've discovered the secret of clowning!" To loosen up his cast during a rehearsal for *A Chaste Maid in Cheapside*, Gaskill had his actors secretly attempt to take each other's hats (and protect their own) as they played each scene. It worked. Keith took Gaskill's initial game and developed it into a series of games and exercises. Benison could take the hat off of anyone and Trent was excellent at guarding his hat, so Keith would often have the two of them play hat-game scenes together. One or more audience members were sometimes invited on stage to play "Taking the Hat with Tony." He was unbeatable until "four immense Germans wrestled him to the floor and flattened him like the Nazis taking Poland," wrote Keith. "[S]o we became more circumspect" (*Newsletter Four* 19–27).

Theatre Machine performing a scene with two masters and their
servants at the Royal Court, c. 1967. John Muirhead (left)
Roddy Maude-Roxby, Ben Benison, and Tony Trent.
Photo Credit: Photo by John Haynes © V&A Images/Victoria and Albert Museum.

Keith might ask for one, maybe two audience suggestions per evening but only to create a benevolent mood. Many improvisers ask for audience suggestions in order to prove they are indeed improvising, but Keith asserts they are "enslaving themselves to the whim of aberrant individuals" (*Storytellers* 26). If the work is good, whether audience suggestions are solicited or not, there will always be someone in the audience who does not believe the performance was improvised. A London critic for *The Stage* accused Theatre Machine of presenting rehearsed scenes "as if" improvised. Keith contested and the critic came back a second time. The critic then admitted the scenes were improvised but added that the improvisation wasn't so hot. The critic's first review, as Keith recalls, was essentially stating that the work was *too good* to have been improvised. Maude-Roxby and Benison say this sort of commenting came up often. Whatever did not work in a performance, audience members saw as improvised, and what did work, they saw as scripted. Moreover, Theatre Machine often had really good sound and lighting technicians improvising the technical elements. They would raise a moon for a night scene or underscore a romantic scene with music or throw in the sound of breaking glass when a player accidentally walked through a previously established window. The effects were sometimes so precise and well-timed that audiences found it difficult to believe it happened *à l'improviste*! "But that was part of the pleasure," says Maude-Roxby. "That you knew you were doing something that people couldn't believe you were doing!"

Before the first European tour, the British press practically ignored Theatre Machine. In the late 1960s and early 1970s, they had fans following them from venue to venue but nobody wrote about them. "Because it was comedy," says Keith. "They don't think comedy is serious and they don't understand it. So they write about all the other groups and there's hardly anything about us in the records."[24] Only after Keith began reprinting foreign press reviews in the programs did the British press began to take some notice.

Theatre Machine after a performance. John Muirhead (left),
Roddy Maude-Roxby, Richard Morgan, and Ben Benison.
Photo Credit: Courtesy of Roddy Maude-Roxby.

---

[24] Keith is correct. In my archival research, I have come across only two or three articles that briefly mention The Theatre Machine.

Johnstone teaches beyond Britain

In the autumn of 1968, Keith took a 3-month sabbatical from RADA to be a guest director at the University of Victoria, B.C. (UVic). His invitation was initiated by Carl Hare, head of the drama department, and by associate theatre professor, Richard Courtney, a fellow Englishman and renowned scholar in drama education who, like Hugh Crutwell, admired Keith's work.[25] Keith directed his short two-man play, *Moby Dick: A Sir and Perkins Story*, originally produced the previous spring by the first lunchtime theatre in London: Theatrescope Original Lunch Hour Plays at the Little Theatre Club in Garrick Yard, off St Martin's Lane.[26] In Keith's version of Melville's classic, the impotent ship captain, Ahab, and his sexually repressed manservant, Perkins, chase the "sperm whale"—literally the captain's runaway sperm matured to immense size and swimming the high seas. Louis B. Hobson, a theatre critic in Calgary, said of the Loose Moose production a decade later: "In *Moby Dick* he [Johnstone] takes impotence, sexual frustration and incest and by superimposing them on the famous Melville tale of a man's obsessions with a killer whale he makes them all seem not only commonplace, but comic" ("Loose Moose and a Whale"). This play is one long master/servant game where status and the pecking-order continually see-saw. Courtney remembered the production at UVic as "one of the funniest performances I have ever seen" (Letter to Dean).

At UVic, *Moby Dick* was advertised as an "outrageous afterpiece" to *The Conspiracy*, Keith's adaptation of the Wakefield Cycle. Keith supposes those working on the mystery cycles during the medieval period were at the edge of their technology, so he decided to utilize every technical device available to him in this production. He used closed-circuit televisions and underscored scenes with music. Jesus was crucified on a telegraph pole. Pontius Pilate was 22-feet high and, as one student critic from *The Martlet* expressed, "awe inspiring" (Burgess). The executioners, in contrast, often just sat around reading horror comics.

Beginning with his children's shows, *Clowning* (later titled *The Defeat of Giant Big-Nose*) and *The Performing Giant*, stilt-walking figures, fake noses, half-masks, and leather-masked executioners became a standard feature in Keith's work. Although all of Keith's short stories could be defined as "dark," *The Conspiracy* marked a transition toward his readiness to allow

---

[25] Courtney published many books, most notably *Play, Drama & Thought: The Intellectual Background to Drama Education* (1968).

[26] Tony Trent directed this production and John Muirhead, who eventually replaced Trent in Theatre Machine, played Sir. Keith, Maude-Roxby, Benison, and Morgan asked Trent to leave the group (c. 1969) because he became more and more difficult to work with. Maude-Roxby says, "He was the most brilliant improviser and solo performer, but like George Best, he'd score goals and never pass. He kept taking over."

his darkest proclivities to play out on the stage. In *Impro*, Keith wrote: "I was so far away from anyone whose criticism I cared about that I felt free to do exactly what I felt like" (28). And so his stilt-walking figures transformed from lonely giants and big-nosed clowns into ominous death figures, and his executioners became progressively viler, albeit absurdly comic. Courtney found the entire production "affecting . . . harrowing and startlingly existential" (Letter to Dean).

Keith's production was at the forefront of where theatre was heading. "The art department was wildly enthusiastic about it," says Keith, "and the stuffy drama department was appalled." Hare and Courtney were not "stuffy" so Keith must be referring to what Judith Koltai called the "American contingent" of new professors. Koltai, a mature student in the department then and a successful authentic movement teacher today, defines the contingent as teachers who had come from a conservative American theatre tradition. "Clearly there was a clash," said Koltai. "In their eyes, Keith was a controversial figure." Keith also maintains that during the 2 weeks he took over a course for a professor, attendance skyrocketed but then dropped off after the professor returned: "It was unforgiveable. I mean they never forgive you for that, especially if you do everything wrong." Soon after Keith's year at UVic, Courtney and Hare left the university and Koltai remembers "the tone, the atmosphere of the department" changing completely.

Keith found out later that the new drama department head alleged that it was a mistake inviting Johnstone to the university. Although I am in no way distrustful of Keith's recollection, there is always another side. Accommodating Keith's inspired but unconventional way of working is not so simple. Gaskill had said Keith was not one to compromise. He also said that Keith "didn't want to exist in the give and take of the theatre as it exists, he wanted to make his own statement" (*World*). Although meant in the best possible way, Gaskill was pointing out that even a professional writers' theatre like RCT was too conventional for Keith's directing.

Theatre Machine back at the Court and Johnstone's courtship

Keith and Theatre Machine just returned from a tour to Yugoslavia, Germany, Austria, Belgium, and Switzerland, when they took part in the "Come Together" festival of fringe groups at RCT from 21 October to 9 November 1970. The Theatre Machine and over 20 performance groups and individual artists performed in the dramatically altered main theatre and the newly added Theatre Upstairs.[27] "If the court had not battled with

---

[27] Four of those groups were: Nancy Meckler's Freehold; Peter Cheeseman's company at the Victoria Theatre, Stoke-on-Trent; The People Show; and The Ken Campbell Roadshow.

the censor," wrote Philip Roberts, "a good deal of what was shown in the festival would never have been allowed" (*RCT 1965* 129). Under Keith's direction, Theatre Machine did their usual improvised short-form, mime, and mask scenes.

Keith doing mask work with Theatre Machine using his handheld mirror technique at Royal Court's Theatre Upstairs, 1970.

Photo Credit: John Haynes.

Benison remembers one performance in particular. Things weren't going so well, so 20 minutes into the show, Keith walked to center stage and asked the audience to take an early interval. "I cannot remember what transpired backstage," says Benison, "but we go back on to do a great show. We play to roars of laughter and when we exit the applause is thunderous. I am so high I swear my feet don't touch the boards!" The Theatre Machine was so popular at the beginning of the "Come Together" festival that an encore performance was scheduled during the final week (Royal Court, *Royal Court Announces*). Maude-Roxby, Morgan, and Richard Pendrey were the other three Theatre Machine members. Pendry toured to Dubrovnik, Croatia, with the group after the festival where Keith remembers him falling off a stage, 9-inches high, dressed as a comfy, human-eating chair: "Poor guy. The lights came up [and] there was Richard deftly trying to move in his armchair costume."

In 1971, Keith was teaching a short course in Fishponds, Bristol, where Ingrid Brind was a student. "We discovered that we lived a few minutes' walk away from each other in London," Keith told me. Fishponds is where

Keith played Group-Yes with three separate "tribes" of sixty students each who "rampaged about the estate, alarming the groundsmen" and had "separate adventures before reuniting and splitting off again" (*Storytellers* 35). Group-Yes is an offer-and-accept game played by large groups. There are no leaders. Randomly, one student will yell out an offer. For example, "Let's walk through the woods!" With enthusiasm, the other players say "Yes" and join the activity. The group's feedback, if all are responding candidly, will teach improvisers to stay within the group's circle of probability, to meet the group's needs and desires, and to make positive, obvious suggestions instead of clever ones. Apparently, Ingrid said "Yes!" to Keith's proposal and they were married in Canada soon thereafter.

Johnstone and Eugenio Barba

In April of 1971, Theatre Machine and several other British companies (e.g., Pip Simmons Theatre Group, Freehold, The People Show, and Theatre Workshop Edinburgh) were invited by Eugenio Barba—considered one of Europe's most influential theatre directors today—to perform at a Seminar on English Fringe Groups at Barba's Odin Teatret in Holstebro, Denmark (Odin Teatret Archives).[28] It was an open course and Barba's students were a part of the course. Upon arrival, Keith and the directors of each fringe group were invited into Barba's office. Barba informed them they would be free to structure the week as they saw fit because he wanted the students to experience the British process. But then, as Keith recalls, Barba immediately followed with something like: "First, we will start each day with discussion." To which Keith and a few others replied, "But we don't discuss." Still, Barba insisted on discussion. "And that's when the English groups suddenly realized that we had a lot in common—the resistance to discussion and analysis. But also a basic anarchy. The British are very good at being naughty. At bad behavior. It's in the culture," posits Keith.[29] Yes, the British can be rather naughty (e.g., The Goon Show, Monty Python, Benny Hill) but Keith's process was not entirely unlike Barba's.

Profoundly influenced by his mentor Jerzy Grotowski, Barba used exercises to train actors to think with their bodies and to develop a "pre-expressive" technique. In *The Purpose of Playing: Modern Acting Theories in Perspective*, Robert Gordon describes the pre-expressive as: "an underlying level of preparedness for performance common to all performers, irrespective of the way that their own cultural identities have determined the particular expressive character of their individual art forms" (340–1). This, to some extent, corresponds with Keith's application of spontaneous improvisations

---

[28] Founded in 1964 by Barba in Oslo, Norway.
[29] Keith recalls the Pip Simmons Theatre Group beginning a discussion session by firing water pistols at each other and shouting, "Discuss this!"

to establish a body-mind connection, to allow space for the imaginative, intuitive, and uncensored self. And like Barba, Keith takes the performer-spectator relationship very seriously. Barba's disciplined actors applied specific exercises to work on individual performance and to discover the self in relationship/confrontation with others. Keith's improvisers applied flexible exercises and techniques to playfully explore their uncensored imaginations and to create stories collaboratively and spontaneously for/with audiences. Perhaps Barba wasn't as playful with his Danish actors (at that moment in time), but Keith and Barba were searching for similar objectives in the classroom.

Keith recalls getting a very positive response from the students in the question-and-answer session following Theatre Machine's performance but he doesn't believe Barba had a good time. Why then would Barba invite Keith to lead *ateliers* (i.e., "studios" or "workshops" in French) and seminars at his second ISTA (International School of Theatre Anthropology) session in Volterra, Italy, in 1981? The central theme of that ISTA session was "Improvisation" and Keith's *Impro*, published 2 years earlier, was growing in popularity, but Barba surely had other options. He didn't have to invite Keith but he did. Grotowski and Dario Fo were listed as the other two "renowned specialists" leading seminars alongside Keith and the "permanent pedagogical team" (Odin Teatret). Over 100 people (participants and artistic staff) representing approximately 19 countries took part in this ISTA session.[30]

The Last Bird in Copenhagen

Returning to the spring of 1972, Keith was invited to teach at the Statens Teaterskole (Danish National School of Theatre) in Copenhagen. Through the mid-1980s, this distinguished school of dramatic arts would invite Keith back to teach graduating seniors for 6 weeks out of every year. In 1972, the senior students wanted to do improvised scenes for their final project so, for the first 3 weeks, Keith gave them classes using the impro techniques he had developed. He also created the game Fast-Food Stanislavsky for this group of Danish students who were more familiar with Grotowski than the Russian master teacher. The game quickly introduced students to the theory underpinning Stanislavsky's "method of physical actions"—if an actor

---

[30] Barba is also credited with identifying and promoting the "third theatre" movement in the 1970s. The third theatre is not the commercial or the avant-garde theatre but rather a performance that is always in process. It is theatre that "lives on the fringes, often outside or on the outskirts of the centers and capitals of culture. It is theatre created by people who define themselves as actors, directors, theatre workers, although they have seldom undergone a traditional theatrical education and therefore are not recognized as professionals [. . . .] But they are not amateurs"—Barba (Gordon 334). Keith and his theatre work, especially after RCT, could be categorized as part of this movement.

truthfully executes a physical action or activity, the emotions associated with that action will naturally follow.

Fast-Food Stanislavsky lists, created by Keith, gave his Danish students permission to do things they wouldn't normally do, to play roles they wouldn't normally play, and to create vibrant characters. Each player selected a purpose or result-oriented direction, written at the top of a strip of paper, such as "To Be Thought Intelligent," "To Be Thought a Hero," "To Flirt with Someone," and "To Accept Guilt." Under the purpose, a long list of suggested actions helped players achieve his/her purpose. For example, under "To Be Thought a Hero," the first five actions a player could choose from were: have a weapon, be on a quest, be attacked, detect dangers, and display strength, athleticism. Under "To Be Thought Intelligent"—correct people, know everything, explain baffling things, use complex sentences, and quote statistics. As players become more competent in this game, lists can be combined to create characters that are complex and/or split, that is, torn between two opposing objectives.[31]

The Danish students thrived on the impro games but, after those first 3 weeks, it was obvious to Keith that these students had not worked together long enough to develop a common technique. They would inevitably fail in front of an audience, which is not a bad thing per se, but the audience for this final project was not going to be a forgiving one. Instructors and directors scouting out talent for the major theatres in Copenhagen would be in attendance. This particular classroom environment necessitated a well-designed playground-like infrastructure for students to safely take risks. So Keith engineered *The Last Bird*, an allegory of an exploitative colonial war, in 3 days. Normally it would take Keith a year or more to write a full-length play of this magnitude, but it was an emergency and he cared deeply about his students and about the topic.

The United States was entrenched in the Vietnam War in 1972, and Keith watched newsreels shown on Scandinavian television of atrocious acts of violence committed against innocent Vietnamese men, women, and children at the hands of US soldiers. These images plus a dream he had about an angel pursued by executioners provided the underpinning for *The Last Bird*. Franz Fanon's *The Wretched of the Earth* (1961), written during and in regard to the Algerian war for independence from France and addressing the psychological implications of colonialism, also inspired Keith's writing. *The Last Bird* is about grieving and the way people behave under extreme duress (or under religious authority) and, for Keith, this often translates into satirical humor. For example, in Scene 13: "Re-Match," Death and Jesus

---

[31] Fast-Food Stanislavsky can be played in a variety of ways (See *Impro for Storytellers*, pp. 285–301 and 343–53). In international workshops, Keith continually expands on the basic structure of this game. For example, in London (2010), he added that a player using a "shadow," that is, another player who holds the list and suggests actions, could say "pass" to a suggested action or "more" if they were ready for another action.

fight for supremacy by creatively killing and resurrecting Grandpa no less than 20 times:

> JESUS. Rise up, Granddad! Rise up!
> WAIF. (Pulling open one of Granddad's eyelids?) He's still in there.
> GRANDAD. (Reviving. Staring around.) Augh! That was t-t-terrible!
>   (Death reentered and killed Granddad again)
> WAIF. Look out!
> JESUS. (TO DEATH) That's enough now!
>   (Death swept out)
>   (Mops brow?) Come back into the flesh! Granddad! Rise up!
> GRANDDAD. Augh! Oh . . . augh!
> WAIF. (Hugging Granddad) Oh Granddad, let's go far away from here.
> GRANDDAD. W-where am I?
>   (Death entered)
> JESUS. (To Death) I won't have this man killed and resurrected like a yoyo!
> DEATH. Try squirting me with Holy Water then!
>   (Death snapped his fingers – Granddad died again)
> JESUS. (He blows into Granddad's thumb) That should do it!
> GRANDDAD. (reviving) Augh!
>   (Granddad dies – Death had stayed on to 'snap' him dead again)
> JESUS. Why don't you give up!
> DEATH. I never give up!
> JESUS. (Furious?) I am the resurrection and the life!
> DEATH. (Leaving) That was then! This is now! (*Last Bird*, Rev. 61–2)

Bits of comic relief like this one—reminiscent of music hall or vaudeville—are necessary in this allegory of a society lacerated by a distorted, nightmarish war.

Six separate story lines constitute the action of the play. The main story line follows a young Waif and her Grandfather on a rescue mission to save the last bird, actually an angel. Both characters are masked. Keith wrote in detail about working with these masked characters in the "Masks and Trance" chapter of *Impro*. The Waif had been brought to life previously by Ingrid Johnstone. This mask induced a "lost child" character with twisting movements which Keith infers were caused by the unevenness of the wide-set eyes. Similar characteristics surfaced from every actress who brought this Waif character to life with this particular mask (*Impro* 174–6).

The play is inhabited by other strange creatures like the "Double Figure," a she-monster monarch with the legs of a man and a vagina that eats her lovers and unborn children. "Headstone," the monarch's head executioner, is inflicted with the stigmata. The violent nature of his job is leaving "scars" internally and externally. In a country ravaged by an illogical war,

Headstone (notice the similarity to "Johnstone") declares he and his gang of executioners cannot be held accountable for their atrocities (e.g., sawing off the wings of the bird/angel and gang-raping the Waif), especially given God's policy of "free will."[32] The compassionate but completely useless Jesus character and his beguiling rival Death provide most of the comic relief. Finally, three happy, "Breugel-type" cripples, a fourth "faking" cripple, a doctor, a bishop, monks, and a variety of peasant characters complete the character breakdown (*Last Bird*, Rev.).

Steen Haakon Hansen was a stagehand and technician on the production at the Statens Teaterskole and Keith's methods and pedagogy had a significant impact on his career.[33] Mask work was not a part of the curriculum in 1972 and Hansen remembered several instructors criticizing Keith's extensive use of masks for the senior production. They did not see the value in presenting masked graduating seniors to potential employers, that is, to the artistic directors/managers of the major theatres in Copenhagen. "Some directors said they couldn't judge the work of the students, they couldn't see their faces when they were wearing masks," Hansen told me. A few actually walked out in protest. Keith tells me each student played a masked character and an unmasked character, but that did not mollify the instructors who were more interested in showcasing their "products" than providing students with a theatrical experience they would never forget. Undeterred, Keith alleged that this production was the most successful production the Statens Teaterskole had ever done. Hansen agrees: "Because it was something completely new, the actors were acting in another way. Maybe not successful for the theatre managers but for others, it was so interesting. For people who were into renewing theatre in Denmark, it was important, yes."

Keith directed *The Last Bird* again in 1974 at the Svalegangen Teater in Aarhus, Denmark, with actress Karen Lis Ahrenkiel, now known as the "grand old lady" of Aarhus Theatre, in the role of the Waif. This time around, the critics were completely divided. Unlike the critical instructors and directors at the Statens Teaterskole, Ivar Gjørup, writing for *Politkken*, one of the largest papers in Copenhagen, was pleased with the mask work:

De syv skuespiller . . . fungerer fortræffeligt som ensemble . . . . Vi ser ikke hyppigt masketeater her i landet, og det gør et fascinerende indtryk i Svalegangens udgave.

The seven actors function excellently as an ensemble . . . We do not see frequent mask theater here in our country and this makes a fascinating impression in Svalegangen's version. (trans. Jeremiah)

---

[32] All of Keith's executioner characters sported black leather helmets exposing the eyes, a grimacing mouth, and chin (*Impro* 176–7).

[33] Soon after this production, Hanson enrolled as a student in the director and actor programs at the Statens Teaterskole, and today he runs the Danish Institute of Improvisation (DIFI) at the Odsherred Teaterskole in Nykøbing with a mission "to keep the work of Keith Johnstone alive in improvised theatre" (Odsherred).

At the other end of the spectrum, Hans Andersen, in his review for *Jyllands Posten*, expressed: "[S]pillets dramatiske og meningsmæssige armod forplanter sig til opførelsen og de medvirkende, således at den rent ud sagt virker uprofessionel og dilletantisk." "The plays' dramatic and thematic poverty spills over to the performance and the performers, so that it, to speak plainly, seems unprofessional and dilettante" (trans. Jeremiah). A third critic writing for *Demokraten* did not judge the opening performance as polished but predicted a bright future for the ensemble:

> [D]er er så meget medrivende teaterleg, så meget talent til stede og mulighed for udvikling i samspil med publikum, at jeg føler mig overbevist om, at der måske kun ved enkelte forestillinger, vil kunne ske spændende og eventyrlige ting på Svalegangen. Prøv selv.
>
> There are so many spell-binding theatre-games, so much talent present and potential for development in the interplay with the audience, that I feel convinced that in maybe a few days, maybe only a few performances, something exciting and fairytale like will happen at Svalegangen. Try it yourself." ("Kristus"; trans. Jeremiah)

A similar divide in critical reception happened when Keith's Loose Moose Theatre Company staged *The Last Bird* in Calgary in 1979 and again when they remounted it for the fringe Festival of Fools in New York City in 1984.[34] "It tends to produce extreme reactions, no matter where it plays, and I really don't understand that," remarked Keith. "I wrote it to be popular theatre. It's got everything in it. It's like a circus" (L. Hobson, "Loose Moose Director"). *The Last Bird* is a circus of the grotesque, a fusion of Keith's memories, philosophy, and his extraordinary imagination. Out of everything he has written, this play and his children's play *The Frog Wife* are his two favorites.[35] Over the years, Keith has continued to revise the dialogue and add elements from various productions, although he leaves the plot unaltered. Like everything he writes or creates, *The Last Bird* will remain a work in progress as long as Keith's mind is imaginatively active.

Emigration

The Theatre Machine finally received an Arts Council grant at some point in 1971 but soon the group would no longer be under Keith's directorship. Constant touring had taken its toll. Keith had not only served as artistic director, but also as emcee, stage manager, off-and-on lighting technician, and teacher, and he wasn't making enough money to justify the work. The

---

[34] Photos and documentation of these productions are in Chapter 5.
[35] Both plays are published in *Wie Meine Frau Dem Wahnsinn Verfiel* (2009) and in *The Last Bird: Stories and Plays* by Keith Johnstone (2012) published by Alexander Verlag Berlin.

profits, actually, were always split evenly. Furthermore, Keith had already accepted a 2-year visiting professorship at the University of Calgary. With a new wife and the thought of starting a family, Keith needed a less nomadic lifestyle and a permanent salary. Canada was ready to offer him both.

Theatre Machine continued without Keith as their director for another decade; however, prior to his exodus, they would never attempt to perform without him. "I was the person they listened to. They were sort of superstitious. But soon after I left, they managed perfectly well on their own," Keith says. It did take some time, however, to learn how to self-direct, self-structure an evening, and to trust that ideas would present themselves. "We worked for awhile with exercises pinned up in the wings, so we could run off and look at an exercise and come back on," Maude-Roxby says. "But as we proceeded, we got better at *not* knowing [and] allowing for awareness that there's a certain pathos if you [don't know] because the audience picks up on that." Although they were very successful on their own, years later, Gaskill told Keith something was missing in Theatre Machine's performances. Keith deduced that they needed an outside eye to force action to happen. Without this side-direction, even professional improvisers are likely to get caught up in the fun and forget that "there has to be some point to things." In other words, a director can remind improvisers to make relationships, to be altered, and to move the narrative forward.

Touring with Theatre Machine, teaching at RADA, and teaching abroad sharpened Keith's skills as a director and teacher of impro and provided embodied experiences which allowed him to develop his theories on audience behavior. A plethora of new games, exercises, and techniques were developed for and with his troupe and students. For Keith, the stages of Europe were also classrooms. No matter how famous Theatre Machine got, the troupe members were always "in training." Maude-Roxby recalls, "In the early days, Keith was very good at taking note of what any individual did instinctively and then giving a resume of that to the rest of the group." He also encouraged the group to visit museums and art galleries in every town they toured in order to observe the vividness, the detail, and the significance of a facial expression or a gesture. "When we were working with Keith, there was a lot of talk about how much you could rehearse in the bath, if you could think yourself through the exercises," Maude-Roxby says. He compares this process to the process a jockey might go through as he walks over and measures the field before a race. It is not preplanning or rehearsing but rather visualizing possible tactics or strategies that can be used in the moment if needed. Metaphorically speaking, it is storing spare keys in case a door suddenly appears that needs unlocking.

Having new improvisers join Theatre Machine from time to time created a necessity for ongoing onstage training, but Keith would have remained a teacher regardless. He never stopped experimenting with, adjusting, or evaluating his own work so why should the improvisers? At the Court, Devine had also worked tirelessly to maintain a theatre-as-classroom environment. He treated every production, whether a hit or miss, as an opportunity for education and he encouraged his artistic staff to mentor others. Keith's way of working with Theatre Machine was a continuation of Devine's legacy.

For the first 2 years, Theatre Machine actually toured and performed scenes with Devine's wonderful collection of masks. Then one day, the Court asked Keith to return the masks. They were to be used in an upcoming production. "I was sure that we'd be able to borrow them again," he wrote, "but I received an anonymous phone call saying that I should come to the Theatre at once. I was too late. The masks had been stamped flat so that they could be crammed into two garbage bins . . . . Spoiled forever" (*Thing* 90). Presumably, from ignorance and/or a lack of communication, Devine's masks were dismantled and demolished during the striking of the set. But Keith would take Devine's mask techniques and his principles with him to Canada. He would also take Stirling's pedagogy, Beckett's advice, and the wealth of practical knowledge collected and discovered during his continuing quest to recapture the spontaneous imagination.

CHAPTER FOUR

The master teacher in the university classroom

Every child is an artist.
The problem is how to remain an artist once he grows up.
PABLO PICASSO

The university should be a place for controversy,
but something's gone wrong.
KEITH JOHNSTONE

Keith remembers most of his childhood as being a nightmare. Although he painted, wrote short stories, and played the piano, his ability to imaginatively and spontaneously respond began to diminish as he reached his preteens. Keith did not rediscover the artist within himself until adulthood. At the Royal Court Theatre and with Theatre Machine, he rekindled a relationship with his artist child and helped others to do the same. His teaching assignments after he left the Court, for the most part, had been opportunities for Keith to continue his explorations in conservatory-like classrooms and on stages with only a modicum of intervention from his superiors. Even the Lord Chamberlain left Keith's public classes/demonstrations alone. But Keith was about to enter a different world—a theatre department in a major university—where seniority, graduate degrees, and procedures could override ideas cooked up by unconventional artists lacking conventional academic qualifications.

This chapter documents Keith's career as a professor of acting at the University of Calgary (UofC) beginning with a 2-year visiting lectureship (1972–74) and ending with his retirement as a professor emeritus in 1995. In 1975, Keith was appointed to a full-time tenure track position. Two years later, with Mel Tonken and a handful of students, he launched the Loose Moose Theatre Company. In the first few years, the Loose Moose did not have a home base and Keith proposed attaching his company to the university to give students professional opportunities. But a few senior faculty members were determined to keep Keith's unconventional company outside of the department. Instead of rocking the boat, Keith quietly acquiesced and detached the work of Loose Moose almost entirely from the university. Although Keith's tenure at UofC chronologically coincides with his artistic direction of the Loose Moose—and the former informs the latter—the focus of this chapter is on the former. It takes a comprehensive look at Keith's Drama 200 and Drama 300 acting classes, his syllabi, his pedagogy, and the four productions he directed at the university using impro methods explored in his classrooms. The Loose Moose Theatre Company is covered in Chapter 5.

O Canada! Johnstone's new home

London had limited opportunities for Keith's kind of writing and directing and he was ready to make a permanent salary, the kind of salary a major university could offer. UofC not only offered him a professorship but an escape from London, the city that was making him ill. For the most part, Keith is a healthy man. He has been a vegetarian since childhood and has had no major illnesses or surgeries. Nevertheless, he is as attentive to his physical body as he is to the observance of human behavior. With his fortieth birthday just around the corner, Keith was ready for a significant change.

In *Impro*, Keith writes about how the status of someone can be altered by the space he is in. For instance, a good or "high-status" view is one in which you can see for great distances. "As people come in sight of a view, it's normal for their posture to improve and for them to breathe better" (60). Kathleen Foreman, a former student in Keith's Drama 300 class, an early Loose Moose Company member, and an associate professor at UofC since 1995, remembers Keith talking about how landscape and space attracted him. "Calgary was a place where there literally, physically, and intellectually was space," reflects Foreman. Keith possibly felt he could breathe better, stand a little taller, and perhaps blaze his own trail in Canada. He also thought he would have more time to write but, with the formation and running of a company, this was not to be. In any case, Canada became home and today, Foreman maintains, Keith Johnstone is "part of the fabric of the wild west ideology in the artistic community in Calgary" (P.I.).

Johnstone's first staging of *Godot*

Keith's visiting lectureship at UofC was arranged once again by Richard Courtney, a full professor at UofC from 1971–74. Keith taught acting and directed a workshop production of *Waiting for Godot* in the wings of the University Theatre.[1] The audience sat in wooden chairs on two levels. Michael McNinch, writing for *The Albertan*, lamented the brief run (only four performances) and declared, "Many drama buffs undoubtedly would have braved the rustic surroundings to watch this excellent production." *The Calgary Herald* critic, Bill Musselwhite, thought the play antiquated but the production a success. "The play is two hours of remarkably well-paced and well-acted entertainment" and "uses all the traditional ammunition of the clown—the pratfall, the sight gag, the inane—and the audience reacts."

As mentioned in Chapter 2, Beckett and *Godot*, in particular, factored largely into Keith's choices as a playwright and as a director; but Keith, who understood Beckett better than most, was never given an opportunity to direct *Godot* during his tenure at RCT. Anthony Page directed a production of *Godot* at RCT in 1964. When I asked Keith why he didn't direct, he did not respond with explanations or any ounce of resentment. He just told me, matter-of-factly, "I do a very good *Godot*. Better than that one. It's a musical piece. All along rhythm. Section after section. But we never blocked it." Keith rarely blocked plays or scenes especially with only two actors. He worked on text and rhythm and then allowed the actors to go where they wanted. "It's only two people. Why should you have to tell the actors where to be?" Over the next 20 years, Keith directed two more productions of *Godot* at the Loose Moose (1978, 1998) and one at the Odense Teater in Denmark (1986).[2]

The University of Calgary

In the fall of 1974, Keith took another year-long visiting professorship at Queens University in Kingston, Ontario, and Ingrid gave birth to Keith's second son, Ben, on November 12.[3] The following fall, Keith embarked on a new chapter of his life as a tenured-track professor at UofC. The most radical playwright at RCT, who consistently fought against authority, social norms, and traditional education in Britain, would spend the next two decades in academia. This move seemed incongruous with Keith's

---

[1] Mel Tonken played Vladimir. Tonken and Keith would coestablish Loose Moose 5 years later. Geordie Johnson, who played Lucky, went on to an extremely successful career in film and theatre.
[2] These productions are covered in Chapter 5.
[3] His first son, Dan Fardell, was born around 1959.

trajectory and, in a way, a step backward in his career, but the university provided a place for Keith to put his theories into practice on his own terms. Foreman describes Keith's acting classroom "as a laboratory for what he was interested in investigating at the time which was an extension of his work from the Royal Court and the Theatre Machine and the creation of his new company." And like other acting professors, he "had absolute freedom to teach in the way he wanted and to teach anything he wanted" (Foreman, P.I.).

Keith had classrooms full of fervent students dying to create something fresh in this conservative city known primarily for its petroleum industry, cattle, and annual Stampede—not theatre. These students needed a rebel leader, a guru such as Keith, to guide them and to give them permission to deviate. With no restrictions and no formal syllabus, Keith could test and expand his Impro System. He also had access to theatre spaces which, at least for the first few years, allowed him to push boundaries. All of these conditions factored into the founding of the Loose Moose Theatre Company and to the creation of Theatresports, Calgary's only indigenous sport.

UofC was and still is a top-ranking research university so it makes sense that Keith was allowed to apply his theories in the classroom. But the drama department had a rather traditional theatre program, so why would they hire a master impro teacher with no formal theatre training? Certainly attracting a big-shot from London to Canada's young city was a major coup and, as a visiting lecturer 2 years prior, Keith had proven himself to be a popular teacher and a worthy director. Also, I deduce that his appointment had something to do with commonalities between the Impro System and educational concepts embedded in Albertan curriculum. Foreman, who grew up in Alberta, told me she had been exposed to improvisation in drama education from an early age; so when introduced to Keith's improvisational methods in 1977, this way of working was not totally unfamiliar to her. Whether or not improvisation/acting was a required discipline in Albertan curriculum guides of the late 1970s when Keith began his tenure, I do not know, but revised curriculum guides in the mid-to-late 1980s suggest that improvisation was a part of the educational landscape.

Alberta *Programs of Study—Fine Arts—Drama* curriculum guides for Elementary (written in 1985) and Junior High and Senior High (both revised in 1989) share the same philosophy on Drama's importance to education and to self-development:

> Drama is both an art form and a medium for learning and teaching. It can develop the whole person—emotionally, physically, intellectually, imaginatively, aesthetically, and socially—by giving form and meaning to experience through "acting out" . . . . The dramatic growth parallels the natural development of the student. This growth is fostered in an atmosphere that is non-competitive, cooperative, supportive, joyful yet challenging. (Alberta, *Elementary* A1; *Junior High* A1; *Senior High* 1)

The curriculum proposes structured dramatic play for grades 1 through 6 to be taught as a separate subject or integrated with other subjects in the Elementary Drama program of study. For Drama Programs at the junior and senior high school levels, the curriculum lists "improvisation" as a required discipline and "spontaneous improvisation" and "theatre sports" as two possible formats (Alberta, *Junior High* C1; *Senior High* 5).[4]

Providing further substantiation that improvisation was part of the landscape, a handful of drama education pioneers who used improvisatory approaches had been influencing Albertan educators since the mid-1960s. Viola Spolin (1906–94), who began her work in Chicago, had and continues to have a huge impact in Canada and the United States. Born in Sussex, Brian Way (1923–2006) was a British educator who, with Margaret Faulkes, founded the Theatre Centre in London in 1953, a professional theatre for young people. On the heels of the publication of his book, *Development through Drama* (1967), Way traveled through western Canada in the 1970s and, like Keith, finally settled there. He served as associate artistic director of the Globe Theatre in Regina, Saskatchewan, lectured, and accepted professorships at various universities. Way also edited Peter Slade's (1912–2004) influential book *Child Drama* (1954) which advocated "play" in British schooling as a means of learning. It was this connection to Slade that encouraged Way to enter the field of what would become known as "theatre-in-education."

Slade, often called Britain's first "drama therapist," confirmed Keith's negative view of traditional British public schooling. At the age of 16, Slade left his beloved prep school where he had been "encouraged and trusted by adults" and entered a public school—"An iceberg of cold grey. No affection, no trust, cold grey" (*Experience* 44). Like Keith, Slade was intuitive, perceptive, but not necessarily clever or good at remembering dates or details that often appeared on exams. He was a misfit, an "outlaw," in public school: "[A]t such places you must conform. If you conform, you are happy. It is easier to be a convergent thinker and unfortunately I have never been that" (*Experience* 44). Dorothy Heathcote (1926–2011), another British-born educator, invented innovative and unorthodox dramatic-inquiry approaches to teaching and learning (e.g., Mantle of the Expert). At Newcastle University, where she taught for 22 years, she developed an Advanced Diploma of Drama Education course of study.

Keith is an extension of these post-war British educators who impacted drama education in Canada. Way, for example, wrote about the need to establish arts as an educational subject concerned with "the development of the intuition" not the intellect and advocated a calm, uncritical environment

---

[4]   Keith should be but isn't acknowledged in the revised 1989 Junior High and Senior High *Programs of Study—Fine Arts—Drama* curriculum guides as the creator of "theatre sports."

where students need not fear failure (4–16). Like Keith, Heathcote believed teachers must not only facilitate but be deeply involved in the process of learning. In her essay on "authentic" teaching, she promoted a pedagogy similar to what Keith advocates: The authentic teacher must assess the reality of every situation, encourage student interaction, be flexible, have the ability to devise a variety of ways to tackle the subject at hand, and must learn the skills that "take their pupils into their subjects through the doorways of attraction—attention, interest, involvement, concern—to investment. . ." (178).

Keith does not mention any of these British-born educators as influential to his work, and he had no knowledge of Spolin's work until after he had developed the core of his Impro System at the RCT Studio. "If I'd known Spolin's work when I started, I probably would've copied her and I wouldn't be here," he said (Stockholm Wksp). Like Keith, Spolin created improvisational games to solve problems that arose during formal theatrical processes and to unleash the imaginative potential of the student actor. Spolin's work, although developed mostly with and for children, also had a profound influence on professional improvisers as it evolved through Paul Sills and The Second City.[5] But Keith and Spolin "differed radically in philosophy and approach," wrote Richard Courtney in his letter to support Keith's promotion to full tenure in 1986. Courtney continues:

> The major difference lies in the inherent creativity in the Johnstone "games": they release a spontaneity unknown to exist in the actor before—a level of the unconscious that is hilarious, bizarre, remarkably fluent and persistent to the end of the task . . . .The effect of Johnstone "games" on undergraduate students can be transformational—dozens of instances at both Victoria and Calgary come to mind. (1)

Spolin, Slade, Way, and Heathcote were also primarily concerned with teaching teachers how to create environments where *children* could playfully interact with and recognize themselves as part of the world. Direct experience, that is, going through the process itself at the child's own pace, is what mattered and theory was left to the educators and to the scholars. At the RCT Studio, patiently waiting for artistic growth through direct experience was impractical for the professional artists who took Keith's classes. They needed practical techniques that they could comprehend and immediately apply to their work in front of and for live, paying audiences. Although Keith writes about primary school education, he developed his Impro System specifically for these professional artists

---

[5] In *Impro for Storytellers*, Keith includes/endorses several of Spolin's games.

and/or for "atrophied" *adults* like himself. This and his determination to get his teachers *and* students to understand the theoretical foundations of every exercise and every technique is what separates Keith from the others.

Keith's methodology is grounded in theory which allows students to not only experience but to understand why the experience matters. His exercises and games have definite form and rules but, for Foreman and for many former students who apply the Impro System to their own processes, the theory makes all the difference. While Keith would be the first to espouse shutting off the rational, intellectual mind when improvising, he is also an adult liberatory educator—like Freire—who comprehends the value of acquiring a critical understanding of reality and the ability to decode "coded" situations. Freire wrote: "When people lack a critical understanding of their reality, apprehending it in fragments which they do not perceive as interacting constituent elements of the whole, they cannot truly know that reality" (104). So they must investigate that reality by decoding it, breaking it into fragments, piecing it back together into a concrete whole, and then returning back again to the fragments. This dialectical reflection allows students to recognize themselves and fellow students as participants of a socially-coded world and as dancers in the kinetic dance. For professional actors, improvisers, directors, and writers with limited time to "experience," critical understanding of coded behavior is essential, not only to re-create normative behavior on the stage, but for deconstructing and exploding those norms.

Frank Totino was a 27-year-old struggling rock musician, not an actor, when he first met Keith in 1976. "I heard from my brother [Tony Totino] that there was an interesting guy and his wife who were teaching in the drama department. I was inspired to join the department based on the fact that this Englishman had actually worked in the real theatre." Frank was especially impressed by the references to Keith in the library. In just a few years, Frank would become a favorite at the Loose Moose, and today he manages Johnstone's Workshops and teaches the Impro System in Brazil and all over Europe. The Impro System made immediate sense to Frank. He had been interested in jazz improvisation for some time and understood what it meant to "groove" or "riff" or "jam." But for everyday spontaneous behavior, no practical vocabulary existed. "Status, accepting ideas, the way one person automatically adjusts to another, you notice it in your life but haven't a clue what's going on," says Frank. Keith took those behavioral clues, decoded them, applied terminology (e.g., status, see-sawing, kinetic dance, offer, block), and created techniques to speed up recognition, dismantling, and re-creation of that behavior on the stage. For the Totino brothers, Foreman, Dennis Cahill (current artistic director of Loose Moose), and other students in Keith's acting classes at UofC, he created a system that was attainable and—as Keith himself often demonstrated—practical to pedagogy, rehearsals, writing, creative collaboration, interpersonal skills, and for sustaining a career in the theatre.

Keith taught Drama 200 (Intro to Acting) and Drama 300 (Advanced Acting I) throughout his tenure at UofC. In the first year, he taught Drama 400 (Advanced Acting II) but, he avows, "They soon demoted me. My teaching was too bizarre for them." Keith never taught a graduate seminar or a course on directing even after the MFA in Directing program was added in 1981. Jim Dugan, Ph.D., was brought in to chair the UofC theatre department from 1983 to 1994, chaired two more times over the next 15 years, and officially retired in 2009. Right from the beginning, it was apparent to Dugan that "the lines had been drawn, so to speak." Dugan is referring to the lines that separated Keith from the two or three "petty colleagues" who were instrumental in setting up the graduate program and dead set against ever allowing Keith near *their* graduate students. "There was a kind of personal antagonism [towards Keith]," Dugan told me. "There was also a professional antagonism towards improvisation when it's an end in itself. . . . So no, in that time and place, Keith would not have found his way into the directing program." Furthermore, when Dugan asked Keith to propose a seminar or course in directing, Keith replied with something like: "No. There's too many people who wouldn't want me to be part of it."

Keith does not like confrontation or arguments. He hardly ever raises his voice even when obviously irritated, and, at UofC, he made an effort *not* to rock the boat. "After a while, I was careful not to express my views to anybody. I just tried to do my work and stay out of it," he says. Still, Keith refused to conform to standard academic procedure if it did not agree with his process-oriented pedagogy. Also, according to former student and colleague Patricia Benedict, "Keith was not much of a socializer with other faculty. He came in, put in his office hours, taught and left." Benedict found Keith approachable, but "he had little time for chitchat and always seemed to be thinking of several things at once."

Before moving to Calgary in 1972 and entering Keith's acting class at UofC as a mature student, Benedict was an actress in Ireland and trained for a year at the National Academy of Drama. From 1980 to 1997, she was an associate professor of acting at UofC and based her curriculum largely on Keith's teachings. While some colleagues like Benedict "adored his eccentricities" and "secretly cheered him on," others found his actions and aloof personality problematic. In faculty meetings, for example, Benedict remembers Keith as "the burr under the saddle of many of the old guard." Only after debating back and forth subsided would Keith offer input. While playing with a pencil, "his hand would rise slowly and . . . in a couple of seconds [he] would annihilate the previous arguments, vanquish the enemy, and make a decidedly good and valid point whether practical or not," wrote Benedict. Dugan confirmed Benedict's exposé: "I don't remember Keith being an aggressive troublemaker, but he would occasionally make a kind of pithy observation which usually resulted in about four seconds of silence, and then a completely new unrelated point would start the conversation up again." Gaskill had called Keith's judgments "raw and penetrating." Arden had labeled him "the unpaid conscience of the Royal Court." Of course, Gaskill also noted, "George [Devine] and Tony [Richardson] ignored most of his advice, but listened to what he said" (*Sense* 25). A similar disregard for Keith's advice happened at UofC. Before proffering why, it is important to take a look at his extremely popular 200- and 300-level acting classes.

Drama 200 and Drama 300

There were four sections of Drama 200 and Drama 300 available to students each year. Sections were taught by the same professor for both the fall and winter semesters. Drama 200: Introduction to Acting met 2 days a week with both a lecture and lab component. Drama 300: Advanced Acting I met 3 days a week with no lecture component. Keith always had a full teaching load. Usually, he would teach one or two sections of 200 and one section of 300. While all professors teaching these courses covered such basics as improvisation, speech, movement, scene study, and various acting techniques, each varied widely on emphasis, recommended reading lists, and structure. Professors were encouraged to develop their courses according to their particular interests. Keith's main interest, of course, was impro—and in impro applied to the acting process—and the nature of impro is spontaneity. In *Impro for Storytellers*, he wrote:

> I visualize myself as coaxing my students away from the rim of the wheel and towards the hub. This makes a conventional syllabus impossible, since any spoke will do if it enthuses a particular group of students. If a spoke gets boring, I just move to a more interesting spoke. When students reach the hub, all spokes seem equally important and exciting. (56)

The only reason Keith created a syllabus at all, he tells me, was to stop students from suing him. It was more of an academic exercise for him, a task that had to be completed in order to maintain a sense of balance. Even so, looking at the consistencies and slight alterations of his syllabi over time is revealing.

Keith's Drama 200 and Drama 300 syllabi were never over a page in length and his statement of purpose varied only slightly: "I'll try to help students be absorbed and truthful while working in front of other people. Emphasis will be on working harmoniously with others, and on clarity of expression." Keith stresses the importance of putting your partner's and the group's needs above your own in his teaching and in his writings. Yet when it came to attendance, Benedict remembered his policy as "more lax" than hers. "I think Keith's view on attendance was such that 'if they wanted to learn they would be there'." He considered students to be adults whereas Benedict viewed them as "adults in training." At some point in the early 1980s, Keith's relaxed approach resulted in a loss of a few students by the end of the school year. Frustrated, he asked Benedict how she managed to keep all of hers. "I never knew how to answer that, but I think they needed to be made more accountable for their actions, and Keith was not that kind of taskmaster," said Benedict. If Keith wasn't a taskmaster, what kind of master was he?

Foreman says Keith was "the force in the classroom that was making everything happen, but he did it in a way that rarely brought the focus to him" (P.I.). Even when he entered the classroom space, before addressing the students, the "master of status" would sit on the floor at a lower, nonthreatening level. As conjectured earlier, Keith's classroom was a laboratory for investigating what interested him, and these investigations carried over into his production work at UofC. He attracted a huge following of dedicated students especially in the first 4 years when Loose Moose was in its infancy and dependent on university talent. Moving into the 1980s, after the initial enthusiasm over Keith's impro methods abated, students may not have been as dedicated to his classes as before, but, by all accounts, Keith remained dedicated to his students.

Vakhtangov and Zen

Who other than Devine, Stirling, and Lao Tzu did Keith specifically consult for pedagogical inspiration? The "recommended reading lists" on his syllabi offer some clues. On a few occasions, he would throw in titles such as *Awareness Through Movement* by Moshé Feldenkrais or *Inner Game of Tennis* by W. Timothy Gallwey and, almost always, he would say "Everything by Stanislavsky." Only three texts, however, consistently made the list: *Impro* by Keith (once it was published), *The Vakhtangov School of Stage Art* (1950) by Nikolai Gorchakov, and *Zen and the Art of Archery* (1953) by Eugen Herrigal.[6] After reading Gorchakov's firsthand accounts of Vakhtangov's process, it is clear why Keith recommended this text.

Vakhtangov's style of teaching and direction has correlations with Keith's. He combined Stanislavsky's realism in acting with Meyerhold's

---

[6] Some professors in the department included Keith's *Impro* in their own recommended reading lists after 1983 and/or, like Benedict and later Foreman, based their improvisational work largely on the Impro System.

stylized physicality to create "fantastic realism" in the theatre. Most of Keith's plays and productions could be categorized as "fantastic realism." Keith often says, "Truth doesn't imply naturalism. Truth is how things really are or the attempt to express how things really are." Vakhtangov also believed a theatre space should be primitive, with "no superfluous decorations," clean, not too large, respected by all company members, and designed so that actors could be easily seen and heard from every seat. "The ideal auditorium is the amphitheatre," declared Vakhtangov (Gorchakov, *Vakhtangov* 32). After their first nonpermanent location at the Pumphouse Theatre, Loose Moose has occupied permanent theatre spaces with amphitheatre-type configurations, with semicircular tiers for audience seating around a thrust stage. Moreover, Vakhtangov would not tolerate disrespect for the ensemble and his method of keeping discipline was humorous and effective. "Bohemianism," that is, pretentious behavior of any sort, was "nipped in the bud." If a young actor at Vakhtangov's Studio displayed this type of behavior, the "man on duty" would simply hang a sign that read: "The Muses Do Not Tolerate Vanity." If an actor joked too often, the "man on duty" would silently carry a jester's cap with bells, stuck on a pole, across the rehearsal room, and so forth (34).[7] Keith's disciplinary measures were in this same spirit. Finally, like Vakhtangov, Keith could be very blunt. At a midterm student evaluation conference, Benedict remembers Keith saying to her, "You know you are not as good as you think you are, however, I think you have more stuff if you could just stop acting so hard." Ann Jellicoe once remarked on Keith's "air of uncorrupted idealism and his sweetness of nature" (Findlater, *At the Royal* 54). These qualities have much to do with why that statement sent Benedict out of the room inspired, not in tears.

    The recommendation of Herrigal's text, *Zen in the Art of Archery*, was not so transparent at first. In the London 2010 workshop, Keith told students that this book helped him as a young adult, and he does allude to it in *Storytellers* and in his other writings. He has integrated the Zen teachings inscribed in this text, and those he has picked up from monks he has taught and from other sources, so thoroughly and successfully into his work that he no longer needs to cite original sources. Nonetheless, in an interview with Hilda Louise Kearley, a former master's student in UofC's Department of Curriculum and Instruction, Keith connected his theories to Herrigal's text. He explained that the theory behind his technique of "overloading"—preoccupying or "screwing up" the verbal mind (a.k.a. the judgmental intellect, the censor, the voice in the head) with multiple tasks so

---

[7] All incidents were then recorded into a daily logbook, so Vakhtangov knew what was going on even when he was absent. If only Keith had kept such records.

the actor's corporeal wisdom can do its thing—is like the philosophy in *Zen in the Art of Archery*:

> [T]he person mustn't fire the arrow, something else must do it. It doesn't mean the actor has to expose all his inner subconscious thought . . . . It means working in non-verbal states. Take riding a bike—if you had to think to ride a bike, you'd fall off. In normal life most choices are not conscious, for example, how to move or how to sound, because you're not self-conscious. It's not a matter of revealing the Freudian unconscious, it's a technique of being "unguarded" so that the body works of its own volition . . . . (Kearley 39)

Keith's students achieve these nonverbal, unguarded states through split-attention techniques and games.

Silently repeating a mantra during a scene disrupts intellectual thinking and prevents students from preplanning. The Hat Game forces students to split their attention by carrying on a conversation while secretly planning to steal their partner's hat. Taking-the-Hat clown games abolish self-consciousness and promote corporeal presence by overloading the students with multiple tasks (e.g., maintaining a pecking-order, throwing and picking up hats, and playing a scene). Shouting out sequential word lists as fast as possible; creating a story with a partner one-word-at-a-time; and interviewing another as if he were an "expert" who is not allowed to hedge can also promote nonverbal states of being.[8] Finally, mask work—using half-masks, false noses, makeup, or alteration of everyday facial expressions and sounds—has the power to release other "personalities" subdued in everyday life. For a student to "leap instinctively into a situation without having to bring it into consciousness," as Herrigel put it, the mask teacher, like the master teacher of archery, must create a safe environment for the masked student to explore these other selves (38).

Archery in Japan and other arts rooted in Zen Buddhism (e.g., swordsmanship, flower arrangement, tea ceremony) are called "artless arts" which denote activities that are free from purpose, aim, and growing from the Unconscious. D. T. Suzuki wrote in the introduction to Herrigel's text:

> Zen is the "everyday mind," as was proclaimed by Baso (Ma-tsu, died 788); this "everyday mind" is no more than "sleeping when tired, eating when hungry." As soon as we reflect, deliberate, and conceptualize, the original unconsciousness is lost and a thought interferes. . . . The arrow is off the string but does not fly straight to the target, nor does the target stand where it is. . . .

---

[8] Keith's Experts game was inspired by Vakhtangov's direction to his actors portraying the wise men in *Turandot*. Vakhtangov asked them to secretly solve impossible problems when onstage (*Impro* 126).

Man is a thinking reed but his great works are done when he is not calculating and thinking. "Childlikeness" has to be restored with long years of training in the art of self-forgetfulness. When this is attained, man thinks yet he does not think. . . . (viiii–ix)

Taking up archery was Herrigel's "preparatory school for Zen." The disciplined practice of this art under the guidance of Master Kenzo Awa allowed Herrigel to reach a state of spirituality where fear and self-consciousness no longer had control. Keith avows that mask work, and all spontaneous acting, restores "childlikeness," silences the voice in the head, and allows students to work in an inspired state, free from stage fright. In his writings and in the UofC classrooms, he espoused and embodied aspects of the teacher to student relationship of Japanese culture. Like Master Kenzo Awa, Keith established trust, convinced "by his mere presence," looked and waited patiently for "growth and ripeness," and, lastly, encouraged students to go further, to "climb on the shoulders" of their master teacher (Herrigel 40–6).

The Japanese pupil, on the other hand, is also expected to have an uncritical veneration of his teacher and, in the beginning, to simply copy what the teacher shows him without question. Keith did not demonstrate in his classrooms so students could not simply "copy," but he was a generator and disseminator of a massive amount of ideas. Most of these ideas trained students to collaborate but that does not mean Keith was good at collaboration. Even during those early years at UofC, when students were actively involved in the formation of Loose Moose and Theatresports, Keith was the captain of his ship, relying on his crew, but ultimately making the final decisions.

Teacher-student interaction

"Keith was always a dedicated teacher," affirms Dugan. And he still is today, but if the teaching profession had not pursued him and had not offered him stability, he would have chosen a different career. Keith approached the opportunity to teach in an academic setting like UofC not for the love of teaching or to collaborate with others but for the salary, to have more time to write, and for the opportunity to test and expand his ideas with university support and funding. It is no different than a scientist supported by university funds teaching classes and doing lab experiments at the same time. The scientist loves his work, needs the students who also need him, but it is the scientist's experiments which are really at stake. Dennis Cahill, artistic director of Loose Moose, original company member, and former student in Keith's acting class, told me: "Keith is willing to accept input if he believes it fits. However, he can be very quick to dismiss ideas he's not interested in. As well, when you work with Keith you do get the feeling he is often way ahead of you and everyone else involved."

Clem Martini, a former student and Loose Moose company member who is now chair of the UofC Drama Department, said Keith remained popular especially when Loose Moose and Theatresports became world famous; but after those first few years, the flock of ardent followers diminished. Martini recalls that a small number of students wanted more text-based, character, and deeper emotional work, and/or felt as if Keith did not have the same kind of passion for the work in the classroom as he had in the early years. A reciprocal relationship, though, is needed to sustain passion. In the beginning, students who were also a part of Loose Moose were spending more than 20 hours a week with Keith. About the time Loose Moose relocated to their own theatre space in 1981, university talent was not needed as before and fewer opportunities were available to UofC students.[9] New students entering the department with hopes of becoming a successful Loose Mooser undoubtedly felt abandoned. The ship had sailed without them, so it seemed, and the classroom probably lost some of its give-and-take vitality. It was not the ideal classroom for Keith anymore because his focus had changed and the environment around him had changed. Dugan's post-1983 viewpoint, however, is that Keith never lost his passion for teaching: "He was always very lively, full of insights, very energetic in his classes." Steve Jarand, a mask teacher endorsed by and working alongside Keith today, found him to be very accessible as a teacher in the late 1980s when Jarand was a student. Jarand just had to locate Keith, walk with him, or sit next to him. Dugan labeled Keith a "blue collar person from the theatre" because he could sit comfortably among a group of students, generate ideas, and essentially "talk shop."

As current head of the UofC Department of Drama, a department facing severe budget cuts, Martini almost certainly needs a faculty of professors who can do a lot of things very well. Unfortunately, these all-too-common conditions do not leave room for eccentric, socially awkward geniuses, like Keith, who are occupied most of the time with their own creative pursuits. No, after the Loose Moose was operating autonomously, students no longer cheered as Keith entered the classroom because the "euphoria," as Jarand put it, of those early years had tapered off. Moreover, unlike the first company members, new students did not get the opportunity to work with Keith in and out of the classroom for 20 or more hours per week. But until Keith retired, UofC drama students *did* have the opportunity to study with a master teacher teaching his own system for an entire school year.

---

[9] Keith says nobody got turned away from Loose Moose but professors at UofC warned their students not to get involved. To this day, an open, free impro class is offered every Friday night before the show at the Moose.

Even Martini acknowledges that Keith was better than anyone when it came to "permitting untrained young people to take some new idea and run with it and having them understand that much of what they need to know they already do."

By the late 1980s and early 1990s, Keith was still the force in the room, using his own status and his Impro System to investigate the nature of acting and spontaneity. Classes were fluid, flexible, and full of energy, and the attendance policy was still simply "show up or fail" (Kearley 150). Process still reigned over product and part of that process was Keith's constant evaluation of his own pedagogy. By 1987, for instance, he no longer advocated, like Stirling, that students should never experience failure. In the first *Keith Johnstone's Theatresports and Life-Game Newsletter* (1987), he wrote:

> I used to think that I should try to prevent the student from ever experiencing failure—I thought I could do this by always selecting exactly the right material, and by grading it in tiny steps. These days I think it's more important to teach ways of dealing with the pain of failure. I tell students, "blame the teacher, laugh, never demonstrate a determination to 'try harder'." Without failure, there can be no real game-playing. (1)

In the classroom, allowing students to blame him for their failure was one of many tricks Keith used to manage fear, but this did not absolve students of responsibility. Master Kenzo Awa did not insist on correct breathing techniques from the start, but instead allowed Herrigel to suffer in his efforts until he was "ready to seize the lifebelt" and to understand its significance (Herrigel 23).

Keith never let his students suffer for long but he was not one to coddle his students either. Like Master Kenzo Awa, he wanted students to find their own power and this could not be if they were slavishly dependent upon his praise. Paulo Freire wrote: "The important thing, from the point of view of the libertarian education, is for the people to come to feel like masters of their thinking . . ." (124). Keith accomplished this. He may have been predisposed to making his own statement, but he did encourage, reflect on, and incorporate others' ideas; and he certainly adopted ideas stemming from his observations of the process unfolding in his classes. Since his days at the Court, Keith has used the theatre, in all of its configurations, as a scientific laboratory to investigate the nature of spontaneous creation. In his production work at UofC, the cast and crew were not only aware of the experiment under way but of their contribution to that experiment. When directing, Keith was very animated and willing to draw focus to himself, but he never treated the rehearsal space as anything other than an extension of the classroom.

Production work at the University of Calgary

Keith directed only four shows at the university after he began his full-time tenured track position: Shakespeare's *The Tempest* in 1977, his own *Live Snakes and Ladders* in 1978 and *Mindswop* in 1983, and Bertolt Brecht's *Caucasian Chalk Circle* in 1989. All were designed by Gavin Semple who Keith met at Queens University in 1974. *Caucasian Chalk Circle* was the only production at UofC that did not leave a lasting impression on anyone, except for Jarand who played the role of Simon Sha Shada, the love interest of Grusha, the heroine. Jarand vividly recollects rehearsing group scenes using partial mask pieces—noses, moustaches, hats, eyeglasses—and mirrors in order to create colorful peasant characters. Additionally, Keith would shape the structure, the "external dynamics," but then he would leave the blocking up to the instincts of the actors. "His directing was daring. It was freeing," maintains Jarand. Conversely, Martin Morrow, drama critic for the *Calgary Herald*, thought Keith's absence of blocking left his student cast "to flounder through the scenes" ("Socialist"). A critic from *Calgary Tonite* found the scenes themselves "so loosely constructed that the plot and purpose of the play are diluted in the wash of text and music" (Rev. of *Caucasian*). Both critics, however, found at least one worthwhile element in the 3-hour presentation. Morrow thought Dennis Cahill brought "confidence and comic flair to the role of Azdak." Cahill, after all, was a seasoned Loose Moose actor brought in by Keith. The latter critic found the production "quite stunning visually" and several performances by the "colorfully costumed array of actors" enjoyable. Both Keith and Semple consider the production a less-than-successful effort, but their other three collaborations were not so easily dismissed and one production, above all, will never be forgotten.

Charles Hayter, critic for *The Albertan*, compared Keith's production of *The Tempest*, staged in the university's main theatre in the winter of 1977, to Antonin Artaud's "total spectacle." Tony Totino, a dance major, was the choreographer and played Ariel. Frank Totino composed music for the production, served as musical director, and had a small role. Ingrid was the mask trainer. Cahill, a student at this time, played Antonio and made an appearance as "Spaghetti," a masked character he had created in class. Martini was the Boatswain. Over 27 actors, singers, and dancers, ten rock musicians, plus huge, fully costumed animal characters (including a lobster and a boar's head), and projection screens filled the stage in this production that held the audience "captive in a circus of earthly delights . . ." (Hayter). Tony told me he could never memorize lines before working with Keith. In rehearsals, Keith would have him translate the lines into gibberish and connect them to physical actions. "Before *The Tempest*, I never understood

Johnstone's Mindswop at University of Calgary, 1983.

Photo Credit: Images courtesy of the University of
Calgary Archives, Department of Drama fonds.

anything about the theatre," but after just eight rehearsals with Keith, Tony professes, "Everything became clear."[10]

In the fall of 1978, Keith wrote and put up *Live Snakes and Ladders* in the main theatre and called it a coproduction with Loose Moose. This section ends with a detailed account of this massive production, so let's first jump forward to the spring of 1983. In the smaller Studio Theatre, Keith staged his three-act, 3-hour, science fiction fantasy—*Mindswop*. Set on a distant planet where everyone learns telepathically, a strange set of characters inhabit this play including a three-legged spacecraft pilot, a professor who lives in a fish tank, and the lobster from *The Tempest* as a gynecologist.

The main plot follows Nova as he searches for and discovers his father on Earth, but his father is lacking telepathic powers and inhabiting the body of a mailman. Years prior, Nova's father had mind-swopped with an infant boy when his aircraft crashed, and Earth's inhabitants deliberately designed an educational system to destroy his and all children's talents. "It's a satire about education," says Keith, "but the theme was not really expressed in the play. It could've been a nice play but I buggered it up. I think it's a nice theme, sure, especially in a university. But you can see how I'm not really popular among academics." *Calgary Herald* critic, Rosemary McCracken, wasn't impressed with the storyline but found the "tongue-in-cheek humor" pleasurable and encouraged readers to see the show "just to view the ingenuity with which Johnstone and his technical designers [Semple and Sheila Richardson Lee] have rigged up the fantasy" ("Sci-fi"). Louis B. Hobson, writing for the *Calgary Sun*, called the production "one of the most exciting and original pieces of theatre Calgary has seen in years." Probably in response to the *Live Snakes and Ladders* uproar, Hobson also advised: *Mindswop* is "bound to anger some of Johnstone's colleagues, several critics, and a good number of audience members who are not used to his lunacy." Indeed, Hobson regarded *Mindswop*, with its 40 scene changes and a range of settings, as "even more ambitious than *Snakes and Ladders*" ("Mindswop's").

"Nothing was more ambitious than *Snakes and Ladders*," Keith declares. Nor were any of the other productions he directed at UofC as unforgettable. *Live Snakes and Ladders* could be equated to something Vsevolod Meyerhold produced during his Constructivism period, that is, when Meyerhold's theory of the theatre as factory and schoolroom inspired him to utilize the most efficient methods to induce audience response

---

[10] Tony Totino resides in Oslo with his wife Helen Vikstvedt, a successful Norwegian film actress and improviser. Tony met Vikstvedt in 1990 at the Loose Moose International Summer School and moved to Oslo soon thereafter. He took over as director of the struggling Oslo Theatresports league formed in 1986. Tony brought in new talent and eventually formed an impro troupe in Norway which included his wife, Harald Eia (a famous comedian), Thorbjørn Harr (star of stage and screen), and Jan-Paul Brekke, Ph.D (a respected sociologist). This troupe still performs about once a month to sold-out houses.

(Law 38–9). "If it was done in Europe, it'd be very famous," contends Keith. He's probably right. Not only did this production rock the boat, for 6 weeks of rehearsal and eight performances, it capsized the entire UofC Department of Drama.

Live Snakes and Ladders

The origins of the children's board game Snakes and Ladders date back to India in the second-century BCE. The British discovered this game probably during their trade operations with India and it was introduced into England in the 1890s. Later on it was marketed as a children's game and, in 1943, Milton Bradley released their version, *Chutes and Ladders*, in the United States. The game is played by two to four players on a ten-by-ten grid with each square numbered from 1 to 100. Some squares are linked by ladders, others by snakes. It is a game entirely of chance in which players take turns throwing the dice, each waiting to throw a six or a pair in order to move his counter accordingly. If a player happens to land on a square showing the bottom of a ladder, he ascends up to a higher-numbered square. If, however, he lands on a square with the head of a snake, he slithers down the tail to a lower-numbered square. Originally, the game had religious significance. A journey through the game represented a moral journey through life to heaven. Ladders, representing virtuous acts, would shorten your journey and snakes, representing evil and vice, would lengthen your journey (Grunfeld 131). In any case, the first player to land exactly on square 100 reaches heaven or, simply, wins the game.

When Keith traveled to Denmark, he would listen to BBC radio game broadcasts and often imagine commentaries for live sporting events that did not exist. One day, he imagined a "live" Snakes and Ladders competition with real snakes and real players and he proceeded to write a 50-minute radio piece describing such a match. This radio play stayed in his files until he needed a production that would give Semple "the opportunity to create something spectacular" in the main theatre ("Stage Directions" 2). While Semple built the model, Keith expanded his radio play and, in fact, did continual rewrites very late into the rehearsal process. Foreman remembers Keith "writing like a mad thing in between rehearsals and then you'd get new sheets. He's always working from the laboratory of the theatre, so I think he must have been working in response to what was happening every day and refining" (P.I.). Foreman, Frank and Tony Totino, Martini, Cahill, Ingrid, several other first-year Loose Moose Company members, and approximately 40 additional performers played 60-plus roles in *Live Snakes and Ladders* (*S&L*). Furthermore, a massive production and running crew were needed to build and operate the spectacular set which looked expensive but did not exceed the budget allotted to all main stage productions.

Semple's set design made use of many preexisting departmental resources. Numerous recycled platforms were connected by rented commercial scaffolding and ladders. Seven gigantic snakes, with papier-mâché heads and mouths that opened 8 feet in height, faced the audience. Their bodies, made of carpet underlay, vanished upstage and were strapped or spiked to the structure.

Competitor Olga Karcinova (Betty McLachlan) just before inserting herself into the snake, Live Snakes and Ladders, *University of Calgary, 1978.*

Photo Credit: Deborah Iozzi.

Department-owned television monitors, cameras, and spotlights were utilized. A simple surgical tent was placed in the center of the structure to treat "injured competitors." A commentator's box on audience right and a Royal Box with puppets operated by strings on the left thrust the action over and into the audience. In his review, Louis B. Hobson called Semple's set a "technical masterpiece" ("Pickle"). Most of the costumes and masks were pulled from stock and/or were remnants from Keith's previous productions. The stilt-walking Death figure and the masked executioners had recently been seen in *The Last Bird* at the Loose Moose. The Lobster used in *The Tempest* and *Mindswop* even made an appearance. "It attacked the Bishop,"

Keith says, "but you had to be looking in that direction to see it. I only saw it once."[11]

Act one opens with a prologue delivered by Death. Bruegel's sixteenth-century painting, "Triumph of Death," depicting an army of the dead assaulting the living, was another inspirational source for the prologue and the play itself (Brennan, "Gone"). In his revised "Stage Directions," Keith compares the symbolic world of the play to "a competitive and greedy and brutal and ruthless social system that everyone seems to accept uncritically" (7). The trapped prisoners at the base of the set represent the bottom of a "lunatic pecking-order," and the King and Queen, literally puppets sitting in the Royal Box, represent the top. The play is "a product of a world in which competition has gone insane," wrote Keith (8). After Death leaves the stage, the other characters are introduced as preparations are made for the next "Live Snakes and Ladders Tournament," including cleaning up leftover blood and slime from the previous game.

Act two is the tournament itself. It opens with the Warmer "warming up" the studio audience: "Ladies and Gentlemen. We'd like to welcome you to Live Snakes and Ladders, and to rehearse some applause and booing so that the viewers at home can get into the spirit of the occasion."[12] This second act is meant to be "psychotic and nightmarish and many layered," wrote Keith ("Stage Directions" 6). Approaching it like a sporting event, Keith wanted to give audience members a choice of what to watch. Still, he used follow-spots guided by sports commentators to bring focus onto the main action when necessary.

Hobson commended the "amount of thought, knowledge of theatre, and absolute discipline" that went into the creation of the show and the "incredible sense of order and structure" maintained in act two by the 50-member ensemble in "constant motion":

> People are dying, striving, climbing, falling, fighting, eating, tossing dice, cleaning, mending and even playing violins. There are contestants, judges, dignitaries, officials, snake trainers, executioners, nurses, doctors, waiters, janitors, mutants, boyfriends, commentators, wrestlers, photographers, reporters, charwomen, groupies and even a gigantic lobster.
>
> What is mind boggling is that every character has been introduced to the audience in act one and no one seems extraneous or insignificant. ("Pickle")

---

[11] Semple told me this story: "In the production weeks before and during setup we painted meters of foam snakeskin, which students glued together with contact cement. Most of this had to be done in the theatre; the only space at the time large enough to layout the "skins" and assemble them into bodies. I remember wandering into the auditorium while this assembly was happening. There seemed to be no one about until I noticed the skin form twitching. The poor students were probably high on fumes even though we had fans ventilating the body."

[12] An emcee for a Theatresports' match warms up the audience in the same way.

Tournament in play, Live Snakes and Ladders, *University of Calgary, 1978.*
Photo Credit: Image courtesy of the University of
Calgary Archives, Department of Drama fonds.

Eric Dawson, a junior critic for the *Calgary Herald*, thought the first act revealed Keith Johnstone "at his best" but called the second act "a long, noisy, only occasionally amusing and frequently gross spectacle" ("Snakes"). The critics were divided, as usual. The conventional theatre-going audience hated it but, according to the UofC Department of Drama's programming manager, students loved it (Brennan, "Gone"). Ultimately, the theatre faculty dismissed the production as "a glorious failure" (Benedict).

The production was a failure only in the sense that it was not perfected before opening night. Keith worked on, experimented with, and made changes to all of his productions up until the opening night and throughout the run. "These productions were our research," stated Semple. "Unfortunately, production schedules and available personnel made that ideal operation difficult." But for Semple, *S&L* continues to serve as a reference for a design process in which director and designer have a "co-creative relationship," and a model of "the scope of production possible under relatively small budgets." A second review in the *Calgary Herald* came out 1 week after *S&L*'s last performance, this time written by senior drama critic Brian Brennan who predicted that Calgary audiences would talk about *S&L* for years to come ("Gone"). Brennan was right. Cast members often encounter folks who enthusiastically describe, in great detail, lingering images of *S&L* decades after attending a performance.

Every cast member I talked to remembers the entire process as not only collaborative but as an extension of Keith's improvisational explorations in the classroom. Martini, who played the Head Executioner, says the script was flexible until the very end because Keith was writing it as he was directing. Martini blames the "sprawling narrative" and Keith's tendency to say "yes" for the chaotic nature of the script: "He threw in everything. Things were always changing. He didn't believe in blocking. So people would try things and, if they tried something better, he'd say, keep that." Keith says the production, however, wasn't chaotic. It may have looked that way but groups were placed under the direction of several group leaders and everyone had very specific jobs to do.

Live Snakes and Ladders *cast with Keith* (upper left) *holding "Cheer" sign, University of Calgary, 1978.*

Photo Credit: Image courtesy of the University of Calgary Archives, Department of Drama fonds.

The show had to be partially blocked for technical reasons but the technical design elements were also subject to last minute alterations. "We would sometimes have conferences among the technical staff to solve problems in the middle of a dress rehearsal," Semple told me. "Keith was open to solutions from everyone [and] he was capable of creating great excitement around finding a solution and having it realized quickly. . . ." Foreman, Nurse I on the Medical Team, recalls time spent on improvising technical elements: how to move contestants "from the head of the snake, out the bum of the snake, and onto the medical cart." Many in the ensemble "were trained [by Keith] to improvise and follow their impulses and to say 'yes and' to the offers," reflects Foreman. "We were just working out of that way of reacting and collaborating with one another" (P.I.).

Keith is fond of saying, "Science works by destroying the past. Endlessly questioning the knowledge. Destroying the knowledge to get more knowledge." For 6 weeks of rehearsal, Keith had converted the main UofC theatre space into a science lab full of fun, spontaneous, imaginative experimentation. But Keith did not lead his team like a "mad" scientist. Although given his bulky physique, long thick hair, oversized spectacles, ballpoint pen-stained shirt pocket, and large brown paper sack of bananas by his side, he might have looked like one (Curry). Keith was animated in the rehearsal space but Foreman said he raised his voice only to deliver instructions across the theatre. The stage may have been covered with fake blood, poop, and slime, but Martini said rehearsals were "never chaotic." And Keith's notes, lasting 40 or more minutes at the end of every rehearsal (and at the end of every performance) "were great," declared Frank Totino, who played Death and a "Live Snakes and Ladders Tournament" competitor. Foreman added that these notes "very clearly told what didn't work and why. . . .There could always be things we could certainly do better."[13]

Keith's pedagogy in the classroom carried over into his rehearsal process. Still using the theatre as a laboratory to investigate what he was interested in, the only significant change was the variables in the experiment itself. In the classroom laboratory, Keith would set up the equation so that the students (i.e., the variables) could experience and he could observe. In the rehearsal laboratory, cast members were still variables, but now the main variable, the main ingredient that made the concoction delicious, was Keith's imagination. With S&L Keith felt a sense of freedom that he had, to some degree, experienced at UVic but never before or since. At the Court, budgets put limits on how many cast members he could employ. In the classroom, he was restricted by time, space, and the curriculum. At Loose Moose, the pressures that came with running a company consistently in debt determined what he was willing to do. But for 6 weeks in 1978, Keith was unleashed.

Like Vassily, the hero in Dovzhenko's *Earth*, who ecstatically walked and then danced into the twilight and into the danger, Keith intellectually knew this production was pushing the department and the faculty to dangerous limits. In an interview for UofC's paper *The Gauntlet*, 2 months prior to the opening and without a finished script in hand, Keith conceded: "The Drama Department is going out on a limb, taking risks, which is okay if I come through. But if I don't come through they won't be taking any more risks like that, which would be a pity" ("Johnstone Offers"). Still, he plowed

---

[13] Notes after every event became and still are standard practice at the Loose Moose and Foreman carries forward this tradition in her production work at UofC.

Keith directing at University of Calgary, 1978.
Photo Credit: Deborah Iozzi.

forward. Fascinatingly, Foreman told me, "During rehearsals it was almost as if Keith was dancing. It's not a thing I saw him actually do, but in the theatre he'd be on his feet, moving through the seats, looking at it from all perspectives, arms out and yelling, really just the most animated I've ever seen him. He was like a conductor!" For once, Keith was the master teacher and the master creator concurrently. In that moment, it was Keith's ideal classroom.

As the confusion at the end of the "Live Snakes and Ladder Tournament" goes into slow motion, Death steps forward and delivers an epilogue, 12 lines of prose that Keith has never been too fond of. He prefers the prologue written in verse perhaps because the prologue marks the beginning of an adventure, and Keith loves adventures. So let's go back to the beginning.

A trap-door is opened by two monks and a medieval Death figure slowly ascends from the underworld first to a normal height, then to a height of 12 feet above the stage. Under his long, black robe there is no support pillar, as the audience assumes. Death is balancing on dry-wall stilts. Suddenly, Death advances toward an astonished audience to proclaim:

I am Death,
Mighty and dreadful Death.
Not Father Christmas, not some plaster saint,
Not some old myth, not something quaint.
I am the skull beneath the flesh,
The carcass in the wilderness,
The shadow on the X-ray plate,

Death (Frank Totino) delivers the prologue, Live Snakes
and Ladders, *University of Calgary, 1978.*

Photo Credit: Image courtesy of the University of
Calgary Archives, Department of Drama fonds.

The pain that never will abate,
The Doctor who avoids your eye,
The patch of skin that's always dry,
The itch that will not go away,
The drunkard on the motorway . . . . . .
Here is my scythe, you'll feel its blade,
Your friend will not come to your aid.
It's no use clutching to your wife,
Not all your wealth will save your life.
Some rage, some plead, some are resigned,
But all must leave their human kind.
Make up your face, take exercise,
Eat vitamins, and live more wise,
But never think I won't surprise,
You as you work, or as you sleep,
At counting change, or counting sheep.
One day I'll quench you, that's for sure,
There is no place where you're secure.

I'll tell you life's great mystery,
That no man thinks he'll sup with me.
He's sure there'll be another year,
And that his world will still be here.
I saw the shells form cliffs of chalk,
I saw the Fish learn how to walk,
I saw the Ape learn how to speak,
And everywhere his Maker seek.
One day I shall explode the sun
And blow all things to kingdom come.
Till then, a play to pass the time,
That may elapse ere you are mine. (1)

Perchance Keith wrote this prologue as a reminder to all that Death will ultimately triumph over and demolish petty rivalries, hierarchies, and unyielding academic structures. Knowing Keith's inclination toward atheism, however, I presume he prefers the prologue because it is a call to live, imagine, spontaneously create, and dance in the corporeal present.

Johnstone's legacy at the University of Calgary

By the late 1980s, Keith had acquired an international reputation as the artistic director of Loose Moose and creator of Theatresports, had published *Impro: Improvisation and the Theatre* and numerous articles, had taught and directed all over the world, and had been a dedicated and popular teacher at UofC for over a decade. Dugan, who worked with Keith on his tenure application, called his promotion to full professor in 1986 a "slam dunk."[14] Keith retired as a professor emeritus in 1995 and, instead of a gold watch, a student close to Keith suggested to the faculty a hot air balloon send off. Ben, 21 at the time, joined his father for this ride over Calgary. "It's a great thing to do. It's like entering a new world," says Keith. "Visually, the sights you are seeing are so unusual and you don't feel the tiniest bit of vertigo which is really odd. You can lean right over and try to get scared and you can't because the balloon lifts so gently. You are in the world of the balloon."

---

[14] Richard Courtney's letter of support was part of Keith's application for promotion. Philip Zimbardo, a leading professor of psychology at Stanford University, sent an unsolicited recommendation letter for Keith in 1982 when he was up for tenure. In the letter, Zimbardo wrote: "His [Johnstone's] original views on the importance of status transactions are only now being introduced into psychology . . . . I not only acknowledge Keith Johnstone's contribution in this area, but borrow heavily from his many perceptive ideas to help bridge what research psychologists are studying in their laboratories and what Keith tells us is happening when actors play roles on the stage—or in everyday life. . . . I hope he is as appreciated at your school as he would be were he here with us at Stanford University."

After Keith retired, he rarely returned to the campus, not because of any lingering hostility from faculty—there had since been a generation turnover—but because he was not invited back. "I never thought to invite Keith," Dugan ponders. "Never even occurred to me that he would even be willing to do it." Moreover, Dugan doesn't recall any other instructor, not even Martini or Foreman, ever inviting Keith in as a guest instructor or lecturer. When I asked whether or not the Impro System influences the curriculum in the department in any direct way, Dugan answered, "No. In indirect ways." Martini told me, "I think that it penetrates through the lessons that those who have studied with Keith pass on. I encourage people in my playwriting classes to read *Impro*." Foreman said, "It's acknowledged. Everybody teaches improvisation in some form or another. I send my students off to Loose Moose or to Rick Hilton's Impro Guild to watch other people work . . . to watch the theory in action."[15] But why isn't the department teaching an Impro System course? After all, for almost two decades the classrooms in Calgary Hall served as laboratories for testing Keith's theories and techniques. Martini's answer to this inquiry was, "I don't think we've had the ability, the budget, [or] the same kind of interest [in improvisation]." On the other hand, Dugan recollects the interest in improvisation increasing around 2004 or 2005, about the time he began serving his final headship.

Even if Martini's rationalization is justified at this moment in time, why isn't Keith's legacy more traceable at UofC? There is no substantial information about Keith on the drama department's website; moreover, on my first visit to the UofC Library, I soon realized that the folks working in Archives and Special Collections had no idea who Keith Johnstone was. Fortunately, Cindy Murrell, the Fine Arts Operational Manager of Visual and Performing Arts, has personally maintained a collection of newspaper clippings, posters, and programs dating back to 1977 documenting Keith's production work at UofC and Loose Moose. Murrell, who is married to John Murrell, a very successful Canadian playwright, seems to understand the importance of maintaining an archive and preserving the legacy of an artist who literally changed the landscape of theatre not only in Calgary but worldwide. "We're all passing along the gift," Foreman told me. The gift (i.e., the Impro System) like the classroom must continue to evolve if a problem-posing pedagogy is the goal but, as Freire proposed, historicity must be the starting point. Students need to be aware of the Impro System's historical reality so they can appreciate their unique point of departure in a process that is, and has always been, in transformation.

---

[15] Rick Hilton and Foreman were part of the second wave of students to join the Loose Moose Theatre Company at the end of 1977. Hilton was also a student in Keith's Drama 200 class.

CHAPTER FIVE

From classroom to world stage: The Loose Moose Theatre Company

I'm all in favour of a dull life.
Who wants to live with the excitement of El Salvador?
There was a Chinese sage who prayed to the gods
that he be allowed to live in dull times, and I'm with him.
Let's have nice, dull, orderly, sensible lives [. . .]
and blow off all our steam with Theatresports.
KEITH JOHNSTONE (Foggo 104)

As early as the fall of 1976, Keith would take a handful of students from his Drama 200 and Drama 300 classes down to small rooms in the basement of Calgary Hall, home of the UofC theatre department, and direct them in impro games, techniques, and mask exercises. Audiences would show up or not. Tony Totino called these "training sessions." As he had done with his professional students at the RCT Studio in the early 1960s, Keith transferred the work from the classroom to the public as a demonstration of sorts, not as an official performance or end-of-the-semester showcase. On a weekly and sometimes daily basis, these training sessions allowed students to ease into working in front of and with audiences without fearing failure.

Secret Impro Shows were eventually advertised by Keith on a piece of paper the size of a postage stamp and pinned to the theatre department's bulletin board. They always took place at noon and, similar to the Theatre

Machine format, Keith directed from the side of but on the stage. Despite
the miniscule advertisements—and the small rooms—these training sessions
became very popular. Keith introduced No-Block Theatresports, a primitive
form, to audiences toward the end of a session. The improvisers would divide
into teams and challenge each other to a "No Blocking" competition. One
team would take the stage and begin a scene. As soon as a team member
"blocked" an offer from another player, the off-stage team would yell
"block!" If the challenge was upheld, the other team got to play. Keith had
previously used "No Blocking" competitions in his classes at UofC and at
RADA to encourage students to accept offers.

This chapter offers a compressed history of the Loose Moose Theatre
Company under Keith's artistic direction (1977–1998). It would be impossible
to document, in one chapter, every project and event this unconventional
theatre company took on during this 21-year time span. Thus, the focus of
Chapter 5 is primarily on the productions directed, written, or devised by
Keith; on the launching and expansion of Theatresports and the highlights
and struggles that resulted; and on the perpetuation of Keith's pedagogy
from the academic classroom to the rehearsal and performance spaces of
his company. As Theatresports took Keith's Impro System all over the globe
and as *Impro: Improvisation and the Theatre* got translated into multiple
languages, the international demand for his teaching and directing increased.
The Swedish theatre community, in particular, embraced Keith's techniques
and this chapter also documents his first forays—some successful and some
not so—teaching and directing in Sweden.

The Loose Moose Theatre Company

In August of 1977, 2 years after Keith began his permanent teaching position
at UofC, he and a former student/veterinarian, Mel Tonken, founded a theatre
company. Keith had the know-how. Tonken, the money to invest. In early
September, Keith and Ingrid invited Tonken, Frank Totino, Dennis Cahill,
Ross Patton, Sandy Carrol, and Veena Sood to their suburban home—6 miles
southwest of downtown Calgary—for tea and dinner. This group, including
Ingrid, became the original Loose Moose Theatre Company.[1] "Loose" means
"spontaneous" and "Moose" is for Canada. "The name is silly and that's
partly why we choose it," said Keith. "[Y]ou can make up catchy sayings
like 'Don't Goose the Moose' and things like that that stick in your mind
whether you like it or not" (Dawson, "A Moose is Loose"). Critics, as Keith
predicted, had a great deal of fun creating titles like "Getting Loose with the
Moose," "Who let the Moose loose?" and "Wine, Women, and Moostro."

---

[1] All but Sood had been involved in Keith's production of *The Tempest* at UofC earlier that
year.

Moreover, the Moose himself became a recognized entity, a member of the company. A large Moose character head was constructed and first worn by Tony Totino on stilts.

Moose Mascot (Tony Totino) with Sue Fitzgerald (left) *and Kathleen Foreman on the lawn of the Calgary Board of Education, 1978.*
Photo Credit: Deborah Iozzi.

At festivals and other events, this tall mascot proved to be quite entertaining. And early program art often included the Moose in whimsical comic strip scenarios hand-sketched by Keith.[2] Yes, this company had a silly name and mascot, but Loose Moosers were primed to do both comedic and dramatic work in earnest.

In September, company members practiced and learned new games and techniques in Keith's small home basement, 1 to 3 nights per week. All were a part of the ongoing Secret Impro Shows at UofC and a few were still in Keith's acting classes. Essentially, all had been trained by Keith in the Impro System. The Loose Moose Theatre Company had its first official performance in mid-October at the Pumphouse Theatre. Built in 1913, this old pump house, southwest of downtown, drew water from the Bow River for citizens of Calgary for many years. It was converted into a flexible theatre space

---

[2] The original/official Loose Moose logo is designed by Gavin Semple.

in 1972, has gone through several renovations, and is still in use today by more than a dozen theatre companies (Pumphouse). Loose Moose secured Sunday nights at the Pumphouse in the fall of 1977 to feature the impro skills of the company and Keith's plays, that is, the ones considered "not tasteful enough" for the university. Once again, Keith found a home for his work on Sunday nights, and in the tradition of Sunday Nights without décor at RCT, his plays often received only one performance.

Similar to a Theatre Machine structure, for the first four or five performances at the Pumphouse, the Loose Moosers performed pure improvisation with Keith directing. Then for about a month, Keith's one-act *Robinson Crusoe* took up the first hour and the troupe would improvise for the second hour. In Keith's dark comedic version of Daniel Defoe's tale, everything is ridiculed—religion, imperialism, stereotypes—and the master-servant hierarchy is not only questioned but reversed by the end when Friday eats his master. Tonken played Crusoe and Patton played Friday in blackface.[3] Keith did not originally intend for Friday to be

The Arms Game with Dennis Cahill using Tony Totino's arms
and Keith using Veena Sood's arms.
Photo Credit: Deborah Iozzi.

---

[3] "Ross with the pointy finger," said Keith. "He used to order energy into his finger and point. I felt like lopping it off."

played in blackface. When first performed in 1969 at the Mercury Theatre in London, Roddy Maude-Roxby played Crusoe and black British actor John Mahoney, born in Gambia, played Friday. In another production spoken in Swahili, a black actor actually played Crusoe in whiteface. A blackface performance in conservative Calgary sounds risky to most, but not to Keith or to his fearless improvisers trained to thrive in risk-taking modes of performance.

The pure improvisational part of the evenings at the Pumphouse clearly revealed the company's training in the Impro System. In response to the third performance, Louis B. Hobson, writing for *The Albertan*, commented, "It is impossible to mention all the beautiful moments in Sunday's spontaneous skits."[4] Hobson acknowledged Frank and Patton's "amazing master-servant routine"; Frank and Ingrid's "intricate and bizarre story of a long-lost brother and sister who find each other through their common speech impediment"; and Patton and Sood's scene with a balloon that "reduced the audience to tears as they discussed their physical beauties and sexual prowess." Hobson went on to praise the improvisers for their trust in/appreciation for each other's talents and declared: "There is no such self-indulgence in the Loose Moose company" ("Loose Moose Galloping"). The basic rules of the Impro System, rules Keith drilled into his improvisers daily—take risks, relinquish control, accept offers, see-saw status, make your partner look good, stay within the circle of probability, reincorporate, and fail good-naturedly— were effective in performance.

In less than 3 months, Loose Moose Sunday night presentations at the Pumphouse were selling out to a younger, nonstandard theatre-going audience for Calgary (Dawson, "A Moose"). Tickets were only a dollar and the company offered refunds when they deemed the performance unworthy. "I know we did offer money back for some performances," says Cahill. "And people did accept the refund, although some would say the performance wasn't all that bad, or no worse than other things they had seen elsewhere. Only a dollar though, but it did create good will." In December, Frank Totino directed and put up Keith's short absurdist play, *The Cord*, for one performance only at the Pumphouse. Written in 1968 and previously produced in London and Sweden, *The Cord* centers around a teenage boy who struggles to cut himself free from the huge umbilical cord that still connects him to his controlling mum, played by Mel Tonken in drag.[5]

---

[4] Louis B. Hobson, a strong advocate for the Loose Moose and Johnstone during those early years, wrote for *The Albertan* until it was replaced by *The Calgary Sun* where he still works as a theatre columnist. Hobson was also the special guest in The Life Game at the Loose Moose on at least two occasions in the 1990s.

[5] *The Cord* is, in part, representative of Keith's relationship to his mum. A short film of this play was produced in 1988 and directed by successful television director and Vancouver Theatresports alumnus Michael Rohl very early in his career.

Mum (Mel Tonken) and her son (Jim Curry) still connected to the umbilical cord in Johnstone's The Cord, Loose Moose at the Pumphouse, *1977.*

Photo Credit: Deborah Iozzi.

The son (right) is no longer attached to mum's umbilical cord, but the daughter (Betty Poulsen) continues to carry her father (Dennis Cahill) on her back in Johnstone's The Cord, Loose Moose at the Pumphouse, *1977.*

Photo Credit: Deborah Iozzi.

As usual, an hour of pure impro followed. By the end of 1977, Keith already wanted to bring more students from UofC into the company.

Beginning of Theatresports

Theatresports evolved from a basic need—to give more improvisers stage time each evening—and from Keith's long held desire to create a "sporting-event-like" excitement among the spectators. As early as 1965, Keith compared his improvisational work at the RCT Studio to pro-wrestling matches in Britain. Professional wrestlers in Britain were actually classified as variety entertainers. Keith, along with John Dexter and William Gaskill, thought it would be great to replace wrestlers with improvisers. Unfortunately, until 1968, censorship laws made it virtually impossible to stage such an event for a paying audience. So Keith took this fantasy with him to Calgary.

The first public Theatresports match took place at the Pumphouse in February of 1978. The Moose Team, made up of four original Loose Moose company members, competed against the Moosettes, made up of newly added company members—Jim Curry, Kathleen Foreman, Rick Hilton, and Tony Totino. All collaborated with Keith on creating the official rules and regulations of Theatresports, but it was Keith's games and techniques that were being adopted into the competitive format. Still, questions of ownership linger and accounts of how Theatresports in Calgary came to be vary according to who is doing the telling. Keith conjectures: "The thing about memory, is every time you remember something, you re-file it and it changes." Nowhere is this more evident than in *Something Like a Drug: An Unauthorized Oral History of Theatresports* (1995) by Kathleen Foreman and Clem Martini. This book provides firsthand accounts by many of the earliest company members of how *they* remember the Theatresports evolution. It is "unauthorized" because, Keith says, his request to proofread and correct any errors in the final draft was denied.[6] "The problem was that not everyone saw things like Keith did," says Martini. Martini is right. In the book, no two accounts are exactly the same.

Tony Totino did not recall an exact structure in place when he joined the Moosettes team, only the basic premise "that you could have two teams vying for possession of the stage" (Foreman, *Something* 41). Frank Totino remembers Keith suggesting status competitions and then everything taking off from there. Without question, "No blocking" (i.e., not killing ideas) was the first rule.[7] A team would lose points for blocking and for boring

---

[6]   Owning the rights to Theatresports, Keith says he wanted the option to contribute a footnote to any portion of the document he felt was inconsistent.

[7]   "No Block" Theatresports was eventually replaced by "Warning-for-Boring" Theatresports (a.k.a. the "regular game") where players were thrown off the stage for "boring" scenes.

or inaudible scenes and gain points for good scenes with good resolutions. Despite its name, the primary goal of Theatresports was and is to engage audiences with skillful, narrative-based impro. In order to encourage longer scenes, teams would multiply their score by the length of time of their scene. The Moose Team and the Moosettes became experts at expanding time. "Tony Totino could wash dishes for ten minutes and get laughs because he was a super mime and dancer," Curry told me. "We would throw Tony out there while we organized." As players became more and more obsessed with the score, Keith limited scenes to 6 minutes. Judges, a scorekeeper, a timekeeper, and a referee were incorporated and other technical aspects of creating a sporting event were collectively agreed upon, but Keith made all final decisions. According to Cahill, the artistic creation, the "how-to-make-it-a-theatre-event" was always Keith's main focus and contribution (Foreman, *Something* 42). Indisputably, Keith's enthusiastic and devoted

The Loose Moose Theatre Company, c. 1978: (back row) *Timothy Lee, Bob Percy, Keith, Frank Totino, Tony Totino, Rick Hilton;* (second row) *Dennis Cahill, Clem Martini, Mel Tonken, Jim Curry, Ingrid Johnstone, Betty McLachlan, Kathleen Foreman;* (front row) *George Curry, Veena Sood, Cindy Neufield, Sue Fitzgerald, Judith Allen, Janne Hicklin;* (on floor) *Cathy Percy and Ben Johnstone.*
Photo Credit: Deborah Iozzi.

students, trained in his Impro System, made it possible to take his Theatresports concept to the next level.

From about mid-March until the end of April of 1978, Loose Moose no longer presented one-act plays during the first hour of their Sunday nights at the Pumphouse. Theatresports and other noncompetitive, purely improvised formats such as "biographies" and "half-mask" sequences now took up the entire 2 hours.[8] In the Sunday, March 5, Loose Moose program presenting *Robinson Crusoe* and an hour of Theatresports, Keith wrote:

> The plays make us too safe [. . .] we always feel that at least we have some text to fall back on when all else fails [. . .] from now on though we will be relying purely on the inspiration of the moment [. . .] only by putting ourselves in this position will we continue to develop new techniques and way[s] of holding the spectator's interest over longer periods.

Keith consistently sought to maintain a "theatre as classroom" environment with his Loose Moosers. All improvised shows were considered "training" opportunities and notes were given after every performance. And in the programs, Keith frequently addressed the audience because he wanted them to know that they, too, were an important part of the Loose Moose process.

On Sunday, March 26, the Moose Team played their first match against an outside competitor, the Eager Beavers team from UofC. Twila Burfield, a critic for *The Albertan*, described a memorable improvised scene which earned the Moose Team a total of thirty points:

> Frank Totino laid two chairs sideways on the stage and sat in one of them. Another member of his team sat in the facing chair and a "normal" conversation followed, rendered absurd by the position of the actors, with the audience looking down, and horizontal becoming vertical. Mel Tonken promptly picked up the cue, lay on the floor and scissored his way across the stage. "Oh, just passing by," he ad libbed. The scene picked up another 10 points for [an] excellent ending when one teammate contrived to shoot the other, who fell up—against the curtain.[9]

Burfield also commented on the spirited audience "shouting out with laughter" for their favorite team or "booing gleefully" at the opponents. The packed houses reacted like fans at a sporting event. Keith's fantasy had developed into a tangible reality.

---

[8] "Biographies" involved players enacting a personal story told by a fellow player. Perhaps this format was a precursor to The Life Game?
[9] The Theatre Machine also played "sideways" scenes.

Waiting for Godot *and* The Last Bird *again*

The company went on their summer hiatus in May of 1978, and Keith traveled again to Copenhagen, Denmark, to teach for the Statens Teaterskole's summer program. He introduced Theatresports to his Danish students and the Turnus Players troupe was formed shortly thereafter. By mid-August, Loose Moose was back in action at the Pumphouse on Sunday nights. In late September, Keith directed *Waiting for Godot* for a second time.[10] Tonken and Cahill portrayed Vladimir and Estragon. Patton and Frank Totino, Pozzo and Lucky.

Vladimir (Mel Tonken) and Estragon (Dennis Cahill) in Beckett's
Waiting for Godot, *Loose Moose at the Pumphouse, 1978.*
Photo Credit: Deborah Iozzi.

Louis B. Hobson admired Keith's well-orchestrated and choreographed direction and likened the actors to marionettes connected to their director via strings "formed from trust and understanding, not blind obedience" ("Waiting"). But Brian Brennan found that Keith's "comic business and music hall gimmickry" failed in "forcing a sense of the desolate upon us" ("Pumphouse"). In response to this, Keith argues, "I didn't put any comic business or music hall gimmicks in. I have too much respect for Beckett. The

---

[10] The first production was at UofC in 1972.

play is actually funny as well as tragic, but the way it is normally done is so miserable, you probably don't notice there's a lot of comedy in it. I think Brennan was misled."

Furthermore, Brennan construed *Godot* as a play of "many intellectual implications," but Keith considers it a play about the human condition, about everyday people waiting for something that will solve their problems. And Keith thinks it is a play people should see not just because of its importance as a literary masterpiece but because it is entertaining. In the program for this first Loose Moose production of *Godot*, Keith wrote:

> Theatre has to be funny, or sad, or awesome. It has to do more than make the audience feel "cultured", or "educated", or "superior". Many people, even in Alberta, will watch any sort of crap as long as it's packaged as CULTURE. . . . Theatre as a "cultural experience" is like a church without God. This is the sort of culture we want to bury—because it's dead.

And just below this weighty declaration—suggestive of statements made by legendary British theatre director Peter Brook in *The Empty Space* (1968)—are four "Culture Stamps" (featuring the Moose drawn by Keith) for spectators to cut out and paste into their "Culture Booklets." One full booklet entitled bearer to miss any cultural event over the next 3 months.

Loose Moose Culture Booklet created by Keith.
Photo Credit: From Keith Johnstone's personal collection.

In the previous chapter, I compared Keith's use of humor in the classroom to Vakhtangov's use of humor in the acting studio. Even if the subject matter is serious, allowing humor to leak into the environment is part of Keith's pedagogical approach. Michael Shurtleff expressed in his book *Audition*

Culture Stamps for the Loose Moose Culture Booklet.
Photo Credit: From Keith Johnstone's personal collection.

(1978)—an acting text Keith often recommends today—that humor is in every scene and in every life situation: "It is the coin of exchange between human beings that makes it possible for us to get through the day" (74). Anton Chekhov said: "First of all, I'd get my patients into a laughing mood, and only then would I begin to treat them" (Gottlieb 11). Through humor and laughter, Keith cures students of stage fright and audiences of the notion that theatre should be a cultural experience only. In 1979, when Keith took his production of *Godot* on tour to the Citadel's Rice Theatre in Edmonton, Alan Hustak of the *Edmonton Sun* found Keith's direction, "stripped" of its "artsy rhapsody," refreshing. Comic business and all, Hustak described the production as "grotesque, garrulous and gratifying."

For the remainder of 1978, Keith and his Loose Moosers were engulfed in *Live Snakes and Ladders* at UofC. Performances on Sunday nights at the Pumphouse were still ongoing, but the company did not really kick into gear again until February of 1979 with their 2-week run of *The Last Bird*. The day after the opening, an extremely sour review by Joy-Ann Cohen appeared in the *Calgary Herald*. Cohen called *The Last Bird* "a snore of a play" with monotonous acting that put the audience to sleep and she criticized the use of masks as "an attempt to build archetypal characters." By now it should be evident that Loose Moose polarized theatre critics in Calgary and diatribes were often personally aimed at their charismatic artistic director. Keith, who does not like one-on-one confrontations, would dismiss personal critiques but would fight back when unfair abuse threatened to disrupt the safe space he had created for his young ensemble-in-training. So he retaliated:

> I don't usually reply to critics because everyone's entitled to their opinion, but my play *The Last Bird* has been seriously misrepresented. I've always thought Joy-Ann Cohen to be a rather conservative and reactionary critic—and why shouldn't she be—but I don't regard her as stupid, and no one could sit in an audience who were laughing, and gasping out loud, and weeping, and then honestly dismiss the acting as monotonous, and my play as a snore. ("Review")

A spectator equally disturbed by Cohen's attack wrote: "Was she [Cohen] really deaf to the laughter around her?" (Birge). Keith has been called a tormented genius, a lone wolf, and other names which tend to paint him as isolated from the "common crowd." And he is often guilty of perpetuating a "me against the system" image. But many Calgarians were cheering on Keith and his unconventional company.

Johnstone's The Last Bird at Loose Moose, 1979. Ingrid Johnstone as the Waif (left), Maggie Clouthier as the Angel, and Tony Totino as Jesus.
Photo Credit: Deborah Iozzi.

The Last Bird *at Loose Moose, 1979. The Doctor (Timothy Lee)*
examines the Double Figure (Judith Allen).
Photo Credit: Deborah Iozzi.

By the end of the summer of 1979, Loose Moose had accumulated a small
debt. A summer series of three shows—Keith's *Moby Dick*, *Robinson
Crusoe*, and Beckett's *Waiting for Godot*—played to small houses and the
tour to Edmonton in August resulted in a $1,100 loss. In September, a return
to Theatresports and purely improvised Sunday night performances seemed
to be the only solution without outside financial support. Not a bad thing
according to Keith who saw this as an opportunity to sharpen performance
skills, create characters, and material for future shows. Except for a successful
holiday performance of Keith's children's play, *The Defeat of Giant Bignose*,
Sunday nights were dedicated to Theatresports for the remainder of the year.
Also, *Impro: Improvisation and the Theatre* was published and released in
London by Faber and Faber, and copies available in the Pumphouse lobby
were selling out faster than Keith had anticipated (L. Hobson, "Johnstone's
Improv").

Theatresports tournaments and
The Loose Moose Hamlet

In February of 1980, Loose Moose hosted the First Calgary Invitational
Theatresports Tournament spanning 5 nights at the Pumphouse. Eight teams
of four competed. "O Canada" was sung before every match scored by three
judges holding big scorecards. A sound technician heightened the excitement

with improvised music cues. Keith missed the first 3 nights of the tournament because he was teaching a workshop at the Vancouver Playhouse Theatre School, but he was there for the final 50-minute showdown between the Moose Team and the Moosettes. The Moosettes took first place and the $250 prize. The following Sunday, the regular season resumed with a competition for the Rubber Chicken prize between the Moosettes and the Warriors, a team made up of members from the Arete Mime Troupe at Mount Royal College led by Ingrid Johnstone.

Theatresports Rubber Chicken Tournament at the Pumphouse with Veena Sood (left), *Frank Totino, Garry Campbell, and Tony Totino.*
Photo Credit: Deborah Iozzi.

Keith returned to Copenhagen to teach in the summer of 1980 and was surprised to find that Theatresports had become a huge hit in the pubs. On his way home, he scheduled a 5-day layover in Chicago to teach at The Second City. Del Close, resident director of Second City (1973–82), an original Second City company member, and creator of "The Harold," a long-form improvisation format, had read and liked *Impro* and initiated the invitation.[11] At Second City, Keith taught a series of workshops: one for

---

[11] Today, Keith's work on "status" is integral to Second City's training program (Libera 40). In *Truth in Comedy* (1994), Close and coauthor Charna Halpern adopt Keith's concepts of reincorporation and tilts (i.e., interrupting routines) for structuring scenes based on storytelling (Halpern 57, 81).

representatives of local professional theatre companies and universities, two open enrollment workshops, and two with Second City actors (Close). In September, Loose Moose traveled to Vancouver for the first Interprovincial Theatresports Tournament against the newly formed Vancouver league. Most significantly, the Canada Council Explorations committee granted Loose Moose a $5,768 grant to expand Theatresports. More tournaments were scheduled and more leagues were formed. Keith also continued experimenting with new formats.

In October, Keith adapted and directed *Hamlet* as Theatresports. Although Shakespeare's dialogue was not altered in the scenes played out by competing teams, transitions in between the scenes were improvised. Also, King Fortinbras, as head judge, consulted with the audience, and the Theatresports commentator kept the audience aware of what was going on at all times. At the end of a regular Theatresports match, members of the audience were invited onto the stage to throw shaving cream pies at the losing team.[12] The pies were also used in *The Loose Moose Hamlet* but every actor got a pie in the face because, Frank Totino reminds me, "It's a tragedy. Everyone loses." Cast members Frank Totino, Tony Totino, and Cahill remember audiences spontaneously leaping to their feet with thunderous applause.

The Loose Moose Hamlet *production poster created by Keith.*
Photo Credit: From Keith Johnstone's personal collection.

---

[12] At first, real whipped cream was used for the pies, but the milk would quickly sour under the hot lights and leave a horrid stench and a sticky mess.

Louis B. Hobson called *The Loose Moose Hamlet* the "most valid comment on Shakespeare's play. He has pointed out the conflicts which exist between Hamlet and his uncle . . . in a way which is immediately clear even to a novice." In this same review, Hobson lashed out at Calgary's professional theatre community for not giving Keith an equal playing field:

> The whole problem with Johnstone and the Moose is time, talent and money. As long as they continue to work under such ridiculous conditions their work will go unnoticed except by their stalwart fans. Johnstone is too good for that. He is one of the most creative minds working in Calgary and perhaps in Canada and still no one is getting to see what he is capable of doing. All we ever get are hints of his genius. . . . The thing that is most intriguing about a Johnstone play is the prospect of what might have happened if all the conditions had been perfect. The budget for the *Theatresports Hamlet* was around $2,000.[13] A normal budget at Theatre Calgary is $40,000. . . . He is not playing in the big leagues yet and Calgary is suffering as a result. ("Let Johnstone's")

Of course, Keith had always been an outspoken critic of Calgary's "legitimate" theatre. Aware of this, Hobson proposed, "all the more reason . . . [they] should use Johnstone. They should make him put his theories into practice." After Hobson's plea, offers did not roll in from the well-funded professional theatres. Even if Keith had been extended an invitation, it is doubtful that he would have accepted. A wave of excitement and possibility was swelling around his amateur company and it wasn't the moment to leave the ship unattended.

In July of 1981, Loose Moose coordinated a Theatresports tournament for the Alberta Summer Games in Lethbridge. Six out of the eight regions sent teams, and during the preceding months, Loose Moose company members traveled to schools to conduct workshops and mini-tournaments in preparation and to give demonstrations. This was also the summer Keith taught workshops at Eugenio Barba's ISTA session in Volterra, Italy.[14] Theatresports leagues were established in Vancouver, Edmonton, and Toronto by the end of this year, and *Impro* came out in its first paperback edition. A wonderful photo by Deborah Iozzi from the Loose Moose production of *The Defeat of Giant Big-Nose* graced the paperback's cover.[15] It is the scene in which Nobody Nose (Tony Totino) wraps the two masked heroes

---

[13] This is not true. The budget for *The Loose Moose Hamlet* was significantly less. Keith and his Loose Moosers were skilled at making the most of limited budgets.

[14] See Chapter 3.

[15] Deborah Iozzi has been taking photos of the Loose Moose productions since 1978. Today she is the business manager of Loose Moose working alongside her husband Cahill, artistic director since 1998.

(Rick Hilton and Ingrid Johnstone) into his magical cloak, which allows them to escape through the walls of the "mime's prison."

Keith and Ingrid divorced in 1981. An affair between Ingrid and Jim Curry began the year prior. These two would eventually move in together and get married, but Curry still censures his own behavior: "I wasn't very generous to Keith at the time but it didn't stop his enthusiasm for me." When one of Curry's plays got a bad review, for instance, Keith wrote a letter to the *Herald* in his defense. Keith concealed his personal pain but Curry saw through the pretense:

> It hurt him. They had much more in common than Ingrid and I ever did. That was really the shame of it. When he'd drop off Ben, they would sit here [at the kitchen table], have tea, and chit-chat about anything. Fuck, they got along famously [and] they always looked so great together. The big guy with the small woman. All of their friends were devastated by the divorce.

Keith, never one to wallow in self-pity, simply moved on to other business. The Calgary Regional Arts Foundation (CRAF) had just awarded the Loose Moose a timely $7,000 operating fund grant, and with the Pumphouse closing down for renovations, the Loose Moose needed to find a new home.

Loose Moose finds a home

In August of 1981, Loose Moose signed a 6-year lease on a former cattle auction house northeast of downtown Calgary and just south of the Calgary International Airport.[16] "It looks and functions very much like the university theatre," Keith said to Louis B. Hobson. "The audience sits in a tight bowl on three sides of the stage. We can seat 270 people but there are only seven rows of seats so it is still a very intimate space" ("Loose Moose has"). And the ceiling had starry lights. Keith finally had his ideal amphitheatre-type structure, dubbed the Moose Simplex (in contrast to the downtown Complex), where actors could be easily seen and heard from every seat in the house. The renovations, however, far exceeded the operating grant received from CRAF. Before the grand opening in September, about $40,000 was spent on lighting and sound systems and other renovation costs (Brennan, "Anyone"). In spite of the fact that senior company members were becoming local celebrities or that Keith—approaching his fiftieth birthday—was internationally known, after the move to the Simplex, Loose Moose found itself in substantial debt each year. "It was a perfect venue," Tonken tells me. "A sound theatrical decision but not a sound financial decision." In the slow summer months, the company would go into the red

---

[16] Physical address was 2003 McKnight Boulevard, N.E.

50,000 or 60,000 dollars and come back to zero in the winter. One of the first expense-cutting measures Keith put into practice was a budget limit of 25 dollars per production. "We had to make enough money to survive the bad times," Keith says, "and we did."

Loose Moose company member, Dave Cameron,
hanging lights at the Moose Simplex.
Photo Credit: Deborah Iozzi.

A Pinteresque season

In November of 1981, Loose Moose presented their first nonimprovised, tightly budgeted production at the Moose Simplex of Harold Pinter's *The Birthday Party*. Under Keith's direction, Louis B. Hobson believed that the actors "captured that delicate Pinteresque balance between comedy and horror" ("Pinter's"). Rosemary McCracken thought the actors were a bit excessive in the first act but called the second act "high voltage" and the cast "confident and in control" ("Birthday"). Although critics, on occasion, compared Keith's own writing style to Pinter's and although the two men had personally known each other, this was the first time Keith had directed a Pinter play.

The following fall, Keith directed a second Pinter play, *The Caretaker*, at the Simplex.[17] Why the sudden interest in Pinter? The Loose Moose was in financial trouble. *The Caretaker* doesn't require an elaborate set design and Keith had actors in the company who could immediately jump into the

---

[17] Tony Totino played Mick, Dave Duncan played Davies, and Mel Tonken played Aston.

three male roles: two brothers—one ill-tempered and the other a mentally unstable recluse living in the dirty old attic—and a manipulative old tramp that comes to live with them. Also, according to Keith the play "was hot" as a result of the success of recent revivals (Interview with Jim Curry).[18] In *The Caretaker* program, Keith shared a personal Pinter anecdote with Loose Moose audiences:

> Pinter came round to my place the morning after the first night [of *The Caretaker* at the Arts Theatre in London] with a handful of reviews—he was being photographed in a room I'd decorated, or misdecorated. I remember his anger at a critic who said that the characters weren't worth writing about. I suppose if you think plays should be about smart middle class people swilling back cocktails it may seem unusual, but Pinter presents wonderfully observed and contrasting characters, and their dialogue now seems to be the way people talk, and always have talked.

Brian Brennan, in his review for the *Calgary Herald*, did not criticize Pinter's characters or the dialogue but the "bad" acting by "the masters of improvisational comedy" who chose to play it "straight" and the director for failing to "underline the comic elements in Pinter's script" ("Adventurous"). Brennan had proven himself to be critical but fair in reviews of Keith's past productions but Keith understood Pinter. The triangular relationship in this absurdist play is complicated to say the least. Critics used words like menacing, cruel, violent, compassionate, and witty to describe the first production in 1960 but rarely referred to it simply as "comedy." An oft-used quote by Pinter from 1960 may explain Keith's direction and selection of this play and Brennan's reaction: "The play is funny up to a point. Beyond that point it ceases to be funny and it was because of that point I wrote it" (Hickling). This financially feasible but complex play gave Keith's actors an opportunity to discover and expand their range.

Bustling and broke

Throughout 1982, the Moose Simplex was abuzz with activity. Theatre-sports was produced 3 nights a week, with ticket prices ranging from $6.50 to $8.00, for audiences three times the size of audiences at the Pumphouse. A recent acquisition of a liquor license allowed wine to be served in the lobby's "Moose Bar" (L. Hobson, "Wine"). Keith's adaptation of *Arabian Nights* and other children's plays were presented on Saturdays. Late Nite Comedy consisting of a lineup of skits, mime, and stand-up routines, was launched. Eager to attract a new audience to their new location, the popular musical revue *Jacque Brel Is Alive and Well and Living in Paris*

---

[18] Keith was likely referring to the 1981 revival at the National Theatre starring his former RADA student, Jonathan Pryce, as Mick. Pryce also played Mick in a 1980 production at The Lyttelton Theatre, London.

was directed by Tonken and put up in the spring along with a large tent, borrowed from the City Parks and Recreation Department, to create "Le Moostro Bistro." At this temporary café, guests could enjoy pastries and cappuccinos before the show and during intermission (L. Hobson, "Wine"). As always, Keith traveled to various locations in late spring to teach workshops. In San Francisco, he taught hat games and other split-attention techniques to a group of monks at a Zen monastery. "There is something religious about spontaneity since it's nonverbal and its relation to Zen Buddhism," said Keith. "Zen Buddhist monks take to it like ducks to water 'cause it's absolutely in their area" (Interview with Jim Curry). Finally, as noted previously, *The Caretaker* was produced in the fall. It was a full and varied season at the Moose Simplex.

In spite of outward appearances, not one of the 70 or so actors, technicians, and artistic staff was making a living at the Moose. They all had day jobs and donated their services at night and on weekends. John Gilchrist, who joined Loose Moose as the business and promotions manager in 1979 for a small salary, had been actively applying for government grants and hoped, by the year's end, the company would break even. Then the Loose Moose could move forward to the next level—to professional status—and finally pay senior Moosers for their contributions. This wasn't to be, and the frustration among those who had given the last 6 years of their life to the company was palpable. All had hoped that Theatresports would really take off in Calgary as it seemed to be doing in Toronto, Vancouver, and elsewhere. "The rest of the world is playing; will it ever take off here?" asked Cheryl Foggo in her article for *Calgary Magazine*. Foggo also dubbed Theatresports "Alberta's only indigenous game." Why were Calgarians slow to catch on? At least London critics took notice of Theatre Machine after Keith began to insert foreign reviews into the program. But in Calgary, Theatresports never enjoyed sustained success like it did in Australia, Scandinavia, South America, or other Canadian cities.

Theatresports did bring large crowds into the Simplex, but accumulated debt plus a freeze on government funding, due to a deep recession that hit Canada in the second half of 1982, kept Loose Moose on a restricted budget. Also, because of their semi-professional status (i.e., they paid some but not all artists), Loose Moose has never qualified for a Canada Council for the Arts' operating grant given to professional theatre companies only. CRAF, now operating as the Calgary Arts Development Authority (CADA), is the only funding agency that has consistently provided Loose Moose with annual operating grants.[19] "The Loose Moose has never been blessed with large amounts of public funding, but I expect that many arts organizations could say that," Cahill told me. "The fact that Keith, and by association the Loose Moose Theatre Company have been very influential in the world of improvisation seems to have no bearing on our status among granting bodies."

---

[19] Except for 1 year. See footnote 35.

Keith often talks about the occasion when actor Peter Coyote, chairman of the California State Arts Council in 1982 and a council member from 1975 to 1983, wrote to several funding agencies in Calgary to tell them that California would fund the Loose Moose, if they could, because the work was so valuable to them. "It's a true story," says Coyote. "Unfortunately the Council was prohibited from sending tax-payer funds to Canada." Keith claims that the local art association's reply to Coyote was something in the nature of: "If you'd seen the work, you'd know it wasn't worth supporting." But Coyote had visited Calgary specifically to see the work. Keith, Gilchrist, Cahill, and others remember this sort of "secret opposition" surfacing now and again during those early years. Although the details are debatable, the struggle for grant money for theatre companies that resist tidy classification seems to be an all-too-common reality.

Jaan Whitehead, former chair of the SITI Company board in New York City, traces the American regional theatre movement from its beginnings (1960s) to its current institutional model in her 2002 essay "Art Will Out." She points out that originally the NEA and Ford Foundation not only funded but actively sought input from regional theatres in order to better assist them. However, in recent developments, theatres often are asked to establish traditionally modeled administrative structures before grants are awarded. Whitehead concluded: "It is very difficult for new theatres that do not have—or want—this institutional structure to break into the funding world, and traditional theatres do little to help them" (34). The Loose Moose, nontraditional in every way, came up against similar barricades in Calgary.

Just like everyone else, Keith kept his day job teaching acting classes 5 days a week at UofC. He donated his time writing and directing for Loose Moose and continued to teach free impro classes to new students who volunteered their time at the theatre. As the demand for him to teach international workshops increased and as more students wanted to take part in Theatresports, core company members like Curry, Foreman, Cahill, Tony Totino, and Frank Totino donated additional time and began to teach. Keith encouraged this. While the rehearsal space at the Simplex was being renovated, Loose Moose secured a small studio on Seventh Avenue across from the York Hotel for classes. This is where Curry and Foreman taught Theatresports to Mark McKinney and Bruce McCullough, half of The Audience Theatresports team and part of the Late Nite Comedy lineup. McKinney and McCullough went on to star in the television sketch comedy show *Kids in the Hall* (1988–1994) produced by Lorne Michaels. A cameo appearance by McKinney as a badly mutilated servant in the Loose Moose adaptation of Lew Wallace's *Ben-Hur* was Louis B. Hobson's favorite moment in this "Monty Python-" like production ("Moose Let").[20]

---

[20] Both McCullough and McKinney were writers for *Saturday Night Live* in the mid-1980s. McKinney joined the cast of *Saturday Night Live* in 1995. In 2003, he co-created, wrote, and starred in *Slings and Arrows* television series.

The popular Audience Team preparing to get pied by spectators after losing a
Theatresports match at the Moose Simplex, c. 1982. Mark McKinney (kneeling
on left), *Bill Gemmil, Norm Hiscock, Frank Van Keeken, and Garry Campbell.*
Photo Credit: Deborah Iozzi.

The Audience Team after getting pied.
Photo Credit: Deborah Iozzi.

For the 1982 Christmas show, Loose Moose did indeed take on the epic saga of Judah Ben-Hur. Several directors were responsible for specific sections of the play and Keith wove it all together into a theatrical tapestry. Critics found it very entertaining. "[A] mélange of melodrama, farce, improvisation, and the popular Loose Moose theatresports events," wrote Rosemary McCracken in the *Calgary Herald* ("Hammed-Up"). As in Theatresports, audiences were encouraged to "boo" and "hiss" at the Romans. The famous chariot race used masked actors in jogging attire as horses. Pontius Pilate, played by Gilchrist, a frequent commentator for Theatresports matches, relayed each moment of the event over a ringside microphone. Gilchrist said the idea for this production came from a previous Theatresports match. A team had asked for movie title suggestions and an audience member shouted out *Ben-Hur*. "The six minute scene which ensued was simply hilarious," recalled Gilchrist. "It put the seed in people's minds that the whole idea could be expanded upon" (L. Hobson, "Moose Let"). In concurrence with what Keith frequently professed, improvisational performances were opportunities to develop characters and material for future productions.

Unsportsmanlike conduct

It mustn't be work. It must be play. It doesn't matter if you win or lose.

KEITH JOHNSTONE (Stockholm Wksp)

Keith turned 50 in February of 1983 and, in the spring, he directed his play *Mindswop* at UofC. Meanwhile on Sunday nights at the Moose Simplex, Theatresports entertained large numbers of devoted fans. At least eight in-house Theatresports teams were competing for stage time—the Moose Team, Moosettes, Gonzos, Polanskis (a team dedicated to bringing Roman home), Mel's Angels, Royal Roaches, and The Audience—and the competition got dangerously real. Curry recollects complaints he made to Keith about The Audience team: "They would stand there and let you take the hat. They'd get huge laughs for making us look stupid. But we showed our true colors, too, and would get angry right on the stage."

In the first year or two of Loose Moose's existence, Cahill equated company members to sheep: "Keith would say when we were going to do a show, and we'd just do it, blindly. . . . We became a group of people who would follow Keith" (Foreman, *Something* 31). In 1983, company members still complained that only Keith's ideas were accepted. At one company meeting, frustrations were voiced and Keith rebutted with something in the vein of: "You kill all of my ideas. You've been taught to have an idea and defend it but I don't do that. I'm not attached to my ideas. For me a good idea is one that inspires you, so I give you idea after idea after idea until there's one you like." Frank Totino, Jim Curry, and new Loose Moose company member Patti Stiles, although not in attendance at that meeting, do remember similar exchanges. "Early in my training with Keith, I remember being so impressed with the amount of ideas he seemed to be able to generate instantly," Stiles wrote to me. "He would put forth such a wide range of ideas, simple to complex, insane to obvious. Through impro I learned that . . . lack of attachment or judgment allows the imagination to let loose. Keith was applying his own impro beliefs." In 1983, Stiles was not the only newcomer. The Loose Moose Company had grown ten-fold, and many of the younger improvisers who had not trained as closely with Keith or at all lacked Stile's sense of commitment to Keith and to the company.[21] For them, loyalty to their Theatresports team superseded their loyalty to Loose Moose.

In the spring of 1983, Keith deliberately didn't show up for weeks, even months at a time. Veena Sood said, "We weren't ready for that yet. So all of a sudden we started to fall apart" (Foreman, *Something* 55). Bitter arguments between teams ensued and the work on stage suffered. "It was aggressive. It wasn't as good as it could be when you're in the other frame of mind," admits Curry. "It got really sexual and Keith noted he heard the word "suck" forty times in one night." Then, some of the more established teams who wanted greater control over the rules, over who got to play when, and a cut of the revenues attempted to form a Players Union. At an emergency meeting convened by Keith, Curry recalls the heated and discomforting argument between Keith and Rick Hilton, an outspoken supporter of the union idea: "You don't see Keith openly angry but he stood up to Rick." Soon Rick and everyone else were silenced. "He read the riot act to us," said Tony Totino. "He said he'd have nothing to do with it [*the Player's Union*], and it would have nothing to do with the Loose Moose Theatre Company . . . " (Foreman, *Something* 59).

Keith had put an end to the union idea before it attained any degree of organization. He uncomfortably stepped out of the "unseen leader" position and asserted his veto power as artistic director. Next, he disbanded the permanent teams for scratch teams to save his company from destructive infighting. But why didn't Keith step in sooner? Was it his intention to allow the situation to intensify so that company members would realize how difficult it was to function without a guiding force in the room? Whatever his motives, when Keith made the decision to act, it was swift, unexpected, and effective.

---

[21] Home base for Patti Stiles is Melbourne, Australia, but she teaches and performs impro all over the world. Her approach to teaching is Johnstonian. She wrote to me: "The simple truth is what I do, teach and perform I learned from Keith. I may have my own extension, interpretation or evolution of certain exercises and techniques. But it was *his* thoughts, *his* observations and *his* creativity that brought this form of improvisation to light. It was *his* ability to teach it, *his* skill in teaching me that has trained me. *He* invented it, *he* laid the foundation, and I get to build, play and create from that. I would be fraudulent to claim it as mine."

Loose Moose moves forward

Take any bunch of human beings, sit one half there (in the audience), the other half there (on the stage), and these (the audience) will want the story to go forward, and these (the people on stage) will kill any chance of it happening. We try to control the future.

We buy insurance but we pay to see things get out of control in the theatre.

KEITH JOHNSTONE (Stockholm Wksp)

From the end of the summer of 1983 and throughout 1984, definite shifts in the company's structure took place. Theatresports continued to be popular even as the competition lessened, but a handful of the strongest players took off to bigger cities and potentially more lucrative jobs. McCullough and McKinney moved to Toronto along with the other players on The Audience team and Late Nite Comedy troupe: Garry Campbell, Norm Hiscock, and Frank Van Keeken.

Cofounder Mel Tonken, who had always been more interested in doing tried-and-true plays rather than Theatresports or controversial material like *The Last Bird*, also moved to Toronto but not because of his preferences. Tonken was bankrupt because of failed investments. So he left Calgary to start another life, to rebuild his veterinary business and his reputation in Toronto. Although Loose Moose was not the investment that put Tonken under, since the company's formation, he had always been the "angel" who supplied the company with money whenever funds were needed. He never bothered Keith with financial details because they both agreed, from the beginning, that Keith would be the artistic force and Tonken the financial backer. At about this time, however, Loose Moose had accumulated a huge debt and half of the debt was owed to the *Calgary Herald* for advertisements. Keith was not privy to this information until after Tonken had left. "I would not have gone into debt to the *Herald*," Keith ruminates. "I understand Mel. He's such a nice person. A good actor, too. The best Vladimir I've ever seen. So humble." Tonken should have been more up front with Keith about the financial health of the company, but Keith, as artistic director, should have also put into place a system of checks and balances.

As others drifted away, Keith made a real effort to shift his focus back to the company and the company's focus back to the classroom, so to speak. In 1984, with the help of an employment grant, Keith hired Cahill as associate director and he established On the Hoof, a paid touring company performing plays and facilitating workshops for school children all over Alberta. Foreman headed this troupe. "I remember doing the Frostbite Festival in White Horse in February at forty degrees below," she said. Wherever they went, they taught the basics of the Impro System as they had learned it from Keith. Keith never told them how to teach or what to teach but, if they had questions, he was very open to offering suggestions. "We had spent so much time with Keith, we knew what the rules were. We knew that any workshop was like a big improvisation" (P.I.). Furthermore, a full lineup for the Theatre for Kids season and tuition-based workshops for children and adults were part of the 1983/1984 itinerary, and veteran company members finally made a little money teaching, directing, and playwriting. Jim Curry, in particular, had several of his plays successfully produced at the Moose Simplex including *Puffballs*, an autobiographical drama about his relationship with his father that Keith encouraged him to write. No longer was Keith the sole Loose Moose playwright-in-residence.

Impro and Theatresports in Sweden

In the spring of 1983, when Theatresports at the Moose Simplex was at its most competitive and just before Keith tightened the reins, he traveled to Sweden to teach a 5-day workshop at Unga Klara ("Young Klara"), an innovative and influential theatre company championing children's issues housed in Stockholms Stadsteater. Notable Swedish director Suzanne Osten created this company in 1975 and still serves as artistic director.[22] In the preface for the Swedish translation of *Impro*, Osten writes about her first encounters with Keith. She was in Copenhagen in 1980 leading a seminar for female actors when she heard roaring laughter from the adjoining room. It was Keith's workshop. Later that summer, she met Keith in Stockholm at the Stadsteater and found him rather sour and difficult to converse with, but she soon discovered his mutual interest in pedagogy and theatre.[23] Keith copied *The Last Bird* on Unga Klara's copy machine, told Osten about his book *Impro*, and went on his way. But the seeds of what would develop into a professional relationship based on mutual respect and admiration had been planted.

While Unga Klara was devising a performance piece about the problems of the Swedish school system for the 1981 season, Osten's copy of *Impro* arrived. She found it to be just what her company needed—"en handbok i skolproblem" ("a handbook in school problems"). In other words, *Impro* was a practical textbook of pedagogical solutions for the formal and informal

---

[22] Two well-known Unga Klara productions are *Medea's Children* (1975), directed and cowritten by Osten, which explored divorce from the children's point of view; and *A Clean Girl* (1983), directed by Osten, which brought anorexia to the public's attention. Other projects tackle serious topics like mental illness, alcoholism, death, and emigration. In 2006, Osten directed *Babydrama*, an interactive play for infants aged 6 to 12 months and their parents. It played to sold-out houses for several seasons. This production was documented in a 2009 film of the same title.

[23] Keith had been teaching in Sweden for several years but primarily at the drama school in Gothenburg.

classroom. Osten systematically led her company through all the exercises in Keith's text, page by page. "Festen varade i 8 veckor" ("the feast lasted for eight weeks"), wrote Osten, and the Impro System not only nourished their controversial project *Fläskhästarna* ("Flesh Horses") with "humor och lössläppta galenskap" ("humor and folly"), but their process of working going forward (Osten 7–11; trans. Bagdade). Well-known Swedish actor, Helge Skoog, was in that production and his introduction to Keith and the Impro System literally changed the direction of his career.

Skoog was a young actor with the Royal Dramatic Theatre in Stockholm from 1958 to 1965 under the artistic direction of important film director, Ingmar Bergman. While there, Skoog was taught that the stage was a sacred, secret space not to be shared with the audience. "They didn't realize a movie could do that. I think theatre should not be like a movie," Skoog said to me. Although Skoog worked consistently in Swedish theatre and television before encountering Keith's Impro System, his early training at the Royal Dramatic Theatre had made him fearful of the audience. After Osten introduced Keith's methods to Skoog and her company, Skoog read *Impro* himself. Then, before embarking with Unga Klara on a US tour in the winter of 1983, Skoog took a side trip to Calgary.

Skoog dropped in on one of Keith's acting classes at UofC and, over lunch, Keith told him about Theatresports. Skoog was fascinated by the idea of performing spontaneously in front of an audience without a script. It was at Skoog's request, not Osten's, that Keith traveled to Stockholm in the spring of 1983 to teach the workshop at Unga Klara. On the last evening of the workshop, Keith and the Unga Klara ensemble surprised the audience at the Pistolteatern with a Theatresports match following the regularly scheduled performance. After the match, Skoog said half of the actors declared, "Never more, this was the worst thing I ever experienced!" The other half cheered, "Wow, let's do it again!" Skoog took the opinion of the "other half."

Keith took a research sabbatical in the fall of 1983 which allowed him to return to Stockholm and teach a workshop at Teatercentrum, an association of free theatre groups. One of the groups challenged Unga Klara to a Theatresports match and they accepted. Skoog was not on the Unga Klara team. He was putting together a cabaret at the Stadsteater and formed a team with three other cabaret actors. A tournament between Unga Klara, Skoog's team, and two teams from the Teatercentrum took place in December. Keith and Osten were two of the three judges. Keith recalled Osten's "amazement at the fury generated by the Stockholm theater goers. I asked her to turn and look at them and she saw all these happy Swedes yelling their heads off" (*Storytellers* 4). Skoog's team beat Unga Klara by one point. Keith went backstage and saw some of the best actors in Sweden in an angry rage. "This is typical of people who are just starting," wrote Keith. "Sooner or later the players have to realize that when it's a great game everyone wins; and when it's a miserable game, everyone loses" (*Newsletter Two* 5). Osten was furious, too. "She didn't realize it was just for fun," muses Skoog with a smile. Skoog opened the Saturday night Cabaret at the Stadsteatern in the winter of 1984 and followed each performance with a Theatresports match. "It soon became very popular among the young people."

In the fall of 1984, Skoog and his team were contacted by Sveriges Television to do a Theatresports series. "We were a bit reluctant," admits Skoog. "Impro is best live, you have to be there and feel the atmosphere. But we were persuaded." *Teatersport Sweden* was a hit and made Helge Skoog a household name. Keith says Skoog lost his stage fright around this time and Skoog concurs: "I was less scared. More confident, as Keith said, and not afraid of the audience. Of course I am a better actor and I've come into more comedy shows on TV."

Skoog launched the Klara Soppteater ("Soup Theatre") in 1989 at the Stadsteater to give Unga Klara ensemble members opportunities to write, direct, sing, and, of course, improvise.[24] This 1-hour lunchtime show attracted people working at the nearby Parliament buildings. The actors actually served soup to the audience in the beginning. Soon, theatres all over Sweden were experimenting with their own soup theatres. Today, the Klara Soppteater is still going strong and so is Skoog's career. In 2010, he had a successful run in Göran Palm's one-man ecopolitical tragicomedy in blank verse, *Sit Down Tragedy*, in the Stadsteatern's 300-seat space. I attended a sold-out performance and, even though I did not understand Swedish, the strong rapport he had with his audience was unmistakable. They laughed and cried and even ate fruit with him. Sara Granath, critic for the *Svenska Dagbladet* ("Swedish daily newspaper"), remarked that Skoog, an actor known for his improvisational skills and public interaction, delivered the verse with a freedom not unlike a skilled Shakespearean actor. Skoog did not hesitate when asked how Keith has influenced his career: "Everything I have done since I started with this [impro] has been grounded in Keith's work."[25] Keith and his Impro System continue to influence Swedish actors and amuse Swedish audiences as the fully booked workshop and the sold-out impro show, both taught/directed by Keith at the Boulevard Teatern in Stockholm in 2010, demonstrated.[26]

Festival of Fools in New York and treated like fools in Quebec

In March of 1984, Keith revived *The Last Bird* at the Moose Simplex for a 3-week run to prepare for the Festival of Fools in April in New York City.

---

[24] Skoog directed Keith's play *The Cord* at the Klara Soppteater in 1985.
[25] Skoog is currently hosting the live television cooking show *Halv 8 hos mig* ("Come Dine with Me").
[26] Keith added 15 minutes of "free impro" before Theatresports matches to warm up the players and to "teach" the audience, in a nonacademic way, about the art of improvisation (*Newsletter Two* 4).

He accepted the invitation to the festival for the exposure and to garner reviews from critics outside of Calgary. Fifteen company members made the trip with Keith.[27] Unfortunately, the festival was unorganized, poorly publicized, and the organizers assumed—since it was an impro company—Loose Moose could work in any space. This included the Port Authority bus terminal where Loose Moosers improvised to commuters and transients one afternoon. For *The Last Bird*, the festival organizers provided the company with an inadequate, very small, fourth-floor studio space just down the road from Times Square. It had sickly yellow walls, a low white ceiling, no seating, and no sound system. Tony Totino remembers the group's disappointment but, being an improvisational troupe accustomed to working with limited resources, they knew they could manage. They bought supplies, painted the entire space black, hung curtains, built risers for seating, scrounged up lighting, and met a guy in a diner who worked for a New York radio station and was able to supply them with a sound system (Zimmerman, "Big Apple"; T. Totino).

The Loose Moosers were ready to go but another glitch rendered this field trip less than ideal. The festival organizers had prebooked youth groups for several performances of *The Last Bird* and did not feel the need to advertise the show further. Sadly, as a result, no critics came and no reviews were written. Furthermore, *The Last Bird* is a dark play, not intended for children, and the content kept some prebooked youth groups from attending. In fact, Keith, Cahill, Frank and Tony Totino all recounted the story of a nun who brought her group of disadvantaged and abused teenagers to a Theatresports match at the Douglas Fairbanks Theatre in advance of *The Last Bird* performance they were going to attend. Before the match and in lieu of advertisement, the company members performed a particularly violent scene from *The Last Bird*. As a result, the nun cancelled the group's booking because she felt the scenes depicted a reality too close to the reality her teenagers faced daily.

In spite of everything, Keith and his Loose Moosers found the entire experience worthwhile. For one, they garnered a new appreciation for their Moose Simplex, the Calgary press, and their own skills in acclimatizing to any situation no matter how chaotic. Furthermore, improvisational companies from all over the city attended workshops and demonstrations given by Keith and the company members. Cahill recalled enthusiastic feedback for their risky, collaborative way of working. Even though most of the improvisational companies based in New York were likely influenced by Second City's sketch comedy style, Keith's status as a pioneer of impro had definitely reached the big apple.[28] Finally, as Tony Totino put it, "Just being

---

[27] Frank Totino, Tony Totino, Veena Sood, Kathleen Foreman, Rick Hilton, Dennis Cahill, Clem Martini, and eight more.

[28] The New York Theatresports League (TSNY) established this year.

in New York for almost three weeks with everybody from the Loose Moose was a catalyzing moment. I loved it."

In June of 1984, Loose Moose was invited to perform with companies from around the world at the first Quebec International Theatre Fortnight festival. In Brennan's review for the *Calgary Herald*, Alexander Hausvater, artistic director of the festival, called the Loose Moose's improvisational performances "old-fashioned" by Quebec and European standards and "the worst disappointment of the festival." Brennan, however, called Comedie Francaise's production of Moliere's *The School for Wives* "the most conspicuous flop" ("Quebec"). But this slight at the famed European company did not appease Keith. Two weeks later, Keith wrote a letter to the *Herald* in his company's defense: "Brennan knows of our work and reputation and I would have hoped he would have defended us against these Easterners" ("Loose"). Keith's rebuke was not so much about defending the Loose Moose performances at the festival, which neither he nor Brennan attended. In fact, Keith was in Europe at the time and only when he returned to Calgary did he discover that *The Last Bird*, the play the Loose Moose was asked to bring to the festival, had been substituted with a one-act by Curry. Keith took issue, rather, with the lack of support from Brennan and the bad manners of the festival director. "We were his [Hausvater's] guests. It's not right that our host should pillory us in this way."

Back home

Back at the Moose Simplex, Keith directed his two-act spoof on the vampire genre, *They Come By Night* (originally titled *Shot By An Elk*), in July of 1984. Keith called the play "frivolous" but "fun" for the summer season and critics seemed to agree.[29] *You Can't Take It With You*, by George Kaufman and Moss Hart, opened the 1984/1985 season. Tonken returned to direct one last time. Frank Totino directed Curry's *Puffballs* in November to critical commendation. Clem Martini's new children's play, *Jack the Giant Killer*, commissioned by the Alberta Playwright Centre in Edmonton, opened in December as a Theatre for Kids production. In January of 1985, Keith directed Christopher Durang's *Sister Mary Ignatius Explains It All for You*.[30] His 10-year-old son Ben played the part of Thomas. Keith also wrote and directed—in under 24 hours—*The Parcel That Nobody Ordered* as a Theatre for Kids production.

---

[29] Rosemary McCracken, critic for the *Calgary Herald*, called it "wacky and mildly titillating" and wrote that "It's significance lies in the fun it affords its audiences" ("Spooky Spoof"). Clem Martini, Frank Totino, and Dennis Cahill played leading characters.

[30] I imagine Keith was attracted to this absurdist comedy because it reveals the psychological damage inflicted on children by Catholicism and by the dogmatic nun who taught them.

In late March, *Mutiny on the Bounty* opened. It was codirected by Keith, Cahill, and Tony Totino and rehearsed (while Keith was writing the script) with an unusually large cast of eighteen playing multiple roles. The lobster from *The Tempest*, *Live Snakes and Ladders*, and *Mindswop* almost landed another cameo role in *Mutiny* in a nightmare scene. But Totino and Cahill did not consider the scene necessary and apprehensively suggested to Keith that the scene be cut. "I believe this was the first time we ever asked Keith to cut a whole scene from one of his scripts," reflects Cahill. "However, Keith did cut the scene with very little discussion." Even with three capable directors working with a script revised throughout the rehearsal process, Kate Zimmerman, writing for the *Calgary Herald*, found the concept interesting but the execution sloppy ("Fuzzy Script"). Louis B. Hobson granted the production had problems but, he wrote: "The Moose's Mutiny doesn't sink. It arrives at the finish line with enough genuine entertainment value still intact to make it a fun evening Moose style." "Moose style" meant unconventional, partly improvised, and surprising. In this production— which unpacks the question "Who are the real savages?"—the British sailors can only speak in gibberish to the Tahitians who respond in a perfect English (L. Hobson, "Mutiny crew").

Beginning of Life Game and other formats

Keith headed to Denmark again to teach workshops including one for the Association of Danish Stage Directors in the spring of 1985. When he returned home, he put his company to work on his new concept, *How It Was* (renamed Life Game later on). As Theatresports continued to spread to places as far away as Australia, the official rules and regulations could not be insisted upon without some sort of oversight committee, and the game got altered in various ways.[31] Also, ComedySportz, an acknowledged rip-off of Theatresports, began its own franchise in Wisconsin. The name ComedySportz alone perpetuated the notion that competitive improvisation is about creating "funny business" not "theatre." Going forth, Keith's approach in his writings and in the classroom is often corrective in nature. For example, he published six *Theatresports and Life-Game Newsletters* (1987–94) ranging from ten to thirty-five pages each. The newsletters contain explanations and historical significance of various Theatresports rules, regulations, and terminology. News on international tournaments is often included. Games and other formats are outlined and,

---

[31] In Australia, the first Theatresports game was played at the Belvoir Street Theatre in Sydney in 1985. Within 2 years, teams were established in five states and a Theatresports television series was launched. Celebrities were known to make guest appearances. Today, Impro Australia, not Keith, holds the trademark for Australian Theatresports.

on occasion, Keith uses the newsletter as a platform for expressing his indignation.

Although he understood the need for Theatresports leagues to vary the structure slightly to suit their particular culture, he takes issue with altering his games or the format simply to make it safer or to avoid failure. "Failure should be welcomed as an essential component of any game, and as an opportunity to show your generosity and good nature," he wrote on page one of the first newsletter. As more and more Theatresports competitions disintegrated into gags and jokes and as filler games began to replace scenes based on storytelling, Keith turned his attention to developing new structures that were dependent upon longer stretches of narrative.

In the Guest Game, one "normal" character is invited to the "abnormal" family home of his/her date. When she arrives, her date is nowhere to be found and she proceeds to improvise scenes with each member of the family. The type of family has to be established as the game goes on (e.g., a military family, a hippie family, a circus family). Short scenes give way to longer ones as the guest continues to actively look for her date and as the family's characteristics expand. "Early form of long-form, if you like," Keith says. "It'll work fine for twenty minutes. I invented it so I could spend more time in the green room having coffee." Keith invented Gorilla Theatre to train proficient improvisers to direct each other in scenes and Maestro Impro (originally spelled "Micetro Impro") as a feedback game that could include a large number of students of all levels.[32] And Keith invented Life Game to guide his improvisers back to the classroom and back to the heart of the Impro System.

Life Game is an improvised format that applies the Impro System to noncompetitively dramatize people's stories, to evoke laughter and pathos, and to create an emotional connection between the improvisers and their audiences. Basically, someone is invited onstage to share their life story in an interview format. A host conducts the interview and, at various moments, a director intercedes and asks the four or more players to improvise a scene about something the guest has just shared. Keith introduced this new format towards the end of a 10-day workshop he taught in Lyme Regis, in county Dorset, England, in 1985. Ann Jellicoe, who had been developing the concept of Community Plays in this area since 1978, arranged this workshop.[33] One of the participants was Phelim McDermott who Keith remembers as "a really bright 22-year-old entranced by the Life Game." McDermott officially cofounded the theatre company Improbable (London) in 1996 and, with

---

[32] See *Impro for Storytellers*, pp. 42–54, for detailed instructions on how to play Gorilla Theatre and Maestro Impro.

[33] Community Plays involve the community in the theatrical event and are usually written for and about the history of that particular community. See Ann Jellicoe's *Community Plays: How to Put Them On* (1987).

Keith's assistance, took Life Game on a successful UK tour in 1998. The concluding chapter documents this tour, ensuing engagements, and the reasons why Improbable keeps Life Game in their repertoire. At Loose Moose, Life Game became a regular part of the late Friday night variety show in October of 1988.

Out of debt but no recognition

Nothing unpredictable or extraordinary happened in 1986 or 1987 at Loose Moose. Theatresports continued to draw enthusiastic crowds to the Simplex on Sunday nights at 8 with ticket prices now at $4.00. On The Hoof continued to entertain at schools throughout Alberta. New plays for the main stage were produced including two by Keith.[34] Seasonal planning kept a "loose" structure, as always, and announcements for the 1986/1987 season relied on phrasing such as "the company's fall production will probably be" or "the last play of the season will likely be" (Zimmerman, "Loose"). The real news was that Keith, with significant help from Cahill and Deborah Iozzi (general manager since 1984), succeeded in finally pulling his company out of debt in April of 1987; and Loose Moose, for the first time, had a surplus fund.[35] The costs of leasing and maintaining the Moose Simplex, however, ate up most of the 1986/1987 $300,000 budget so company members were still unable to make a living at the Moose. Times were desperate and Theatre for Kids productions, which sold very well, took on greater importance.

In an interview for *Calgary Magazine*'s April 1987 issue, Keith told reporter Ron Shewchuck that he felt like "an aardvark among camels" in this city. He had just returned from directing a well-received production of his adaptation of Georg Büchner's *Woyzeck* at the Odense Teater, one of the oldest and most important theatres in Denmark. The Odense provided Keith with whatever he needed because his production of *Godot* the year before had been extremely successful. It was Keith's third staging of *Godot* but the first time the Odense produced Beckett's classic play, and the critics loved it. Sisi, drama critic from the *Jydske Tidende*, wrote:

> Den engelske instruktør Keith Johnstone har set mere humor og håb midt i absurditeten . . . . Men trods optimismen rammer spillets piskesnert os

---

[34] In 1986, Keith wrote and directed *The Secret Life of Doctor Watson*. In 1987, he wrote and directed *The Beast with Five Fingers*, a sci-fi political thriller with thirty or so characters.

[35] One year, when the company accumulated a surplus of funds, CRAF cut their grant. Cahill said CRAF's reasoning was that Loose Moose managed their finances so well that they didn't need the grant. Keith claims, "CRAF wanted us to be in debt so they had power over us. It was very annoying." CRAF did reinstate the grant, however, and funded the Loose Moose even when they were without a theatre space for 3 years (2001–04).

lige ætsende, når vi opdager, at også vi er blevet vældig gode til at slå tiden ihjel og har affundet os med ventepositionen.

   English director Keith Johnstone has set more humor and hope in the middle of absurdity . . . . But despite the optimism, the play hits us like a corrosive crack of a whip when we discover that we too have been very good at killing time and resigning ourselves to waiting (trans. Hansen)

Peter Ferm, writing for the large Swedish paper *Dagens Nyheter*, said Keith's production was not as anarchistic as he would've expected given his reputation in Sweden as the creator of Theatresports:

   Nej, det är det gedigna hantverket det lätta handlaget som talar ur hans regi. Förmågan att ge var sak dess betydelse, förmågan att inte ge efter för ingrodda uppfattningar om Becketts absurditet och tyngd. Kanske är det tiden som arbetar för en realistisk "Godot."
   No, it is the superb craftsmanship, the gentle touch that speaks in his staging. The ability to give each thing its importance, the ability to not succumb to the ingrained perceptions about Beckett's absurdity and gravity. (trans. Hansen)

Other reviews found the production "warm and funny," "as good as new," "juicy," and "worth waiting for." This positive feedback from the professional theatre community abroad only heightened Keith's sensitivity to the lack of recognition he and his 10-year-old, internationally known company had received from local Calgarians. Shewchuck wrote: "Keith Johnstone, bespectacled, ironic professor of drama at University of Calgary and artistic director of Loose Moose Theatre Company has become a world figure, a famous guy. The strange thing is that the inventor of Theatresports is famous just about everywhere but here." It is the same issue Louis B. Hobson had with Calgary in 1980. The city was not taking full advantage of Keith's talents.

   Michael Dobbin, artistic director of Alberta Theatre Projects, blamed Keith's low profile and his lack of presence in the theatre community in Shewchuck's article for the lack of recognition. As the article's title—"Loose Moose Recluse"—suggested, Keith came across as a lone artist. He was also soft-spoken, not a great socializer, and often lumbered about looking down at his feet, but this did not prevent international theatres and communities from reaching out to him. Then again, Keith was an outspoken critic of theatre and audiences in Calgary even though he rarely attended theatre events beyond the Moose Simplex. One of his theories was that Calgarians were too dependent on imported culture and, therefore, unable to imagine Calgary as a place of innovation. With hard-hitting, unsubstantiated opinions like these, who could blame theatre organizations for not wanting to invite Keith to their parties? If Keith had really wanted more recognition in Calgary, he would have shoved himself through that door, leaped over that abyss, and latched on to that precipice. Instead, over the next decade, Keith put more focus into teaching and fine-tuning the Impro System. Clearly, where he really wanted recognition was in the classroom.

(Re)Teaching Theatresports

Keith took on more and more international workshops and launched the first Loose Moose International Improvisational School in the summer of 1989. This intensive 2 to 3-week training program continues to attract participants from all over the world. Also in 1989, Eva Mekler's *Masters of the Stage* was published. This text is a collection of interviews from influential teachers working at the time in Britain's foremost theatre schools. At least four teachers from three different schools specifically said they applied Keith's techniques to their actor training processes.[36] Even as teachers around the world found the Impro System invaluable, a handful of teachers in Calgary responded negatively to Keith's games. Kathleen Foreman faults the teachers. She says students would see a show at Loose Moose and bring the games, or their limited understanding of the games, back to the classroom. Their teachers would then allow the games to be played but, without knowing the theory or the "secret language," they were unable to sidecoach effectively.[37] Thus students became competitive, wanting to be more clever, funnier, and quicker than the next guy. "Keith had to do a lot of remedial work," maintains Foreman (P.I.).

Keith taught the first teacher's workshop in 1993 and continued writing *The Theatresports and Life-Game Newsletters* until 1994 when Loose Moose published his *Don't Be Prepared: Theatresports for Teachers*. This manual was Keith's attempt to reteach and re-explain Theatresports and the Impro System to any ill-informed teachers. On page one of the introductory chapter, one can almost hear Keith's frustration. He stresses that all of his games come from theory: "[We] have to know why the games exist, or they'll be misused, and after being misused they'll be rejected (or they'll deserve to be) . . . . [J]ust as every scientific theory implies a range of experiments, so each improvisation theory implies a set of games" (1–2). Keith identifies not only the theoretical foundation of each game (or set of games) in this manual, but also the game's origin (i.e., when it was invented, why, and by whom if by someone other than Keith) and whether or not he recommends using it. Alas, Loose Moose no longer prints this manual.[38]

---

[36] John Abulafia from The Drama Studio (London); Michael Gaunt from The Guildford School of Acting and Dance; Edward Argent and Peter McAllister from The Royal Scottish Academy of Music and Dance.

[37] Steen Haakon Hansen says this still happens in Denmark. Just a few years ago, for example, his two daughters would come home from high school doing exercises invented by Keith but they were not taught the theory and had no idea why the exercises were important.

[38] Most of this information can be found in *Impro for Storytellers* (1999) but the information targets a larger audience, not just teachers.

Between 1988 and 1994, Keith had many obligations to fulfill which further informed the nature of his teachings and writings. He traveled to major cities around the world to teach workshops and/or to establish new Theatresports leagues; although, by this time, he tried to avoid Theatresports as much as possible. Still, he found himself settling disputes among groups in the same city wanting to form a league (only one league per city) and serving as a judge for international tournaments. In 1988, for example, Calgary hosted the XV Olympic Winter Games and an Olympic Theatresports Tournament, organized by Cahill and Iozzi, was included in the conjunctive Olympic Festival of the Arts.[39] The tournament sold out, a live goat made an appearance, and during the medal ceremony, Roger Fredericks, a player from the winning Vancouver team, slowly began to eat his bouquet of flowers to everyone's delight (Johnstone, *Newsletter Two* 6).

Another International Theatresports Tournament took place from July 11–15, 1988, as part of the World Expo in Brisbane, Australia. Keith was scheduled to present workshops and judge the event but he had family issues to deal with at home, so he sent Cahill in his place. The Concert Hall of the Performing Arts Complex was converted to a theatre-in-the-round for the sold-out competition. Calgary's Loose Moose team took the top prize, the Kiwi Cup. "That's bad news for Australia," wrote Martin Portus, a journalist for the *Sydney Morning Herald*:

> In no other country has theatre sports been so enthusiastically played, fueling teams across Australia, in theatres, in schools, on television and even in the corporate world. We have taken this game of improvisation and fashioned it into a theatrical production somewhere between a revivalist meeting and a football orgy. Australian theatre sports has played to full houses since Belvoir Street first discovered it in 1985. And now we have lost, again. The good news is that is just doesn't matter . . . .The Expo miracle is that all the teams talk not of winning, but of how different countries had extended the possibilities of the game. The evangelism of a true theatre sporter is unstoppable.

Australians and New Zealanders took to Theatresports in a way Loose Moosers could only dream about and it has everything to do with their evangelistic attitude. Over the last few years, Keith's Impro System in Brazil and other Latin American countries has enjoyed a similar surge of excitement. Like the teams in the Australian tournament, a handful of the most successful improvisers in Latin America want to draw practitioners and audiences into their impro world not through domination but through persuasion—via presentation of quality impro-based theatre and reciprocity. Teaching, for one, is a strategy adopted by these improvisers in their effort to inculcate in the artistic culture impro's importance. The

---

[39] Teams from Loose Moose, Australia, Denmark, Sweden, Edmonton, England, Halifax, New York, Seattle, Toronto, and Vancouver took part (Johnstone, *Newsletter Two* 1).

Latin American impro movement is briefly explored in the concluding chapter.

In October of 1989, Keith directed *Caucasian Chalk Circle* at UofC and in November, funded by a grant from the Canada Council Explorations Program, *How It Was* (i.e., The Life Game) officially premiered under Keith's direction and ran for 6 months at the Moose Simplex. On the other hand, Cahill had gradually assumed more and more responsibility over the day-to-day operations. Cahill's primary goal then and now is to keep the Loose Moose solvent. In 1989, that meant elimination of the costly main stage season of plays. "The amateur company, which once mounted a six-play season at its northeast theatre, is now reduced to doing only its cheapest forms of programming," wrote Martin Morrow for the *Calgary Herald*. Shelving more "ambitious" projects was the cause, according to Morrow, for the decline in the theatre's status in the local community ("Loose Moose Founder"). Although a handful of plays were mounted over the next decade, the main stage season was never reinstated.

Conflict and closure—Beyond and within

Keith went back to Stockholm in the fall of 1991 to direct Chekhov's *The Seagull* at the Stadsteater. He took Gavin Semple with him and it is an experience both would like to forget. When he arrived at the theatre, Keith agreed to move the production to a larger theatre in order to accommodate a company of established actors, many who were famous, including Skoog who played Trigorin. Keith had originally hoped for a small space and a younger cast, but the established actors wanted to work with him. While Skoog and assistant director Martin Geijer were prepared to work in Keith's improvisational style, the other actors were not.

Geijer remembers the first few weeks of rehearsal as "a very pleasant period" in which Keith would introduce impro exercises, games, and techniques and then merge them into the story. When the rehearsal period was almost complete and Keith, as usual, insisted on keeping the scenes unblocked, some actors responded apprehensively. About a week before opening, an audience was invited to watch a run-through and Geijer hails this as the best performance because it was alive and enthusiastically received. Regardless, the anxiety felt by cast members—who did not trust Keith's or their own improvisational processes—was expressed to the artistic director and the opening was postponed. Suddenly, a famous Chekhovian director from Finland, Ralf Långbacka, who had recently directed another production at the Stadsteatern, was brought in to set some of the scenes. Geijer and Skoog were despondent over Keith's situation. As Långbacka took over, Keith stood in the back of the theatre and quietly said things like, "This is not what I wanted." Skoog can barely speak about this painful experience: "It was awful. Yes."

Although a practitioner of and an advocate for Keith's improvisational methods, Geijer believes a failure of communication and lack of preparation on Keith's part played a role in the debacle. "From the start, Keith should have let the actors in on his mind set. He should have been more prepared to work with actors who did not know his process." Keith, too, blames himself. His theory is that a lack of fear on the part of the director creates a theatre that is living and breathing. When Keith was given a group of "very good" but inflexible actors, he succumbed to the fear. "I was trying to get *The Seagull* right, so I gave up and tried to do a conventional production," he confesses. "It was a catastrophe." Semple's account concurs. Keith, uncharacteristically, asked Semple to design the set as Chekhov had written. "Normally we would have discussed setting it on Mars and gone from there," says Semple. "However, we blundered on, but found it difficult to arrive at satisfactory solutions. I'm not sure why we were doing it."

After the opening, the headline in Stockholm's biggest paper, *Dagens Nyheter*, read: "The Seagull Lands Like an Albatross." Skoog, Geijer, and Semple all had high expectations going into this production and were greatly disappointed with the outcome. "He loved that play," said Skoog. "But he had ideas that he didn't dare fulfill and the production became very old-fashioned and formatted like normal theatre." Keith had previously expressed (and still expresses) his admiration for Swedish culture and for the Swede's willingness to try new things, so his disheartenment, in this case, was particularly heightened.

In 1993, Keith came under attack again but this time he did not concede. He chose to use his words as weapons and the *Theatresports and Life-Game Newsletter* as the battle ground. Here are excerpts from his essay "Smoke Without Fire (Or: Who Really Invented Theatresports, Daddy?)" included in *Newsletter Five* from April, 1993:

> Imagine that you had enrolled in an acting course at Calgary University, and suddenly found yourselves playing Theatresports in public amid huge enthusiasm and acclaim—interviews in the newspapers and on television; people cheering you in the street; lots of glamour. And imagine that you had achieved this by using ideas that were the opposite of everything that you had previously accepted. This would have been one of the most amazing things that ever happened to you, and after such excitement, such ecstasy, how could you not feel that you had contributed to the invention of this wonderful game while it was being assembled around you?
>
> I shared these feelings, and I feel in my bones that those first players of Calgary Theatresports were united with me in an extraordinary adventure; and yet, when I look back and remember why I invented each detail, and that I had directed such games long before I arrived at Calgary, I have to say that the idea that the first players in Calgary "created Theatresports" is an illusion.

Rumours reach me, about the way that I "cheated the people who really invented Theatresports". You might consider that these accusations are too sordid to deserve a reply—after all I came to Calgary as one of the leading authorities in my field—but if just one disgruntled person nags on for year after year, the wounds, imaginary or real, will never heal. So here are seven "grumblings" about the "rat Professor who climbed to fame on the shoulders of his students" . . . . (22)

Keith lists and then refutes each of the seven grumblings and then concludes his essay with a conjectural reflection on why the ownership issue kept surfacing. "The answer may lie in anthropology," he continued:

For example, Malinowski wrote that "[. . . . .] *the whole of tribal life is permeated by a constant give and take*; [. . . . . . .] every ceremony, every legal and customary act is done to the accompaniment of material gift and counter gift [. . . . .]

Many (or all) human societies have complex behaviour relating to gratitude . . . . A gift can be a barbed hook driven deep into the gullet: a way of forcing an unwelcome tie between the giver and the recipient. . . .

Consider the one-sidedness of my relationship with Loose Moose. I have given my life's work freely to the players at Calgary, believing that if I can "empty myself" without reserve, new ideas will rush in to fill the vacuum. I'm the unpaid President and Artistic Director of the company (this can eat up acres of time), and I give free classes here, and I write and direct plays, and so on, but I receive nothing in return. And unlike the players (who may be geologists, or mail-carriers, or cooks, and so on) I do not find this a refreshing change—because improvisation is what I do all day long anyway!

I don't want to be a guru—because once you're a guru people start to rely on you instead of searching into themselves—but I can't avoid the role entirely, and transactions with gurus are supposed to involve the exchange of some sort of gift. . . . But I don't receive anything back, or expect to receive anything, and this breaks the rule that there should be "reciprocity", and perhaps gives a few people an intolerable feeling that they rationalize as injustice. (25–6)

Paying it back or paying it forward is how Keith chooses to deal with his own feelings of indebtedness. Mark McKinney, it seems, gave something back when he showed up unannounced one day, tuned a piano in Keith's living room, and walked away. A random act of kindness that resonated with Keith: "I still feel differently about Mark than about the people who give nothing in return" (26).

Keith does not name those "people" targeted in his essay. Likely the attack was, in part, a reaction to the project Foreman and Martini had recently undertaken—to document the history of Theatresports—but they were not the targets of Keith's bitterness. In any case, Keith never brought up this issue again, at least not in a public forum. Not even in *Impro for Storytellers* (1999) does Keith make reference to these so-called grumblings. But back in April of 1993, just weeks after his sixtieth birthday, Keith felt the need to set things straight from his point of view, once and for all.

Around this time, Keith was falsely diagnosed with something like low-pressure glaucoma and told he was going to go blind. Doctors said it might take up to 10 years but it could also happen immediately. Keith always had a difficult time remembering faces, so he began to draw faces from photographs because, without sight, he would at least have a sense of what people looked like. Inspired by Kimon Nicolaïdes, the artist and art teacher who wrote in his book, *The Natural Way to Draw*, that one must make 5000 mistakes before one can be adept enough to correct them, Keith drew 5000 faces in exactly 1 year, 3 months, and 3 days. During this process, he never felt like he was improving but he did not look back. He stayed the course following his own pedagogical advice: "Don't get too pleased with yourself. Don't get depressed. Don't punish yourself. And know that it won't always work." Sitting on his living room bookshelf in his home in the suburbs of Calgary, four binders containing 5000 drawn faces in chronological order, prove that perseverance *does* work. "I did learn to copy faces rather well," says Keith, "but it made no difference whatsoever to remembering them."

Everything Keith reads finds its way into the classroom. Today, Keith tells students they must do something 5000 times to become skillful, but he never intended on showing his drawings to students. The act of drawing 5000 faces was a personal struggle in his ongoing battle with memory, and an opportunity to observe the details. With the production of *The Seagull* in Stockholm, Keith lost faith in his own pedagogical principles. Rumors about the ownership of Theatresports spawned him to uncharacteristically scold, in a newsletter, ungracious students. These incidents imply a drift away from the theatre-as-classroom environment, an environment Devine worked tirelessly to maintain at RCT. In those days, Keith observed everyone and everything in great detail and created the basics of his Impro System from those observations. Now in his 60s, it was time for Keith not only to remember but to observe his own creative processes once again; to pay attention to *his* insecurities and to *his* fears in order to move in the direction of the next classroom.

Transitions

In 1996, Keith traveled to London to facilitate a Life Game workshop with Phelim McDermott and Improbable in anticipation of their 1998 UK tour. Why did Improbable and not Loose Moose take the Life Game on tour? For two main reasons: Loose Moose was not financially willing to take risks and they no longer had an ensemble of dedicated performers willing to donate their lives to such a project. Conversely, McDermott and Julian Crouch, two of the three artistic directors/founders of Improbable, were having huge success in 1998 with their codirection of the ambitious musical *Shockheaded Peter* and were ready to launch a new project. Life Game was the vehicle of choice. It was as simple as that.

All of the original Loose Moose company members, except for Cahill, had moved on by 1996, so daily training in the Impro System by those who embodied the "secret language," not only in performance but in everyday life, was no longer available to new performers. As stated before, Cahill, as associate director, had assumed more responsibility since the late 1980s, and his approach was more cautious than either Tonken or Keith's and not as loosely structured. It is because of Cahill's business savvy that Loose Moose is still operating today albeit in a formulaic, predictable way. In the early years, Keith was a dynamic leader who held himself accountable for risk-taking and failure so his improvisers could experience walking the edge of chaos without fear. However, he entrusted others with decisions that should have been made by him. His artistic direction was *too* loose, and often *too* remote, to accommodate the growth and accumulated expenses of a pioneering theatre company. Instead of finding a happy medium, from the mid-1990s forward, Loose Moose played it *too* safe.

A Christian school took over the building that housed the Moose Simplex in 1998. Although the owners of the school invited Loose Moose to stay, it was clear to Cahill they would have to leave in the long term. Cahill also recalls the power randomly shutting down and theatre volunteers being told by Christian school folks that what Loose Moose did was essentially evil. Moreover, it was getting more difficult to attract audiences to their location by the airport, and a move to a more central location had been part of discussions for some time. The Garry Theatre in Inglewood, built in the 1930s as a cinema and located 1 mile from downtown Calgary, became the home of the Loose Moose from 1998 to 2001.

At the end of 1998, just 3 years after his retirement from UofC, Keith handed over the artistic direction of Loose Moose to Cahill. He also set up the not-for-profit International Theatresports Institute (ITI) to handle licensing of his other trademarked formats: Theatresports, Maestro Impro, Gorilla Theatre, and Life Game. Of course, Keith never made much money off of licensing. The minimal per show percentage fees were/are used primarily for legal expenses and for maintaining the copyrights. "But the Dutch keep complaining," he says with a fetching smile. "They think I'm on a yacht in the Mediterranean." Before officially stepping down from the artistic director position, Keith guided the Loose Moose Theatre Company through his fourth and final production of *Waiting for Godot* at the old Garry Theatre.

Always keeping in mind Beckett's description—a stage is a place of maximum verbal and corporeal presence—Keith worked to achieve both in every production of *Godot* he directed. This last production was no different. "You can feel it [the corporeal presence] in this play," Keith said in a preopening interview for *Fast Forward Weekly*. "It's the flesh [Beckett is] trying to get to and the physical images of people clutching each other and trying to build each other up" (Sheppy). Beckett, of course, supplied the verbal presence and Keith the corporeal by giving Calgarian audiences a "broadly physical interpretation," according to Martin Morrow, drama critic for the *Calgary Herald* ("Loose Moose Offers").Cahill, who portrayed Estragon 20 years earlier at the Pumphouse, played Pozzo this time around. He was the old hand in this cast of mostly young actors which included Derek Flores and North Darling of The 3 Canadians, a popular improvisational troupe in the 1990s. No doubt Keith took pleasure in the *Calgary Herald* review. Not only did Morrow award this production with a "Critic's Pick," he advised readers:

> Don't imagine that because the play is being done by improv comedians at the home of Theatresports, it is in any way slighter than a "serious" production. In fact, Johnstone's approach is far closer to Beckett's absurdist spirit than the dull, dutiful Godot seen at Theatre Calgary a few years back – and twice as lively.

The 3-week run of *Godot* at the Garry Theatre ended on November 7, 1998, and then Keith quietly took his leave from Loose Moose only to return now and then to teach a workshop, judge a tournament, or host an evening of Life Game. He had a book to edit (*Impro for Storytellers*) and workshops to teach that, for the next decade, would take him away from Calgary 3 to 6 months out of every year.[40]

The Loose Moose today

Today, the Loose Moose Theatre Company produces improvisational shows and a Theatre for Kids season at their current 200-seat venue on

---

[40] On February 20, 1999, Keith and Phelim McDermott codirected a night of Maestro Impro (advertised as "Micetro Impro") at the Hackney Empire Theatre in London. The Spontaneity Shop, an impro company founded on Keith's work, arranged this benefit performance to help the Royal Court raise funds for the refurbishment of their Sloane Square theatre. The cast of players included actor Jonathan Pryce—a former student of Keith's at RADA; Improbable's coartistic director Lee Simpson; Channel 4's *Whose Line Is It Anyway?* original cast member Tony Slattery; novelist Stella Duffy; and a handful of other established British performers. Keith remembers Pryce wanting to be eliminated in the first round because he was hosting a party on the same evening. But when an improviser doesn't care about winning, they often do their best work, and so Pryce advanced to the very last round and was likely late to his party. It was London's Comedy Store Players' founding member Neil Mullarkey, however, who took home the title of "Maestro."

the second floor of the Crossroads Market, southeast of downtown and 1.3 miles from the Calgary Stampede. Maestro Impro and Gorilla Theatre, not Theatresports, are the formats Loose Moose continues to produce on a regular basis. Cahill still serves as artistic director. Free impro classes are still given, to volunteers on Friday nights and the International Improvisational School, continues to welcome new students each summer.

In the fall of 2012, Loose Moose celebrated their 35th Anniversary Homecoming, and alumni living and working in every corner of the world came home to Calgary for 2 weeks of sold-out shows and festivities. Keith judged a night of Theatresports commentated by John Gilchrist, spent time with his former company members, and reunited with his old partner Mel Tonken after many, many years. Tonken was astounded to see such a vibrant organization still in existence. Yet he also noted that some of the most basic rules of impro (e.g., know your status and pay attention to your partner's needs) were wanting in the three performances he attended. "When you are training with Keith every day, that is a miracle," says Tonken. "He is a master at what he does. He is brilliant. It is just different with him not being there [at Loose Moose]. The basic training suffers. For me, the quality of the improv showed a lack of direction."

The intensity of training received by that first wave of Loose Moosers has never been repeated. Without an ensemble training and performing together daily under the directorship of someone who is willing or able to take risks, both artistically and financially, Loose Moose is no longer a force to be reckoned with in Calgary theatre. Critics don't rave about or slam this company anymore because they simply don't care. Keith says, "If you go to a theatre company and it's alive, you know it at once. You know there's someone there stirring it up. The Loose Moose needs someone." The decisions Keith made—or did not make—as the first artistic director of the Loose Moose, however, are partly to blame for its current status. Keith could have laid a more solid foundation for Cahill. On the other hand, it has been 14 years since Keith stepped down as artistic director, plenty of time to restructure. Cahill agrees but he doesn't know quite how to proceed when the financial obligations of the company take up most of his time. It may take a new generation of artists to concurrently loosen up and restructure the old Moose, or maybe Cahill simply needs to guide his company back to the classroom. The 35th Anniversary Homecoming celebration was a good start. It allowed old and new company members to reunite, perform together, and share ideas. Perhaps reapplying the Impro System in a concentrated way to training and performance is what Cahill needs to do next.

The Loose Moose's current home at the Crossroads Market, Calgary.
Photo Credit: T. Dudeck.

Dennis Cahill and Keith Johnstone at Loose Moose
during the 35th Anniversary Homecoming, 2012.
Photo Credit: Kate Ware.

CHAPTER SIX

What now? What comes next? What classrooms still remain?

I'm still moving. I'm still breathing. I'm still teaching.

KEITH JOHNSTONE

Since Keith stepped down as artistic director of Loose Moose in 1998, he has continued teaching at home and internationally. For the first decade, he would easily spend anywhere from 3 to 6 months abroad each year. Even in 2010, the year he turned 77, he was away from Calgary for 3 months teaching 5- to 10-day workshops in eight American cities, and in London, Stockholm, Graz (Austria), Rotterdam (Holland), and Cologne and Wolfenbüttel (Germany). In 2011 and 2012, however, Keith spent only 2 months abroad, but he taught five intensive workshops in Calgary at Loose Moose. The first intensive was for professional improvisers from Chili and Argentina; the second was an intensive for artistic directors of Theatresports leagues; the third, a 10-day summer intensive for 25 international students, 14 of which hailed from Latin America; the fourth, for 29 Japanese students from Toho Gakuen College of Drama and Music (Toyko); and the fifth, in July of 2012, another 10-day intensive which again attracted students from all over the world—from Norway, Germany, Switzerland, Netherlands, Australia, Japan, Brazil, the United States, and Canada.

Keith says he's like a "deflated sex doll" after a long day of teaching. He relies on humor, once more, to deal with another inevitable factor of life—growing old. At the 2011 10-day summer workshop, for the first 3 days, a stronger prescription of medication threw Keith off-balance. Each morning he looked awful, drained of energy, and in need of a bed.

Keith teaching in Holland, 2010.
Photo Credit: Erik van der Liet.

I kept him hydrated with hot watered-down green tea because he was also losing his voice.[1] But by the second hour, Keith not only sounded better, he had vigor. For the remaining 5 hours, Keith was alert, spry, and inspired. On the third morning, his voice was weak again and he informed the group: "Went to Safeway and they helped me with my bags. Treated me like a really old person. You speak like this, they think you are close to death." Everyone laughed with a sense of relief. Keith is still committed to creating a safe space where students can take risks. Worrying about the well-being of their teacher is not conducive to risk-taking and, therefore, he puts everyone at ease with self-disparagement. At the Boulevard Teatern in Stockholm, after Keith tripped on the lip of an unlit step while making his way to the seat next to mine, he alleged matter-of-factly, "Swedes have this sense of humor," and proceeded to brush off what could have been a fatal plunge.

Gaskill once said that Devine was "a different man" when teaching, less stressed, and almost youthful (*Sense* 54). It is no different with Keith. Teaching is the pinnacle for him because it offers a perpetual mystery, daily challenges, and a journey that never ends. That is why Keith advises students not to take what he says too seriously, to test everything out, and find out if the opposite could also be true. Keith wants students to think on their feet and for themselves.

---

[1] Keith was diagnosed with Type 2 diabetes approximately 15 years ago which can cause fatigue and other side effects.

Johnstone—The reluctant guru

He is wary of the guru status that many in improvisation have given him.

MARK RAVENHILL

He's had an incredible influence but he sort of ducks that a bit and I wish he didn't.

PHELIM MCDERMOTT (World)

Yes, Keith wants students to make their own discoveries. Conversely, students travel great distances and pay large sums of money to receive advice from the wise old master of impro. During breaks, students often gather around Keith for a personal chat, sometimes sitting at his feet if chairs are not available. After pointing this behavior out, Keith replied, "They actually do now [sit at my feet]. Bloody hell."

Keith talking with students during a break. Guilherme Tomé
(on couch), *Marcio Ballas and Andrei Moscheto*
(sitting at Keith's feet). *2011 workshop at Loose Moose.*
Photo Credit: Daniel Nascimento.

Kathleen Foreman remembers students sitting at his feet as far back as 1984 during the Festival of Fools in New York. Yet back then, Keith was physically able to slide onto the floor with them in an attempt to lower his status. As Ravenhill and McDermott expressed, Keith deflects his guru status but he is also aware it exists. Australian articles dating back to 1995 refer to Keith as "the Theatresports guru." In 1998, the year Improbable took Life Game on a UK tour, "impro guru" or "improvisation guru" was the new brand name of choice. Viola Spolin, her son Paul Sills, and Del Close, have also been called gurus of improvisation. In contrast to these others, Keith's status owes less to the formats, games, and techniques he invented or to the companies he launched and more to his embodied pedagogy. Keith has been teaching adults of various professions and from all over the world continuously since 1963 using his own espoused, always evolving pedagogy. Spolin, Sills, and Close were all teachers but not for 50 years uninterrupted. Moreover, Close was primarily known as an improviser and director. Sills was an influential director and teacher, but his volatile temperament often generated a less-than-ideal classroom environment. And Spolin's work primarily focused on children and on further development of her improvisational exercises through the work of Second City, not on discovering better methods of teaching.

The Oxford English Dictionary defines "guru" as: "A Hindu spiritual teacher or head of a religious sect. Also in general or trivial use: an influential teacher; a mentor; a pundit." Keith has definitely changed people's lives on a spiritual level but he is not Hindu or in any way religious. So, for now, let us focus on the second "general or trivial" definition and the three words—influential, mentor, and pundit. Unpacking these operative words, it seems a guru has embodied wisdom, that is, a wisdom born from experience and reflection, and has the ability to adeptly disseminate that experience, in the moment, in a way that is reassuring and effective for those who need guidance. A guru, therefore, does not have to be an inventor of original ideas or even a great collaborator. He does not have to write books or launch famous careers. In many ways, the guru is like a teacher of one of the artless arts of Zen. He must create a safe environment for students to "leap instinctively." He must establish trust through "his mere presence." He must wait patiently for students' "growth and ripeness," and he must encourage students to go further, to "climb on the shoulders" of their teacher (Herrigel 38–46).[2]

Conversely, guru status can be problematic. In an academic theatre setting, for example, working with a guru can be difficult, not necessarily because of what he or she does but because of what followers will do in pursuit of the guru. When students admire one professor above all others, faculty morale inevitably suffers. This behaviour can also disrupt curriculum and production planning, because students will opt to be in the guru's class or production if they are given the choice. Again, even if the guru teacher/director does nothing to exploit his or her status—and I presume Keith fought and continues to fight against his own and anyone else's exploitation of their social positioning—working alongside or with a guru can be debilitating. Followers often follow their guru with blind obedience. In the first year or two of Loose Moose, Cahill said company members, himself included, did

---

[2] See also Chapter 4.

whatever Keith told them to do without question. Whether Keith promoted this or not is beside the point. Followers will follow a guru, communities will form around one, and some will be so dependent on this person, they will cease thinking for themselves. This last undesirable effect is why Keith dodges the guru label even as he continues to do all the things a guru does.

Keith has been Steve Jarand's guru, in the best sense, since 1988. For the last decade, Jarand has taught mask-making workshops and Keith's mask techniques all over the world. As his mentor, Jarand says Keith is supportive and nonjudgmental but his counsel is occasionally "cryptic." Keith once advised him, for instance, "Maybe you should take martial arts. Sometimes you need to be aggressive."[3] If not cryptic, his advice to Jarand is infrequent, succinct, often takes time for Jarand to absorb, but is almost always applicable. "[Keith's counsel] somehow makes you independent," Jarand said to me. "It empowers you to ask the right questions and to answer them yourself." Keith is a master teacher in the Zen tradition *and* a guru. Not "the guru of improvisation." Just a guru, period, and his continual evasion of that title is a conscious component of his pedagogy.

It is also because of his guru status bolstered by the careers he has launched and his famous creations that Keith has had such a rewarding and enduring career as a teacher. Whether he likes it or not, his name will always be attached to Theatresports and to the Theatresports-inspired television show *Whose Line is it Anyway?* or what Keith calls "light entertainment" or "padding between commercials." Although Theatresports-inspired television shows all over the world have introduced a new generation to comedic impro, these shows have also perpetuated the misconception that impro is always fast, funny, and antinarrative. "Television improv isn't really a good fit," said Colin Mochrie, a regular on the American version of *Whose Line is it Anyway?* "Because of the time constraints, everything has to happen really quickly. You don't have time to build your character, to build a scene. Everything sort of has to be there" (*World*). The content and quality of the impro is also regulated by television ratings and commercial sponsors. Daniel Nascimento, an original cast member on *É Tudo Improviso* ("It's All Improvised")—essentially the *Whose Line* of Brazil—alleges, "Television needs formula and impro is not about formula."[4] Neither is Theatresports, but leagues located in every corner of the world are frequently found guilty of submitting to similar pressures.

Keith does not watch Theatresports competitions anymore because he perceives most improvisers as trying too hard to win. No longer protected

---

[3] Jarand said this using his best "Keith" impersonation beginning with Keith's habitual palatal click of the tongue and proceeding with a mild Devonshire dialect. In every workshop, at least one student will attempt an impersonation of Keith to everyone's delight.

[4] Nascimento is also a member of Barbixas, a popular three-man impro company from São Paulo, Brazil.

by one's mentor or the safety of the classroom, professional Theatresports teams cease to see failure as an option when ticket sales are at stake. Paradoxically, a fear of losing creates watered-downed and self-absorbed performances because improvisers are afraid to take risks (e.g., accepting offers and abandoning control). Keith views improvisers unwilling to fail or to trust their audiences to empathize with their failure probably in the same light as teachers unwilling to learn from their students. Keith's workshops afford him an opportunity to transport students from all over the world back to the reciprocal classroom.

Johnstone's international workshops— Ideal for who?

I wanted to die at 72. I thought that was a very good age.

KEITH JOHNSTONE

If Keith had died at 72, I would not have studied with him for the past 7 years all around the world or spent hours in conversation with him. I would not have witnessed this man releasing over a hundred students of various professions and nationalities into states of blissful childhood or getting a Swedish audience of over three hundred to talk in one voice. Although I was initially inspired by the ideas he set forth in *Impro*, a book does not replace embodied knowledge. I have become a better teacher of improvisation because I have been in the same classroom space with Keith time and again. I have participated, observed, and learned from his pedagogical process. Since 2010, I have also enjoyed a privileged position as the observer/assistant who Keith seeks out during breaks, shares lunches with, and often engages in a discussion about the workshop in progress. And at the beginning of 2012, Keith asked me to be his Literary Executor, so I will continue to organize, document, and preserve his personal archive for future scholarship. My particular association with Keith and his work allows me to experience compressed, 4 to 10-day workshops, in a comprehensive way. Thus I am reminded, once more, to consider the experience others might have and whether or not these workshops are ideal for them. Not only do the workshops span, on average, less than 10 days, 5 to 7 hours a day, they also admit 20 or more participants, some who speak little or no English. This structure does not allow for much in-class or individual experimentation or for inclusion of the Impro System's more complex games. Students cannot take just one workshop and expect to walk away with a deep understanding of the Impro System. No, this final classroom is not ideal for everyone, but it is ideal for Keith at this moment in his life.

"It's good for the students to get a burst of ideas and then to go away and think about it," Keith said to me recently over a cup of tea. "Probably the same with you. Once you've seen it, you go away and think about it and then you come back and you see it in a different way because you've been organizing it in your mind. And you see things that you missed the first time." During hiatuses, Lee Simpson, coartistic director of Improbable, will often return to Keith and/or to the basics of the Impro System only to discern greater clarity and depth in the "simple and elegant rules, guidelines, and parameters" he has developed for creating "endlessly and infinitely complex" theatre. "You see greater universality in what he teaches than you saw before." As stated in Chapter 4, Keith's objective is to guide students down various spokes from the outer edge of the wheel toward the hub, that is, toward the heart of the Impro System. Given a short amount of time, Keith works fast using foundational games and techniques that convey his theories in a straightforward way. Students should leave each workshop with a basic, corporeal knowledge of how the Impro System can be used as a whole to create and convey good stories and authentic relationships through collaborative, spontaneous means. From that point, students can choose to advance (or not) in various directions, or down different spokes.

The inherent danger in this simple, compressed pedagogical approach is not every student receives information in the same way or has the inclination to advance beyond the one classroom. So if students do not see the hub as a starting point to a process that is endless, or if they mechanically follow Keith's advice without deeper reflection, they might advance in a way that is less-than-ideal or in a way that perpetuates those well-worn misconceptions about impro (e.g., it is formulaic, not applicable to real theatre, only a tool for training, just games, antinarrative, only used for comedy, and so on). I suspect, though, that the majority of students who make the expensive pilgrimage to a Keith Johnstone workshop are ready to advance down a productive spoke. Most have already read *Impro* and/or have taken another workshop with Keith or with a Johnstone-inspired teacher, have reflected, and have returned to the classroom to fill in the gaps.

These ideal students are often committed to teaching and executing the Impro System in a way that honors Keith's pedagogical process—a Freirean process. "The most important connection I see between Paulo Freire and Keith," reflects Andrei Moscheto, general director of Antropofocus theatre company in Curitiba, Brazil, is the theory that "the responsibility of the teacher is not to *do* the process, it is to *start* the process." Moscheto was a participant in Johnstone's 2011 Calgary workshop and he detected Keith's dislike for formulas and for those who follow formulas without question. "When Keith says 'apply this to what you are doing', he is also saying 'please keep this going further'. . . Things start with the teacher, they don't end with the teacher." Although the games and techniques used in each international workshop vary only slightly, Keith does indeed re-form his reflections and fine-tune the tenor of his teaching in accordance to the needs of the students in each particular workshop. Likewise, he is always ready to try something he has never tried before, an adjustment to a game perhaps or a combination of two techniques into one. As posited in the introductory chapter, Keith's pedagogy cannot be separated from the rest of the system without compromising the system's efficacy. To see the pedagogy in action, one only needs to watch him teach.

What may (or may not) happen in a Johnstone workshop

Following is a look at what a student may or may not experience in a Keith Johnstone workshop today. I was not physically present in Keith's classrooms at the Royal Court, at RADA, at UofC, or at Loose Moose, but I have been a part of his current—and possibly final—classroom environment since 2006. These workshops have shown me, beyond a doubt, that Keith does put into practice the pedagogy he advocates. I may be experiencing the simple, compressed version of the classrooms of Keith's past, but this is his classroom now. It has evolved over half a century and, I suppose, will continue to evolve until Keith ceases teaching.

On the morning of the first day of a Keith Johnstone workshop, students mingle and introduce themselves over a cup of coffee or tea and perhaps a *kanelbulle* ("cinnamon bun") if we happen to be in Stockholm. The excitement is palpable as all anticipate Johnstone's arrival. Finally, the tall, silver-haired master teacher enters, wearing his usual black buttoned-down shirt tucked into his black pants, a black sweatshirt draped over his shoulders, white tennis shoes, a large wristwatch, and wire-rimmed spectacles. My portrayal may seem a bit intimidating but Mark Ravenhill's is not. Ravenhill, a prolific British playwright, attended a workshop in London in 2009, and his depiction of the first in-the-flesh encounter with "the man who made me a playwright" captures the quintessential image of Keith today:

> He arrives, a natural clown. His teeth sit widely and uncomfortably in his mouth, his trousers are high on a generous belly, his trainers are unfeasibly large. He's carrying a plastic bag full of balloons, hats and cards containing lines of dialogue in gobbledegook. He grins, sighs and blinks at us through thick glasses.

Although Keith was a handsome young man, he spent a large portion of his youth feeling like a misfit, uncomfortable in his own body, and embarrassed by his bad posture and awkward gait. Still, after years of self-guided analysis and improvement, certain characteristics linger but Keith no longer seems to care.

It is time for the workshop to begin. All 20 or so participants take their seats in the house (or on one side of the studio) and Keith takes his seat

Jorge Rueda and Rhena de Faria on a "Keith Sofa" taking direction from Keith. 2011 workshop at Loose Moose.

Photo Credit: Andrei Moscheto.

center stage, sometimes on a "Keith sofa"—a sofa that suddenly sucks improvisers into or out of the concealed slit in the middle.

He commences every day of every workshop with about 10 minutes of impromptu discourse on failure, relationships, being clever, accepting stupid offers, creating a safe space, giving your partner a good time, and making use of scenography (e.g., props, furniture, doors, sound effects, and costume accessories). Keith might start with maxims like: "Please don't do your best. Trying to do your best is trying to be better than you are"; "Go onto stage to make relationships. At least you won't be alone"; "Shout 'Again!' if you're not having a good time!"; "Screw up and stay happy"; "You can't learn anything without failing"; and "Improvisation should be the art of good nature." A personal anecdote or two will be thrown in to support his declarations. Then, spontaneously, he will enthusiastically call for one, two, four, or more improvisers on the stage for the first game or exercise.

Keith sometimes begins with a scene in which three girls speak in "one voice" with three boys. Or he might have the entire front row play a round of Group-Yes. With a more advanced group of improvisers, he often jumps right into What Comes Next? What Comes Next? trains improvisers to develop stories collaboratively, paying attention to the needs of their partner and to the audience. This game can be played several ways but Keith usually begins with the two-person version. Improviser A will ask Improviser B, "What Comes Next?" and B will offer a suggestion, for example, "We enter the forest." If A likes the suggestion, they both enter the forest. Improviser A continues asking for suggestions until B gives an offer she doesn't like. Then A will politely say "nope" and B will then ask A, "What comes next?" "Nope" communicates what the other wants which is why this game is important. And like Group-Yes, this game often unveils students' fear of meeting the unexpected, even in the safety of the classroom. "By nature we don't want the story to go forward. We fear the future," theorized Keith. "But we were little kids once and we didn't fear the future. It can be taught" (London Wksp). In the 2010 London workshop, two beginning students demonstrated this theory. For the first round of What Comes Next?, Improviser A kept accepting B's offers but every offer was negative or prevented the story from advancing—they looked for a magician but couldn't find him; the door opened by itself so interaction with another being was impossible. Finally, Keith interjected, "The magician answers the door!" But the next offer by B was "The magician shrinks and we can't hear him." Fascinatingly, in Stockholm, San Francisco, and Calgary, the instinct was always the same—not to go forward, not to interact, and not to get into trouble. In all workshops, Keith returns to What Comes Next? at least once a day.

Word-at-a-time games also prevent students from controlling the future.[5] Keith coaches two players to enter the forest, meet a bad thing, and then run away, and they must narrate this encounter alternating one-word-at-a-time. The first round is quick and painless. For the second round, however, Keith does not allow players to escape from the bad thing and they must define it. Soon, pairs of improvisers are running throughout the theatre, meeting monsters and other nasty creatures, and taking each other on wild adventures. Group-Yes, What Comes Next? and word-at-a-time games also train improvisers to stay within the circle of probability, that is, to move the story forward according to the logic of the imaginary world that has been established.[6] Essentially, these games train improvisers to be more obvious.

Once students meet a bad thing, interact, and come out unscathed, Keith might move on to status exercises. Or he may try split-attention techniques which preoccupy or completely screw up the verbal intellect allowing the body to make its own decisions. Repeating the mantra "I love you" or "I hate you" while playing a love scene, for example, has the power to pull a performance that is captivatingly subtle out of the most inexperienced student. The mantra can be anything, it does not necessarily supply a purpose, but it gives actors subtext, substance, and can interrupt a nervous actor's self-censor so they can be in the moment.

---

[5] Keith's "Meet the Monster" experiments at Dartington College and at RADA in the late 1960s evolved from word-at-a-time games. See Chapter 3.
[6] Keith's "circle of probability" concept is described in Chapter 1.

Status work, mantras, and all split-attention exercises and games are good introductions to Keith's concept of the kinetic dance.[7] Party Endowments is a split-attention game in which four players secretly endow each other with predetermined qualities like sexy, funny, or repulsive, and attempt to establish a relationship based on their chosen endowments. The other player's choice of endowments also creates strong obstacles. For example, A might find B sexy but B finds A repulsive and has her eye on C who thinks B is funny and D is sexy. This game requires such involvement that players don't have time to worry about their performance, and the kinetic dance prevails.

Keith may proceed with several rounds of Fast-Food Stanislavsky, first in its party version, then in groups of four with two playing the scene and the other two shadowing them.[8] Or he could move into "tilt" scenes.[9] Two students begin a scene, establishing a stability or platform. After about 30 seconds, Keith suggests a tilt that changes the stability of the scene, or at least it should. "A tilt is just an offer of a tilt until it's validated by someone being altered," he wrote in *Impro for Storytellers* (354). Keith, like most audiences, would like to see actors altered on the stage, to do things most are inhibited from doing in everyday life, to walk over the abyss.

As explained in Chapter 3, Keith used to call the work of a clown "the abyss" because the clown must step over one precipice after another, but if the clown looks down, he falls. Pecking-order clown games and master-servant scenes—often utilizing hats and/or long airship balloons—train students to walk over the abyss and are included in every Keith Johnstone workshop. In the 2011 Calgary workshop at the Loose Moose, the professional improvisers from Brazil, Uruguay, and Spain excelled at the Hat Game, a split-attention game that skirts the edge of chaos. Keith, as always, started this group off with the basic Hat Game, because stealing a hat off another student's head can be dangerous and certain rules of safety must be established. The basic game begins with two players sitting side-by-side on a couch, bench, or on two chairs. After several minutes of alternately practicing taking off each other's hats, Keith side-coaches: "You are two monks" (or two teachers, gardeners, demons in hell, superheroes, beekeepers, chickens, etc.). The players start a scene as their designated characters, but the scene ends as soon as one player takes the other's hat or attempts to take the other's hat. If a player succeeds, she stays onstage. If her attempt is blocked or if she does not hang on to the hat, she is replaced by another player. Keith has taught this game to Zen Buddhist monks in San Francisco because it is a game about mindfulness and perception. If you assume the other person in a hat game, you will lose your hat. If you are anywhere other

---

[7] "Kinetic dance" is defined in Chapter 1.
[8] See Chapter 3 and *Impro for Storytellers*, pp. 285–30 and "Appendix One: Fast-Food Stanislavsky Lists."
[9] "Tilts" are defined in Chapter 1.

than the present, you will lose your hat. "Hat-Games demand a split in the players' consciousness," wrote Keith. "[P]art of the mind plays the scene, while another part watches attentively. Until players can make this split, their hats are vulnerable" (*Storytellers* 162).

The professional improvisers from Latin America were able to make this split quickly. In no time, Keith had this group on their feet playing the Hat Game during scenes just as Theatre Machine had done 40 or so years prior. Then Keith added a third player to the scenes and the "best out of three" rule, specifically, the first player who takes the hat off of either of the other two players two times out of three wins. The next day, Keith asked three players to choose a status position/number between 1 and 3 (1 = most dominant; 2 = less dominant; 3 = least dominant) and apply that to their best-out-of-three Hat Game scene. Finally, he invited everyone on stage for a Hat Game elimination party. Andrei Moscheto and Marco Gonçalves, a regular on *É Tudo Improviso* and a clown/improviser in Jogando no Quintal ("Playing in the Yard"), one of the oldest professional impro companies in Brazil, were the last two standing. Within a minute, Gonçalves brilliantly swiped the hat off his much larger opponent, Moscheto, and the group appropriately cheered like sporting fans.

Keith working with students. Jorge Rueda (left), Daniel Nascimento, and Lucia Dotta. 2011 Johnstone workshop at Loose Moose.

Photo Credit: Andrei Moscheto.

Throughout a workshop, Keith will share anecdotes or recommend outside source material that illuminates the theories of the Impro System. "I talk more than most teachers," he confessed to the students in the Stockholm workshop, "but you need insight into how it works and you learn the game."

Keith talked much less in Calgary in 2011 not because of his weakened voice but because he had recently observed himself teaching on film. For several months, he and Frank Totino had been editing footage from the 2008 Calgary workshop. Distressed by the amount of time he spent talking in that workshop, Keith consciously decided not to repeat this behavior in 2011. After the first few days, though, the *students* began asking questions about his personal and artistic life. So for approximately 30 minutes, he addressed their inquiries but then got right back to work. Keith was certainly less verbose but he still managed to offer the students a "burst of ideas," that is, anecdotes and recommendations in conjunction with the practical work. The subsequent rundown of what Keith talks about and recommends is in no way exhaustive, but it does catalogue the most recurrent offers given by him in the workshops I have attended from 2006 to 2012.

Keith talks about growing up, about his experiences at RCT, RADA, with Theatre Machine, Loose Moose, Pinter, Beckett, or anything else that is appropriate to the moment. He offers stories from and recommends books like *Surely You're Joking, Mr. Feynman*!, a selection of autobiographical stories from Nobel Prize-winning physicist Richard Feynman, stories like how he learned to pick up show girls; *Zen in the Art of Archery* by Herrigel, the book discussed in Chapter 4; *Audition* by Shurtleff; *The Inner Game of Tennis* by Gallwey; *The Body Has Its Reasons: Self-Awareness Through Conscious Movement* by Thérèse Bertherat; and the *Tao Te Ching*. Keith will quote passages by William Blake, Quintilian, and Goethe. He will recommend a variety of films based on a single actor's performance, the plot structure, on one particular scene, and/or on his knowledge of the director's process. A few of his favorite films are: Akira Kurosawa's *Ikiru* (1952) and *The Hidden Fortress* (1958); Mike Nichol's *The Graduate* (1967); Wolfgang Petersen's *Das Boot* (1981); and Carl Theodor Dryer's *The Passion of Joan of Arc* (1928) starring Maria Falconetti who Keith finds "amazing from the moment you first see her." He refers to the work of theatre practitioners – specifically Stanislavsky, Vakhtangov, Feldenkrais, Michael Chekhov, and Rudolf Laban. In any given moment, he might talk about a comedic performance by Rowan Atkinson, Bob Newhart, Lord Richard Buckley, or George Burns and Gracie Allen. Or dramatic performances by Laurence Olivier, Ralph Richardson, Vanessa Redgrave, the great Greta Garbo, among others.

Keith will advise improvisers to try something 5000 times to become skillful, to read comic strips for a better understanding of "tilts," to observe human and nonhuman animal behavior, and to keep up with the latest discoveries in cognitive science because these are the things he has done and/or continues to do.[10] Keith asserts, "The brain is an amazing machine

---

[10] On several occasions, Keith has told me the story of Sharon, a former student of his from Liverpool, who had a hole in the middle of her brain the size of a grapefruit. Her case was featured on an episode of *Nova* on PBS. Even in her condition, she scored better than average on O-Level exams in England.

that creates the universe for you, so the idea that anybody should be dull is ridiculous. Even half a brain can achieve amazing things. When you switch off bits of the brain, other things are released." Finally, a workshop would not be complete without Keith's recommendation of comedies of the silent film era. In fact, he often equates various components of the Impro System to the antics of Stan Laurel, Oliver Hardy, Buster Keaton, and, most of all, to Charlie Chaplin.

Keith did not watch Chaplin as a kid. He watched cowboy and Keaton films. Today, he will say he prefers Keaton to Chaplin because "Chaplin really wants you to like him" (Stockholm Wksp.). This is one of those moments in which Keith contradicts himself, where he does "the opposite of the opposite of the opposite," as Nascimento articulated. Keith wants audiences to want to take the improvisers home and "feed them grapes." He wants improvisers to treat audiences benevolently and like large, intelligent beasts that need to be tickled. For Keith, the audience is why improvisers and storytellers do what they do. The audience must never be ignored nor taken for granted.

Chaplin did not take audiences for granted. He did not trick the audience with cinematic devices or elaborate setups. He would use up reels of film on a bit or gag, but no matter how funny, he would scrap it if it interfered with the logic of events (Chaplin 318). I sense Keith prefers Keaton as a director to Chaplin's directing which often required a great deal of patience from his cast and crew. Chaplin was a perfectionist in every way and would "write" his stories with the camera, improvising until it felt accurate (Milton 129).[11] Moreover, Chaplin feared failure and had dark moods that became more pronounced as sound films came into vogue (Lynn 360). Chaplin's Tramp character, conversely, did not fear failure, and it is the Tramp—the masked Chaplin—that Keith finds captivating.

The ending of City Lights makes Keith emotional; the first 25 minutes of The Circus is worth watching because the Tramp gets into so much trouble; the pathos in The Kid works perfectly, it is beautiful storytelling; and parts of The Gold Rush are inspired—Keith makes declarations akin to these in every workshop. Toward the end of the 10-day workshop in Calgary in 2008, the students were lucky enough to spend an evening with Keith watching clips from Keaton and Chaplin films. We began with Keaton's The Navigator and Steamboat Bill, Jr., and ended with Chaplin's The Circus (the first 25 minutes!), The Kid, and The Gold Rush. Watching Keith watch these silent film comedians is, in itself, captivating. Watching Keaton's thrilling stunts, Keith is transported back to his childhood. He becomes a restless 10-year-old-boy in a grown man's body. Watching

---

[11] Chaplin used over 90,000 feet of film stock for the two-reel short, The Immigrant. This plus postponements and Chaplin's indecisiveness cost the Mutual Film Corporation more than they had anticipated (Lynn 194).

Chaplin, Keith balances on the edge of his chair with a twinkle in his eye, his mouth slightly agape, in blissful anticipation of what comes next. He takes such delight decoding the Tramp's language. It is a language Theodor W. Adorno recognized as "common to the clown and to children, a language distanced from sense.... Nature, so pitilessly suppressed by the process of becoming an adult, is, like that language, irrecoverable by adults" (Schickel 270). Well, not irrecoverable by all adults, as Keith exemplifies and teaches in his workshops.

Finally, at the end of the last hour of the last day of a workshop, Keith will bid the class farewell: "Thank you for entertaining me this week. It has been a pleasure" (S.F. Wksp. 2009). But the conversation continues at the closing party, the pub, and via the Internet, and students take what they learned back to their groups and their classrooms around the world.

Improbable's Life Game and Rebecca Northan's *Blind Date*

If theatre did not exist then perhaps this [Life Game] would be a good place to start if we wanted to invent it from scratch.

KEITH JOHNSTONE

Keith began developing Life Game (i.e., *How It Was*) at the Loose Moose in the mid-1980s because, as stated in the previous chapter, he needed to guide his company back to the classroom and back to the hub of the Impro System. Yet it was Improbable that took Life Game all over the United Kingdom and to America.[12] Cofounded in 1996 by Phelim McDermott, Lee Simpson, and Julian Crouch, Improbable theatre company has become known for their innovative, visually stunning projects that often combine impro and storytelling with music, masks, and puppetry. After taking Keith's workshop in Lyme Regis in 1985, "I vowed to myself that we would put on Life Game," McDermott told me. "But not above a pub or in a small fringe venue. We would aim for it to be taken seriously as a theatre show." Over 20 years later, the Arts Council funded Improbable's project. "This is, to my knowledge, the only time the Arts Council has given full support to an improvised show." And Improbable returns to Life Game every few years because it is like returning to the classroom. "It's not so much a show as it is a practice in the way that meditation is a practice," Simpson explains to me. "It is an infinite game, a game that exists in the playing not in the outcome." Life Game, in Improbable's capable hands, is an ideal demonstration of the Impro

---

[12] The official name today of Keith's format is "The Life Game" but the name has gone through several transformations. Early on, Keith sometimes hyphenated the name—"Life-Game." Improbable has always used the compound "Lifegame."

System's power to create profound and engaging narratives spontaneously during performance—within the onstage classroom.

Life Game takes the interview to new heights. A host interviews a recognized guest or a member of the audience on stage and, at various moments, a director stops the interview and asks the team of four or more improvisers to improvise a scene based on something the guest has just shared. Before the first scene, the guest selects an improviser to portray him/her. In Improbable's slightly altered version, the host also doubles as a director and all players collaboratively codirect scenes. Because a stranger is introduced into the mix every night, the dynamics change, so no one can or should claim they know exactly how to play Life Game. Still, you can play it well if you notice and welcome what Simpson calls "the process that's unfolding." Following is a look at the unfolding process of five past performances of Improbable's Life Game.

"Lifegame combines theatre's depth and poignancy with the improviser's here-and-now creativity," wrote Andy Lavender in *The Times* after catching a performance at the Lyric Hammersmith Theatre, London, in June of 1998. Several nights later, actress Joanna Lumley, best known for her television roles in *The New Avengers* and *Absolutely Fabulous*, was the celebrity guest; but McDermott, as host and director, did not ask Lumley about her career. "If Neil Armstrong is the guest, you don't ask him about the moon landing," admonishes Keith (S.F. Wksp. 2009). No, McDermott asked Lumley about her earliest memories and soon, as Dominic Cavendish, critic for *The Independent*, recalled, "[T]he sheer force of the Lumley personality began to infect the acting area." Illuminating how imaginative and poignant Life Game can be, here is Cavendish's summary of the rest of the evening:

> Before we knew it we were being whisked headlong into her nascent consciousness: imagining her mother and father's first meeting; joining her at table with all the family; sharing her days at boarding school (a mini-puppet show conveyed a teacher's closet ballet dance). With a mock-delicacy that admitted the approximate nature of impro, the actors went on to tackle her first crush (rendered as a Shakespearean pastiche) and her first love, transformed into a musical number. . . .That Lumley is a star became irrelevant: she even admitted to being unfulfilled as an actress, hankering after the life of a linguist. We left her "on a high bright hill" (well, atop a ladder) smoking, drinking and defying death.

Cavendish's synopsis implies a performance full of laughter, surprise, and impro similar to—but not exactly like—impro seen before. *The Guardian* critic, Lyn Gardner, supposed a performance at the Tron Theatre in Glasgow, Scotland, successful because the improvisers resisted "the temptation to play for laughs." Following a performance at the off-Broadway Jane Street Theatre, Ben Brantley of the *New York Times* dubbed Life Game "as selfless-seeming a slice of show business as I have ever witnessed." When Improbable produced another 2-week run of Life Game at the Lyric Hammersmith in the summer of 2010, Henry Hitchings, critic for *The Evening Standard*, called the tone "warm and humane," the approach "carefully exploratory," and the impro "neatly accomplished."[13]

Simpson has noticed that Improbable's approach to Life Game has evolved over the years. In the beginning, they tried to select guests they could work with, guests who would make their job a little easier. Today, Improbable is much more interested in "unsuitable guests," namely, in guests whose unfolding process offers a challenge to their expectations. "Life Game should be a show that says, 'You can't just look at someone and judge them', but we judge them anyway," confesses Simpson. Instead of getting irritated with a guest who might be considered less-than-ideal, Improbable welcomes the opportunity to practice patience and to deliver a broader point-of-view. For Simpson, this is "the deeper expression of accepting an offer."

In 1988, 16-year-old Rebecca Northan joined the Loose Moose and never left, except now and again to appear on a television sitcom or to tour her successful improvised show *Blind Date*, a show Keith thinks is absolutely perfect. Northan created *Blind Date* in 2007 as a ten-minute piece for the Spiegeltent at the World Stage festival in Toronto. It became a tent favorite. Back at Loose Moose, under Dennis Cahill's direction, Northan turned *Blind Date* into a full-length show. It was a success and picked up by World Stage again, enjoying a sold-out run at the Harbourfront Centre in 2009. Then, Broadway producer Kevin McCollum (*RENT*, *Avenue Q, The Drowsy Chaperone*) brought Northan to New York City for another sold-out, 3-week run at the off-Broadway Ars Nova Theatre in December of 2010. And *Blind Date* has been selling out at various venues ever since.

In *Blind Date*, Northan plays Mimi, a French temptress who sports a red clown nose. "The clown nose gives permission and protection at the same time," says Northan. "It really is the smallest mask in the world." The audience first meets Mimi in a café. She is waiting for a blind date that never shows. So she proceeds to select a man from the audience to take his place. Over the next 90 minutes, it is Mimi's job to fall in love with a stranger, to make the audience fall in love with him, to encourage him to play the romantic hero, and to make him fall in love with her. Apparently,

---

[13] Improbable opened Life Game at the Brewery Arts Centre, Kendal, in March of 1998 and toured it to the following theatres: The Tron Theatre and Tramway Theatre in Glasgow, Scotland; The Theatre Royal in Bath; The Lyric Hammersmith Theatre and Purcell Room in London; The Newcastle Playhouse (now called Northern Stage) in Newcastle-Upon-Tyne. In 2000, they did a 5-week run of Life Game at the La Jolla Playhouse, California, followed by a 3-month off-Broadway commercial run at the Jane Street Theatre in New York City. In May of 2004, Improbable performed Life Game for 2 weeks at the National Theatre's Cottesloe venue, London.

Rebecca Northan as "Mimi" in Blind Date.
Photo Credit: Greg Tjepkema.

she succeeds. Critics have called Northan's *Blind Date* "absolutely magical," "a blind date you'll actually enjoy," "a high-wire act of improvised theatre," and "hilarious and heartening." Like the host in Life Game, Mimi interviews her guest, asks him nontrivial questions, and makes him feel comfortable enough to elicit truthful responses. "There are a lot of Life Game elements in *Blind Date*," says Northan. And it is her impro training that makes the show work. For Northan, the Impro System functions in a way that parallels how she functions when she is in love:

> When I am totally in love with someone, I'm at my charming best. I listen to everything they say. They make a suggestions and I go "Yes! Let's do it! Because I love you and I can see that lights you up." If every time I stepped on the stage to improvise I allowed myself to fall in love with the other improviser, I would never block them. I would never do anything at their expense. And we would go on an adventure together.

As Improbable's performances of Life Game and Northan's performances of *Blind Date* have shown, Keith's Impro System can create theatre that is corporeal, verbal, humorous, poignant, infinite, courageous, and most important of all, benevolent.

Impro hot on stages and in classrooms of Latin America

It was amazing to meet the man who created the thing that I earn money doing.

DANIEL NASCIMENTO

Whereas most Loose Moosers were never able to give up their day jobs, Nascimento and at least 7 out of the 14 students from Latin America in Johnstone's 2011 Calgary Workshop are famous and earning a significant income performing in impro-based shows. An impro renaissance is happening in Latin America but why? Frank Totino believes it is because of their inherently positive natures. Loose Moose company member Shawn Kinley, who teaches impro in Columbia, Peru, Chili, Argentina, and Brazil, says, "In Latin America, the culture bends and moves on the dance floors with Salsa, Tango, and other dances that reflect their passion for interaction." Jorge Rueda, an improviser with Spain's Impromadrid Teatro, a company well-known to impro festival audiences in Latin America, deems "impro is healthy" there and in his home country because "people are willing to take risks." Nascimento thinks their Brazilian audiences are better than Calgarian audiences in the early days of Loose Moose: "They want to see new things, they challenge us." Apart from the positivity, passion, and audience, why is the impro renaissance in Latin America happening now?

While impro as solely a medium of theatrical entertainment is in its early stages in Latin America, Brazilians, for one, have a rich history of improvisational theatre through the work of Augusto Boal. Inspired by Freire, Boal founded Theatre of the Oppressed and began developing techniques in the 1950s which allowed participants to witness and practice liberation from oppressive social situations. This current generation of improvisers, obviously, is not oppressed by a military dictatorship as Boal's generation was. Still, every Brazilian improviser I interviewed did express an aversion to their educational system calling it formulaic, repressive, and imaginatively stifling. Apparently, Freire's espoused pedagogy, like Keith's Impro System, has had more influence beyond the borders of the country he called home. In response to my inquiry on Freire's legacy, Moscheto said: "We have a saying in Brazil. In the blacksmith house, wooden sticks." That is to say, in Brazil, as in America, Canada, and other countries, citizens are often guilty of failing to acknowledge their own homegrown innovations. But the impro-based work of Moscheto, Nascimento, and the other improvisers from Latin America is being acknowledged at home. I tender it has a lot to do with this group of improvisers' dedication to creating quality impro-based work and in their overall attitude toward impro as a medium of expression. Following is a brief look at the paths taken by these popular improvisers from Latin America, how their paths connect to Keith, and how their dedication and attitude perpetuate their success and inform their expectations of what comes next.

Marcio Ballas, the veteran of the group who came to the 2011 Calgary workshop, cofounded Jogando no Quintal ("Playing in the Yard") with César Gouvêa almost a decade ago. This very popular company of 12 combines clowning and impro in a competitive format like Theatresports called "match d'impro" or "match."

Popular Brazilian troupe Jogando No Quintal. *Marcio Ballas* (top left),
Rhena de Faria and Marco Gonçalves (front row, left) *were students in
Johnstone's 2011 workshop at Loose Moose.*
Photo Credit: Edson Kumasaka.

In Montreal, the late Québécois actor and director, Robert Gravel, began developing this tightly structured improvised competitive format based on ice hockey around 1977.[14] The Ligue Nationale d'Improvisation took this match format to France, other francophone countries, and eventually to Latin America via folks like Ballas. In 2007, Nascimento, Anderson Bizzocchi, and Elidio Sanna wanted to put together a show similar to *Whose Line is it Anyway?* for their fledgling company Barbixas. Bizzocchi

---

[14] This was the same year Keith launched his loosely structured Theatresports at Loose Moose in Calgary. So far, I have found no evidence that Gravel knew of Keith's work or vice versa.

and Sanna were also participants in the 2011 Calgary workshop. Through Doutores da Alegria ("Doctors of Joy"), a nonprofit organization that sends clowns to visit hospitalized children, Nascimento met Ballas and asked him for guidance. Ballas gave Barbixas an impro workshop based, in part, on the Impro System and, soon after, Barbixas performed their first purely improvised show in the theatre of their old high school in São Paulo. The performance was filmed, uploaded onto YouTube, and Barbixas became famous almost overnight.[15]

Elidio Sanna, Anderson Bizzocchi, and Daniel Nascimento of Barbixas, *a celebrated Brazilian impro troupe. All were students in Johnstone's 2011 workshop at Loose Moose.*

Photo Credit: Barbixas.

In 2008, with Ballas as their onstage impro-director, Barbixas performed 10 times to sold-out houses. In 2009, they performed 170 times—7 shows a week, 1 each week in São Paulo and 6 on the road. The same year, MTV Brazil hired Barbixas to join Marcos Mion, a famous television personality, on *Quinta Categoria. Quinta Categoria* literally means "fifth category" but is also an idiomatic expression for something that is poor or cheaply produced. This program began as a sort of talent show but, once Barbixas signed on, it became the first improvised show on Brazilian television. Adopting a *Whose Line is it Anyway?* format, it aired live on Thursday nights. By the end of 2009, however, Mion was picked up by another network and Barbixas was asked to join one of the biggest networks in Brazil. Ballas and Barbixas, along with Marco Gonçalves (the winner of the Hat Game elimination party) and two female improvisers, made up the original cast of *É Tudo*

---

[15] "Barbixas" loosely translated means "goatee" and all three members have one.

Improviso ("It's All Improvised")—yet another *Whose Line*-like television show launched on Band Network in 2010.[16]

Ballas and Gonçalves are still on *É Tudo Improviso* but all three members of Barbixas left the show within the first 3 or so months of 2010 because they wanted more variety. "Every show ended with a Helping Hands game," Nascimento tells me. "It's funny but every day? But it was very difficult to fight against the dogmas of the old guys [the producers] who were telling us what we needed to do." Even though Ballas stayed on the program, he continues to work with Barbixas, with his company Jogando no Quintal, and has recently developed *Caleidoscopio*, a long-form impro format with four actors and one musician. Ballas is also the one who introduced Barbixas to the Impro System. Fundamental to his own practice, Ballas, like the others, feels a responsibility "to teach and pass that 'language' on." Still, prior to the 2011 workshop in Calgary, not one of these Latin American improvisers had worked with Keith Johnstone himself.

Barbixas did study with Sergio Dominguez Molina, cofounder of Mamut Colectivo Teatral ("Mammoth Theatrical Collective") based in Chili, just after Molina had returned from a 10-day course with Keith in Calgary in 2008. Nascimento recollects: "It was the first time someone came to us and said you can say "no" [to offers]."[17] Between the summer of 2008 and the summer of 2011, almost all of these Latin American improvisers had also studied with Frank Totino or Shawn Kinley. But finally getting to study with Keith was like meeting "The ultimate boss. The pope of impro," declares Nascimento. By contrast, Andrei Moscheto did not find Keith's manner bossy in the least: "He doesn't show tattoos of himself. He doesn't wear t-shirts saying, 'I invented improvisation. Worship me'. That tells me a lot." Nevertheless, coming to Calgary was not solely about "meeting the man" for these Latin American improvisers. With Frank Totino participating and observing in the same space, it was an experience that revealed to everyone that this pedagogy can and does flow from teacher to teacher and from one culture to another.

All the participants from Latin America feel a personal responsibility to make impro a respected part of their culture by bringing it back to the classroom using a Johnstonian pedagogy. "We have a huge responsibility, a problem to solve in Brazil. We became popular playing games and everybody thinks that impro is games. How do you say that impro is much more than that? It's very important for us to build that foundation," insists

---

[16] Ballas says they draw in approximately 2 million viewers for every episode of *É Tudo Improviso*.

[17] In the summer of 2008, Molina and I both learned to say "no" politely to offers that did not inspire us or to those that did not move the narrative forward. It was also the first time I had heard Keith give students permission to shout "Again!" if they were not having a good time.

Nascimento. Rueda, although from Spain, made a statement that had his Latin American friends—Moscheto, Nascimento, and Elidio Sanna—all nodding in agreement:

> We are the generation who are saying, "It's not mine." And it's the most important thing. In every country there was one man saying, "Impro's mine. I am the man in this country." We are the first generation who is saying, "Fuck you. It's not yours. It happens in Argentina, in Spain, in Columbia, in every country. This show is my show, maybe this is my idea, but impro is not mine. You can do it." We are all together in this feeling. It's not my impro but we are saying, "Do the work, do it well, please respect impro."

Over the years, this particular group of improvisers has worked hard to maintain a selfless attitude toward impro. They have supported each other's work and have taken classes from one another. They share information and ideas every time they meet at festivals. They blog and Twitter about their work. They upload videos on YouTube and maintain multiple websites. These Latin American improvisers consider their relationship to improvisers all over the world as one of reciprocity because, like Freire and Keith, they understand that impro needs to evolve from classroom to classroom or else it will languish.

Impro beyond the theatre classroom

Applied improvisation—improvisational theatre methods and theories used for human development and training in communities and within organizations—is expanding all over the world and into various fields. For many years, Keith's theories and techniques have found their way into the social sciences and education.[18] Today, more and more business consultants are applying his techniques. Large corporations such as Disney, Nike, and

---

[18] See Daniel H. Pink, *To Sell Is Human: The Surprising Truth About Moving Others* (2012). Pink draws from the social sciences to illuminate the changing world of business. He writes, "If improvisational theater has a Lenin – a well-spoken revolutionary who provides a movement its intellectual underpinnings – that person is Johnstone" and advocates applying impro methods to negotiations in Chapter 8 (204). See also Patricia Ryan Madson, *Improv Wisdom: Don't Prepare, Just Show Up* (2005). In this self-help guide, Madson, professor emerita at Stanford, combines Keith's theories and exercises with Dr. David K. Reynolds' ideas in the field of psychology to help others pay attention and respond spontaneously to the present moment. And psychotherapist Daniel J. Wiener, who attended Keith's workshops, adapted many of Keith's techniques for his approach to psychotherapy in *Rehearsals for Growth: Theater Improvisation for Psychotherapists* (1994). Finally, *Blink: The Power of Thinking Without Thinking* (2005) by Malcolm Gladwell, the best-selling author of *The Tipping Point*, references Keith's work in Chapter 4 as relevant to skilled and spontaneous decision-making.

Intel, and business schools in major universities all over the country are hiring more and more impro-trained consultants to teach managers and students to do what they do—to thrive in spontaneous, collaborative, risk-taking environments. David Zinger, founder of the online Employee Engagement Network with 5,800 members and counting, studied with Keith in Calgary in 2008. Zinger often applies impro theories and techniques in workshops he facilitates with leaders and managers. He gets his clients to recognize status transactions, for example, and to think of themselves as cocreated by the people they lead. And "What comes next?" he says, "is such a great tool for career and personal decisions. It is a wonderful question to ask a group that is collaborating."

Because Keith based his Impro System on a broad range of nontheatrical sources and experiences, it is adaptable to classrooms beyond the theatre as the workshops at the Applied Improvisation Network (AIN) annual conferences often demonstrate. AIN is a network of over 2,600 members from around the world who apply improvisational techniques and theories in some of the ways I mentioned above. Each year AIN holds a conference offering workshops and networking opportunities. In 2012, the conference was in San Francisco and, in 2013, it will be in Berlin. In every workshop I participated in at the 2009 conference in Portland, Oregon, Keith's theories and techniques were applied in some shape or form. More explicitly, some-times they were used very effectively, at other times not so. Many games and techniques were adapted versions of the original and, more often than not, Keith was not acknowledged as the source of inspiration. Still, most members in attendance at the Portland AIN Conference seemed committed to applying impro to business consulting in a way that did not reduce it to a formula or to something unrecognizable to those who use impro to create powerful theatre.

Bay Area Theatre Sports (BATS), founded in 1987, hosted the 2012 AIN Conference in San Francisco and company members offered workshops and performances before, during, and after the conference for conference attendees. Rebecca Stockley, a cofounder of BATS and long-time student of Keith's, is an active member of AIN, and she has been teaching impro skills to employees at Disney's Pixar University (PU) since 1997. She calls herself a PU trainer, or rather "a secret agent of improvisation," because if she uses "impro," "improv," or "improvisation" in workshop announcements, folks might shy away. But the employees at PU know Stockley and they know she applies impro tools in workshops to develop soft skills (i.e., skills that help people authentically engage, collaborate, take risks, motivate others, be spontaneous, and effectively deliver a story or idea) and various impro structures to deal with specific company issues. When working with animators, Stockley will often bring in professional improvisers because animators want to watch the behavior, the status, and the kinetic dance: "With animators, I apply all the impro work that helps us get in touch with our imagination and body language. Animators are genius at what they do, and they are working at making the acting more truthful, more realistic, and more honest."[19]

The most interesting way in which the Impro System is being applied beyond the theatre classroom, however, has to be in the training of Zen Buddhist monks and priests. As mentioned earlier, Keith has taught hat games and other split-attention techniques to monks. Celebrity actor Peter Coyote also uses the Impro System in workshops for senior priests-in-training in the Zen Buddhist lineage of which he is a member. Instead of paraphrasing and possibly misrepresenting Coyote's process, I have included unedited portions of his letter to me here:

> As you might know, the fundamental insight of the Buddha is that a fixed, permanent "self" is an illusion. . . . Buddha's observation that our idea of the self as separate from the rest of the world, generates fear of obliteration, and leads us to try and "protect" it in numerous ways, most of which are unhealthy. . . .
>
> For senior priest training, I start people on something easy and fun, like imitating one of their parents (which everyone can do). It's amazing to watch them "inhabited" by that persona, and they see it too—see their voices, posture, intentions, everything change.
>
> Then. . . following Keith's teaching, I put them in the mask, and then hold a mirror up in front of them. I urge them to take whatever impulses they receive from the mirror and let them play on their bodies. The transformations are astounding. Characters emerge and I follow them, putting the mirror back in front of them when I feel them "lost" for a moment. After putting people in touch with this new character (a completely arbitrary, but whole self), I put them together in improvs very often related to Zen practice—teacher-student conversations for instance. Zen priests are very brave and fearless about leaping into these identities whole-heartedly.
>
> It's a revelation to see just how quickly an alternate personality can be developed, intuited, and deeply understood. It's very moving and I credit Keith with all of it. . . .

Coyote distinguishes Keith as an "unrecognized" genius. Not wanting to perpetuate that notion, Coyote is passing along the gift without forgetting the gift-giver. But Coyote, who only worked with Keith on intermittent occasions, is not necessarily referring to Keith as a personified genius. He is pointing to the genius that lies in the pedagogy and in the process Keith has passed on through *Impro: Improvisation and the Theatre*, a book Coyote has personally gifted to 15 friends and continues to recommend to others.

---

[19] When Stockley taught workshops in India for DreamWorks Animation Boot Camp, each animator created their own "Animator Tool Kit" which included impro rules, tools, and even Fast-Food Stanislavsky lists!

What comes next? What classrooms still remain?

In 2006, Phelim McDermott was devoted to and also disgruntled about theatre in the United Kingdom and so he and Improbable took action. They launched the first Devoted and Disgruntled meeting attended by 220 artists from the theatre community to address this vast question in an Open Space format: "What are we going to do about theatre?"[20] Since then, monthly forums have taken on a multitude of big issues affecting the theatre community at large. The question proposed at the 15 September 2011 forum held in the Battersea Arts Centre's main theatre space was: "What are we going to do about Impro?" About 60 members developed working sessions around questions like "How to start an impro school?" and "*Impro* or *Improv*—what does the *v* mean?" Other sessions unpacked more serious questions similar to the ones Lee Simpson posted on the meeting's announcement e-mailed to 884 Devoted and Disgruntled members: "Why is it [impro] still treated with suspicion and derision by many people? Why do different improvisational philosophies feel more like religious schisms than a healthy diversity of practice? Why is the press still so weird about it? Should we, could we, have a greater sense of community?" (Devoted). Although transcriptions of what transpired at that meeting were never posted, the questions Simpson proposed are the questions Keith has been asking and answering for over 50 years. Isn't it wonderful, and at the same time disgruntling, that others besides Keith devoted to impro-based theatre processes are addressing these same questions today? Of course, no simple answers exist nor would it be in impro's best interest to intellectualize over any question for too long. Anyone devoted to carrying forward impro in a way that honors the process Keith began at the Royal Court Theatre in the 1950s should implement a no-discussion policy, get on their feet, and try one idea after another.[21]

Nonetheless, those who are genuinely dedicated to impro and especially to the Impro System have every right to ponder over the question: What comes next? More specially, what classrooms still remain? That is, what other academic and artistic disciplines and/or organizational structures might profit from a system that inspires creativity and innovation through collaboration and assists in the development of interpersonal and leadership skills? Keith's story is not complete and his circle of influence will go on indefinitely, although no one knows for sure how his legacy might play out.

---

[20] Open Space format comes from Open Space Technology, a flexible, democratic approach to hosting meetings and conferences. The purpose of the meeting is articulated beforehand but the working sessions are created and managed by the participants in the room.

[21] Another Devoted and Disgruntled forum addressing the same question—"What are we going to do about Impro?"—took place at the Slapdash Festival in London in June of 2012.

Still, as history has shown, patterns exist across time which allow us to anticipate with some faith the possibilities for Keith's work in the future. Therefore, before considering the question proposed above, let us revisit the historical landscape of Keith Johnstone's classrooms, keeping in mind that he is a complex system himself, a multifaceted human being who has situated his experiences, imagination, triumphs, and failures into his work. It is this human component—the Johnstonian component—that makes the Impro System complex and endlessly applicable.

As a young boy, the world was Keith's classroom and it was one where anything was possible if you could only imagine it. Then his primary school classroom attempted to destroy his imagination and he went into survival mode. Survival mode for Keith meant privately questioning everything, reading anything he could get his hands on, and, essentially, educating himself. A self-taught student, however, was not university material so Keith reluctantly enrolled in a teacher-training program because he needed a job and an escape. An art teacher released him by showing him a classroom environment that encouraged imagination and inspired creativity with a modicum of adult interference. Keith successfully applied this type of pedagogy in his first teaching assignment. But this was not an ideal working environment for him. So he moved on, floundered about for a year or two, and landed unexpectedly in a school for playwrights and for creative misfits like himself.

The Royal Court Theatre gave Keith the education he needed: a 7-year "undergraduate" classroom where he could declare one major and then another and then another; and a 3-year "master of fine arts" classroom that allowed him to discover, develop, and teach his own system, in his own way, on a professional level. Keith entered the Court's classroom spaces in 1956 adrift and graduated in 1966 as a ground-breaking teacher and director of improvisation. Accordingly, he took a teaching job at RADA and went on the road with Theatre Machine as their director into classrooms and onto stages all over Europe. For 7 years, Keith taught, directed, created, managed, and wrestled with his own fears until he, too, could leap spontaneously into the unknown.

In the early 1970s, Keith took a huge leap across the Atlantic and landed in Canada where he began a long tenure teaching in conventional academic institutions analogous to the ones that had denied him access two decades prior. At UofC, his classroom space, which included the rehearsal space, was unconventional in almost every way—a laboratory for Keith to explore and expand his Impro System. The students latched onto him and his methods with zeal, but some faculty members found Keith's popularity, his Impro System, and his reclusive nature problematic. This made it difficult for Keith to develop projects on a bigger scale using university resources. His Loose Moose Theatre Company, therefore, operated autonomously from the university. But Keith remained as dedicated to his students at UofC as he was to his company members, and his pedagogical principles carried over to the rehearsal and performance spaces of the Loose Moose.

For the first decade, Loose Moose under Keith's artistic direction was a force in Calgary's theatre community. It seemed this avant-garde troupe of improvisers could not be stopped. They launched Keith's Theatresports, the format that took the Impro System all over the globe. In 1983, though, the company had grown too big, too in debt, and during the most volatile moment of the company's 6-year history, Keith distanced himself for months. This strange behaviour and his choice to completely entrust others with the financial affairs of his company were illogical. Furthermore, when international teaching and directing obligations rendered Keith unavailable to make important artistic decisions, the work occasionally suffered as a result. It is also *because of* the decisions Keith made over his 21-year tenure as artistic director that the Loose Moose Theatre Company is still around.

In the professional theatre world of today and of yesterday, Keith would not be and would not have been considered an ideal artistic director. He lacks the required social skills and business savvy among other things. Yet no one can deny he was and still is a masterful teacher who can deftly lead a group of creative artists back to the classroom and back to the hub of the Impro System as he demonstrated with Life Game. Keith will probably not be remembered for his plays or his productions. His games no longer belong to him. They belong to the globally connected world of impro. Even though his simple and, at the same time, profound theories and techniques for re-creating complex human behavior on the stage and structuring narratives will continue to be applied, Keith will not always be recognized as the source. Still, for years to come, students will remember Keith Johnstone as the teacher who could generate ideas and start a process; who established a safe classroom space where they could spontaneously and collaboratively create stories using their uncensored, unique imaginations; who told them to take risks and gave them the right to fail because, having tried and failed so many times himself, Keith understood that failure is a component of a problem-posing pedagogy.

Now let us revisit that question: "What comes next? What classrooms still remain?" When I proposed this immense question to Rebecca Stockley, she replied: "World leadership. I'd like to think the principles of improvisation would have the same effect on people who create policy that I've seen it have on individuals, groups, and organizations. If everybody were doing improv, we might have world peace!" Caspar Schjelbred, artistic director of the Improfessionals in Paris, responded with: "There is but one classroom— anywhere humans meet—and Keith's lesson is never over." Schjelbred also dreams of a day impro theatre classes become a required discipline in every school. "Can you imagine what society would look like if everyone had had impro classes in school? More so, it seems to be the 'natural' destination of Keith's work – that's where it originated." Lastly, Lee Simpson did not distinguish impro in any tangible form or in any specific classroom. He said the practice of improvisation is simply, "An invitation to become aware. In this it sits alongside many other forms of practice. The story of the universe will unfold whatever we do. Keith, alongside the other great teachers, wonders if we might at least pay attention as it does so." Working on this critical biography compelled me to pay attention to the story of one of the finest teachers of the twentieth *and* twenty-first centuries. My journey has been exhilarating and will undoubtedly continue down various spokes for years to come. This particular spoke afforded me the opportunity to honor my teacher, Keith Johnstone, by situating his name into our histories of theatre.

BIBLIOGRAPHY

Alberta. Department of Education. *Programs of Study – Fine Arts – Elementary, Junior High, and Senior High Drama*. Edmonton, AL: Alberta Education, 1985, 1989. Web. 12 September 2011. <http://education.alberta.ca/teachers/program/finearts/programs.aspx>.

Alvarez, A. "The Rehearsal Rehearsed." Rev. of *Eleven Men Dead at Hola Camp*. Royal Court Theatre, London. *New Statesman* 1 August 1959. ESC/RCT Archive, 1934–2007. V&A Museum, London. Print.

Andersen, Hans. "Et lille voldsteater." Trans. May-Britt Jeremiah. Rev. of *The Last Bird* by Keith Johnstone. Svalegangens Teater, Aarhus, Denmark. *Jyllands-Posten* January 1974. Print.

Applied Improvisation Network Conference. Portland, OR. November 2009.

Aristotle. *Poetics*. Trans. Gerald Else. Ann Arbor: University of Michigan Press, 1970. Print.

Ballas, Marcio. E-mail interview. Trans. Cinara Diniz. 24 October 2011.

Barker, Felix. "Carrier-Bag Drama Rivals The Dustbin." Rev. of *The Knack* by Ann Jellicoe. Royal Court Theatre, London. *Evening News* 28 March 1962. ESC/RCT Archive, 1934–2007. V&A Museum, London. Print.

Beckett, Samuel. Letter to Keith Johnstone. 4 April 1957. Keith Johnstone's personal collection. Print.

—. Letter to Keith Johnstone. 7 March 1958. Keith Johnstone's personal collection. Print.

—. *Waiting for Godot*. New York: Grove, 1954. Print.

Benedict, Patricia. E-mail interview. 21 July 2010.

Benison, Ben. Messages to author. 29 October 2012–16 November 2012. E-mails.

Bertalanffy, Ludwig. *General System Theory: Foundations, Development, Applications*. New York, NY: Braziller, 2009. Print.

Bertherat, Thérèse, and Carol Bernstein. *The Body Has Its Reasons: Anti-Exercises and Self-Awareness*. New York: Pantheon Books, 1977. Print.

Birge, Susan. "Last Bird Audience Laughed." Reader response to Cohan's review of *The Last Bird*. *Calgary Herald* 20 February 1979. Print.

Blake, William, and Geoffrey Keynes. *The Marriage of Heaven and Hell*. London: Oxford University Press, 1975. Print.

Blake, William, Frederick Tatham, and Archibald G. B. Russell. *The Letters of William Blake: Together with a Life*. London: Methuen, 1906. Print.

Blewett, Denis. "A Far-out Farce." Rev. of *Day of the Prince* by Frank Hilton. Royal Court Theatre, London. *Daily Telegraph* 15 May 1963. ESC/RCT Archive, 1934–2007. V&A Museum, London. Print.

Bogart, Anne. "Terror, Disorientation and Difficulty." *Anne Bogart Viewpoints*. Ed. Michael Bigelow Dixon and Joel A. Smith. Lyme, NH: Smith and Kraus, 1995, pp. 3–12. Print.

Brantley, Ben. "Your Story Transformed on the Spot into Theater." *New York Times* 29 September 2000: E3. *LexisNexis*. Web. 31 October 2011.

Brennan, Brian. "Adventurous Local Theatre Troupes Revive Two Modern British Classics." Rev. of *The Caretaker* by Harold Pinter. Loose Moose Theatre Company, Moose Simplex, Calgary. *Calgary Herald* 30 October 1982. Print.

—. "Anyone for Bingo or Mud-Wrestling?" *Calgary Herald* 6 March 1982. Print.

—. "Gone (for Now) but the Memory Will Linger for Some Time." Rev. of *Live Snakes and Ladders* by Keith Johnstone. University of Calgary. *Calgary Herald* 2 December 1978. Print.

—. "Pumphouse Version of Godot Staged for Comedy Effect." Rev. of *Waiting for Godot* by Samuel Beckett. Loose Moose Theatre Company, Pumphouse Theatre, Calgary. *Calgary Herald* 21 September 1978. Print.

—. "Quebec Festival Gamble Pays." Rev. of Quebec International Theatre Fortnight Festival. *Calgary Herald* 26 June 1984. Print.

Brien, Alan. "The Man Within." Rev. of *The Performing Giant* by Keith Johnstone. Royal Court Theatre, London. *Sunday Telegraph* 6 March 1966. ESC/RCT Archive, 1934–2007. V&A Museum, London. Print.

Brook, Peter. *The Empty Space*. New York: Atheneum, 1968. Print.

Browne, Terry Westfall. *Playwrights' Theatre: The English Stage Company at the Royal Court Theatre*. London: Pitman, 1975. Print.

Burfield, Twila. "Who Let the Moose Loose?" Rev. of Theatresports. Loose Moose Theatre Company, Pumphouse Theatre, Calgary. *Albertan* 31 March 1978. Print.

Burgess, Robin. "The Wakefield Crucifixion." Rev. of *The Conspiracy* adapt. Keith Johnstone. Phoenix Theatre, University of Victoria, B. C. *Martlet* 29 November 1968: 1. *Archives: UVic Newspapers*. Web. 8 September July 2011.

Cahill, Dennis. Messages to author. 31 August 2010–September 2011. E-mails.

Cavendish, Dominic. "A Life with Lumley: First Night Lifegame." Rev. of Life Game. Improbable Theatre Company, Lyric Hammersmith Theatre, London. *Independent* 25 June 1998: 7. *LexisNexis*. Web. 1 November 2011.

Chaplin, Charlie. *My Autobiography*. New York: Simon and Schuster, 1964. Print.

Close, Del. Letter to Keith Johnstone, 1980. Keith Johnstone's personal collection. Print.

Cohen, Joy-Ann. "Loose Moose Turns Last Bird into Monotonous 'Snore of a Play'." Rev. of *The Last Bird* by Keith Johnstone. Loose Moose Theatre Company, Pumphouse Theatre, Calgary. *Calgary Herald* 15 February 1979. Print.

Colman, Andrew M. *A Dictionary of Psychology*. Oxford: Oxford University press, 2009. Print.

The Conspiracy. Advertisement. *Martlet* [Victoria BC] 29 November 1968. *Archives: UVic Newspapers*. Web. 8 September 2011. <http://archives.library.uvic.ca/featured_collections/uvic_newspapers/martlet_1960/1960.html>.

Courtney, Richard. Letter to Dean of Faculty of Fine Arts, University of Calgary, in support of Johnstone's promotion to Full Professor. 20 February 1986. Keith Johnstone's personal collection. Print.

—. *Play, Drama & Thought: The Intellectual Background to Dramatic Education*. London: Cassell, 1968. Print.

Cox, Frank. "Actor in the Studio." *Plays and Players* December 1964: 8–11, 50. Print.

Coyote, Peter. Messages to author. 18 April 2011–20 April 2011. E-mails.

Curry, Jim. Personal interview. 16 July 2011.

Darlington, W. A. "Heavy Handed and Imitative." Rev. of *Day of the Prince* by Frank Hilton. Royal Court Theatre, London. *Daily Telegraph* 15 May 1963. ESC/RCT Archive, 1934–2007. V&A Museum, London. Print.

—. "Miss Jellicoe has a Feeble Third Act." Rev. of *The Knack* by Ann Jellicoe. Royal Court Theatre, London. *Daily Telegraph* 28 March 1962. ESC/RCT Archive, 1934–2007. V&A Museum, London. Print.

Davies, Andrew. *Other Theatres: The Development of Alternative and Experimental Theatre in Britain*. Totowa, NJ: Barnes & Noble, 1987. Print.

Dawson, Eric. "A Moose is Loose in the Structured Experience of Play-Going in Calgary." *Calgary Herald* 28 January 1978. Print.

—. "Snakes and Ladders Shows Johnstone Being Naughty Again." Rev. of *Live Snakes and Ladders* by Keith Johnstone. University of Calgary. *Calgary Herald* 24 November 1978. Print.

Dent, Alan. "Born Actors – But Let's Hear Them." Rev. of *Eleven Men Dead at Hola Camp*. Royal Court Theatre, London. *News Chronicle* 20 July 1959. ESC/RCT Archive, 1934–2007. V&A Museum, London. Print.

Devoted and Disgruntled.ning.com. Improbable: Devoted & Disgruntled. 15 September 2011. <http://devotedanddisgruntled.ning.com/>.

Doty, Gresdna, and Billy Harbin, eds. *Inside the Royal Court Theatre, 1956-1981: Artists Talk*. Baton Rouge: Louisiana State University Press, 1990. Print.

"Double Bill at the Court: New Author on Fresh Ground." Rev. of *Brixham Regatta* by Keith Johnstone. Royal Court Theatre, London. *Times* [London] 24 June 1958. ESC/RCT Archive, 1934–2007. V&A Museum, London. Print.

Dugan, Jim. Personal interview. 6 July 2011.

Earth. Dir. Alexander Dovzhenko. U.S.S.R: Zemlya, 1930. Film.

English Stage Society. "Press Release." *English Stage Society announces Eleven Men Dead at Hola Camp*. London: July 1959. ESC/RCT Archive, 1934–2007. V&A Museum, London. Print.

Esslin, Martin. "Hit and a Miss." *Plays and Players* June 1964: 28–9. Print.

Feldenkrais, Moshé. *Awareness through Movement: Health Exercises for Personal Growth*. New York: Harper & Row, 1972. Print.

Ferm, Peter. "Beckett's Godot som kram." Trans. Steen Haakon Hansen. Rev. of *Waiting for Godot* by Samuel Beckett. Odense Teater, Denmark. *Dagens Nyheter* [Sweden] September 1986. Print.

Feynman, Richard Phillips, Ralph Leighton, and Edward Hutchings. "*Surely You'reJoking, Mr. Feynman!*": *Adventures of a Curious Character*. New York: W.W. Norton, 1985. Print.

Findlater, Richard. "At Last: A Theatre for New Plays." *Tribune* [London] 13 April 1956. ESC/RCT Archive, 1934–2007. V&A Museum, London. Print.

—. *At the Royal Court: 25 Years of the English Stage Company*. New York: Grove Press, 1981. Print.

Foggo, Cheryl. "The Highest High." *Calgary Magazine* June 1982: 88–90. Print.

"For Children." Rev. of *Clowning*. Royal Court Theatre, London. *Observer* 2 January 1966. ESC/RCT Archive, 1934–2007. V&A Museum, London. Print.

Foreman, Kathleen. P.I. (Personal interview). 21 April 2010.

Foreman, Kathleen, and Clem Martini. *Something Like a Drug: An Unauthorized Oral History of Theatresports*. Red Deer, AL: Red Deer College Press, 1995. Print.

Freire, Paulo. *Pedagogy of the Oppressed*. 30th Anniversary edition. New York: Continuum, 2004. Print.

Frost, Anthony, and Ralph Yarrow. *Improvisation in Drama*. 2nd edition. New York: Palgrave Macmillan, 2007. Print.

Gallwey, W. Timothy. *The Inner Game of Tennis*. New York: Random House, 1974.

Gardner, Lyn. Rev. of *Life Game*. Improbable Theatre Company, Tron Theatre, Glasgow, Scotland. *Guardian* [London] 1 April 1998: 12. *LexisNexis*. Web. 1 November 2011.

Gaskill, William. *A Sense of Direction*. London: Faber and Faber, 1988. Print.

Gaskill, William, and Keith Johnstone. "Report on *Eleven Men Dead at Hola Camp*." July 1959. Keith Johnstone's personal collection. Print.

Gaskill, William, Iain Cuthbertson, Keith Johnstone, et al. "Three at Court." Interview by Peter Roberts and Simon Trussler. *Plays and Players* November 1965: 8–12. Print.

Geijer, Martin. Message to author. 3 May 2011. E-mail.

Gibbs, Patrick. "Human Being in Menagerie." Rev. of *Brixham Regatta* by Keith Johnstone. Royal Court Theatre, London. *Daily Telegraph* 28 June 1958. ESC/RCT Archive, 1934–2007. V&A Museum, London. Print.

Gjørup, Ivar. "Husk at være et godt publikum." Trans. May-Britt Jeremiah. Rev. of *The Last Bird* by Keith Johnstone. Svalegangens Teater, Aarhus, Denmark. *Politiken* [Copenhagen] 19 January 1974. Print.

Gladwell, Malcolm. *Blink: The Power of Thinking Without Thinking*. New York: Little, Brown and Co, 2005. Print.

Gorchakov, N. M. *Stanislavsky Directs*. New York: Funk & Wagnalls, 1954. Print.

—. *The Vakhtangov School of Stage Art*. Moscow: Foreign Languages Publishing House, 1950. Print.

Gordon, Robert. *The Purpose of Playing: Modern Acting Theories in Perspective*. Ann Arbor: University of Michigan Press, 2006. Print.

Gottlieb, Vera. *Chekhov and the Vaudeville: A Study of Chekhov's One-Act Plays*. Cambridgeshire: Cambridge University Press, 1982. Print.

Granath, Sara. "Skoog har full koll på Palm." Rev. of *Sit Down Tragedy* by Göran Palm. Stadsteater, Stockholm. *Svenska Dagbladet* 13 August 2010. Web. 14 September 2011. <http://www.svd.se/kultur/scen/skoog-har-full-koll-pa-palm_5128575.svd>.

Grunfeld, Frederic V. *Games of the World: How to Make Them, How to Play Them, How They Came to Be*. New York: Holt, Rinehart and Winston, 1975. Print.

Hall, Peter. "Godotmania: Its premiere 50 years ago was ignored. When it arrived in London, it was derided. But, says Peter Hall, since Waiting for Godot, theatre has never been the same." *Guardian* [London] 4 January 2003, Sat. Pages: 16. *LexisNexis*. Web. 2 September 2011.

Halpern, Charna, Del Close, and Kim Johnson. *Truth in Comedy: The Manual of Improvisation*. Colorado Springs: Meriwether Publishing, 1994.

Hansen, Steen Haakon. Message to author. 25 January 2011.

—. Personal interview. 7 October 2012.

Haynes, John. Message to author. 14 November 2012. E-mail.

Hayter, Charles. "The Total Tempest." Rev. of *The Tempest* by William Shakespeare. University of Calgary. *Albertan* 18 February 1977. Print.

Heathcote, Dorothy, Liz Johnson, and Cecily O'Neill. *Dorothy Heathcote: Collected Writings on Education and Drama*. London: Hutchinson, 1984. Print.

Heilpern, John. "Look Back at Osborne." *American Theatre* January 2007: 80–6. Print.

Herrigel, Eugen. Trans. R. F. C. Hull. *Zen in the Art of Archery*. New York, NY: Pantheon Books, 1953. Print.

Hickling, Alfred. Rev. of *The Caretaker* by Harold Pinter. Octagon Theatre, Bolton, Manchester. *Guardian* [London] 13 March 2009. Web. 14 September 2011. <http://www.guardian.co.uk/stage/2009/mar/13/theatre-review-the-caretaker-bolton>.

Hitchings, Henry. "This Is Your Life." Rev. of *Life Game*. Improbable Theatre Company, Lyric Hammersmith Theatre, London. *Evening Standard* [London] 9 July 2010: 32. *InfoTrac Newsstand*. Web. 26 March 2011.

Hobson, Harold. "A Private Kind of Tyranny." Rev. of *The Knack* by Ann Jellicoe. Royal Court Theatre, London. *Sunday Times* [London] 1 April 1962. ESC/RCT Archive, 1934–2007. V&A Museum, London. Print.

—. "The Screw Turns Again." Rev. of *The Birthday Party* by Harold Pinter. Lyric Hammersmith, London. *Sunday Times* [London] 25 May 1958. Web. 17 November 2012. http://www.haroldpinter.org/plays/plays_bdayparty.shtml.

Hobson, Louis B. "Johnstone's Improv 'is Not A Cookbook'." *Albertan* 13 September 1979. Print.

—. "Let Johnstone's Moose Loose." Rev. of *Theatresports Hamlet*. Loose Moose Theatre Company, Pumphouse Theatre, Calgary. *Calgary Sun* 26 October 1980. Print.

—. "Loose Moose and a Whale of a Tale."Rev. of *Moby Dick* by Keith Johnstone. Loose Moose Theatre Co., Calgary. *Albertan* 24 January 1978. Print.

—. "Loose Moose Director Off to the Big Apple." *Calgary Sun* 1 March 1984: 31. Print.

—. "Loose Moose Galloping Fun." Rev. of *Sunday night presentation*. Loose Moose Theatre Company, Pumphouse Theatre, Calgary. *Albertan* 1 November 1977. Print.

—. "Loose Moose has New Home." *Calgary Sun* 11 September 1981. Print.

—. "Mindswop's Mind-Boggling." Rev. of *Mindswop* by Keith Johnstone. University of Calgary. *Calgary Sun* 25 March 1983: 51. Print.

—. "Moose Let Loose to do Ben Hur." Rev. of *Ben Hur*. Loose Moose Theatre Company, Moose Simplex, Calgary. *Calgary Mirror* 14 December 1982. Print.

—. "Mutiny Crew Keeps Tight Ship." Rev. of *Mutiny on the Bounty* by Keith Johnstone. Loose Moose Theatre Company, Moose Simplex, Calgary. *Calgary Sun* 29 March 1985. Print.

—. "Pickle the Snakes, Climb the Ladder." Rev. of *Live Snakes and Ladders* by Keith Johnstone. University of Calgary. *Albertan* 24 November 1978. Print.

—. "Pinter's Party Worth a Look." Rev. of *The Birthday Party* by Harold Pinter. Loose Moose Theatre Company, Moose Simplex, Calgary. *Calgary Sun* 6 November 1981. Print.

—. "Waiting for Godot Isn't Time – Wasting." Rev. of *Waiting for Godot* by Samuel
  Beckett. Loose Moose Theatre Company, Pumphouse Theatre, Calgary. *Albertan*
  22 September 1978. Print.
—. "Wine, Women and Moostro." *Calgary Mirror* 18 May 1982. Print.
Holdsworth, Nadine. *Joan Littlewood*. London: Routledge, 2006.
Hustak, Alan. "A 'Godot' Worth Waiting For." Rev. of *Waiting for Godot* by
  Samuel Beckett. Loose Moose Theatre Company, Citadel's Rice Theatre,
  Edmonton. *Edmonton Sun* 21 August 1979. Print.
"Intestinal Lessons." Rev. of *The Performing Giant* by Keith Johnstone. Royal
  Court Theatre, London. *The Observer* [London] 6 March 1966. ESC/RCT
  Archive, 1934–2007. V&A Museum, London. Print.
Jarand, Steve. Personal interview. July 2011.
Jellicoe, Ann. *The Knack; and, The Sport of My Mad Mother*. London: Faber and
  Faber, 1985.
—. *Community Plays: How to Put Them On*. London: Methuen, 1987. Print.
—. P.I. (Personal interview). 15 September 2012.
Johnstone, Keith. "The Abyss." *Programme 2: Royal Court* December 1965–
  January 1966: 27–8. Keith Johnstone's personal collection. Print.
—. "An Approach to *End-Game*."Royal Court Theatre publicity brochure for
  End-Game and *Krapp's Last Tape*. London: 1958. Keith Johnstone's personal
  collection. Print.
—. *Brixham Regatta*. London: Keith Johnstone. c. 1958. Keith Johnstone's personal
  collection. Print.
—. Calgary Workshop. Loose Moose Theatre. July 2011.
—. Calgary Workshop. Loose Moose Theatre. July 2012.
—. Calgary Workshop. Mount Royal University. July 2008.
—. *Don't Be Prepared: Theatresports for Teachers*. Calgary: Loose Moose Theatre,
  1994. Print.
—. Drama 200 and Drama 300 Syllabi. 1977–95. University of Calgary Library
  Archives and Special Collections. Print.
—. "Improvisation and All That Jazz." *Plays and Players* April 1965: 14, 46. Print.
—. *Impro: Improvisation and the Theatre*. 1979. New York: Routledge, 1992.
  Print.
—. *Impro for Storytellers*. New York: Routledge, 1999. Print.
—. Interview. "Johnstone Offers Unique Theatre Experience." *Gauntlet* [Calgary]
  15 September 1978. Print.
—. Interview with Jim Curry. *Now Show*. 1982. *YouTube*. Web. 21 April 2011.
—. Interview with William Hall. Bay Area Theatresports, San Francisco. 16 August
  2009.
—. *Keith Johnstone's Theatresports and Life-Game Newsletter One*. Calgary:
  Keith Johnstone, 1987. Print.
—. *Keith Johnstone's Theatresports and Life-Game Newsletter Two*. Calgary:
  Keith Johnstone, 1988. Print.
—. *Keith Johnstone's Theatresports and Life-Game Newsletter Four*. Calgary:
  Keith Johnstone, 1992. Print.
—. *Keith Johnstone's Theatresports and Life-Game Newsletter Five*. Calgary:
  Keith Johnstone,1993. Print.
—. *Keith Johnstone's Theatresports and Life-Game Newsletter Six*. Calgary:
  Keith Johnstone, 1994. Print.

—. *The Last Bird*. Rev. edn. Calgary: Keith Johnstone, c. 1972–2011. Keith Johnstone's personal collection. *Microsoft Word* file.

—. *The Last Bird*. 1972. First ed. Toronto: Playwrights Canada, 1981. Print.

—. Letter to G. Gould. 23 February 1966. ESC/RCT Archive, 1934–2007. V&A Museum, London. Print.

—. Letter to Harold Pinter. 9 March 1966. ESC/RCT Archive, 1934–2007. V&A Museum, London. Print.

—. *Live Snakes and Ladders*. 1978. University of Calgary Library Archives and Special Collections. Print.

—. London Workshop. Bloomsbury Baptist Church, UK. August–September 2010.

—. "Loose Moose's Honor is Dear." Response to Brennan's Rev. of Quebec Festival. *Calgary Herald* 7 July 1984. Print.

—. "Meeting Beckett." English MS of "Begegnungen mit Beckett." *Wie Meine Frau Dem Wahnsinn Verfiel* ("My Wife's Madness"). Berlin, Germany: Alexander Verlag, 2009. 15–31. Print.

—. *The Performing Giant*. 1966. ESC/RC Theatre Archive, 1934–2007, V&A Department of Theatre and Performance, London, UK. Print.

—. Messages to the author. 16 July 2010–February 2013. E-mails.

—. Personal interviews. August 2009–January 2013.

—. "The Return."*New Writers 2*. London: John Calder, 1962. 77–93. Print.

—. "Review Misrepresents The Last Bird." *Calgary Herald* 21 February 1979. Print.

—. San Francisco Workshop. Bay Area Theatresports, CA. August 2006.

—. San Francisco Workshop. Bay Area Theatresports, CA. August 2009.

—. "Stage Directions for *Live Snakes and Ladders*." Calgary: Keith Johnstone, c. 1978–2011. Keith Johnstone's personal collection. *Microsoft Word* file.

—. Stockholm Workshop. Boulevardteatern, Sweden. September 2010.

—. *The Thing in the Mirror: Trance and Masks*. Calgary: Keith Johnstone, c. 2011. Keith Johnstone's personal collection. *Microsoft Word* file.

Jones, Peter Lloyd. *Come Back That Boy! An Evacuee's Tale*. Intract, 2012. Kindle Ed.

Kearley, Hilda Louise. "The Pedagogy of Keith Johnstone: The Role of Improvisation in Teaching and Acting Training."MA thesis. University of Calgary, 1992. *ProQuest Dissertations & Theses*. Web. 29 September 2011.

Kinley, Shawn. E-mail interview. 1 October 2011.

Koltai, Judith. Personal interview. 5 November 2012.

"Kristus Tog På Fisketur." Trans. May-Britt Jeremiah. Rev. of *The Last Bird* by Keith Johnstone. Svalegangens Teater, Aarhus, Denmark. *Demokraten* 18 January 1974. Print.

Lau, D. C. *Lao Tzu: Tao Te Ching*. New York: Penguin Books, 1963. Print.

Lavender, Andy. "Whose Show Is It Anyway?" Rev. of *Life Game*. Improbable Theatre Company, Lyric Hammersmith Theatre, London. *Times* [London] 19 June 1998. *LexisNexis*. Web. 1 November 2011.

Law, Alma, and Mel Gordon. *Meyerhold, Eisenstein and Biomechanics: Actor Training in Revolutionary Russia*. Jefferson, NC: McFarland, 1996. Print.

Libera, Anne. *The Second City Almanac of Improvisation*. Evanston: Northwestern University Press, 2004. Print.

Loose Moose Theatre Company. *Program for Robinson Crusoe and Theatresports at the Pumphouse Theatre*. 5 March 1978. Visual and Performing Arts Collection, University of Calgary Library. Print.

—. *Program for The Caretaker at the Moose Simplex*. October–November 1982 Visual and Performing Arts Collection, University of Calgary Library. Print.

—. *Program for Waiting for Godot at the Pumphouse Theatre*. September 1978. Visual and Performing Arts Collection, University of Calgary Library. Print.

Lorenz, Konrad. *King Solomon's Ring: New Light on Animal Ways*. New York: Crowell, 1952. Print.

Lynn, Kenneth S. *Charlie Chaplin and His Times*. New York: Simon & Schuster, 1997. Print.

Machlis, Joseph. *Introduction to Contemporary Music*. New York: Norton, 1961. Print.

Madson, Patricia R. *Improv Wisdom: Don't Prepare, Just Show Up*. New York: Bell Tower, 2005. Print.

Marowitz, Charles, and Simon Trussler, eds. *Theatre at Work: Playwrights and Productions in the Modern British Theatre*. New York: Hill and Wang, 1967. Print.

Marriot, R. B. "A Macabre Farce of English Family Life." Rev. of *Day of the Prince* by Frank Hilton. Royal Court Theatre, London. *Stage* 16 May 1963. ESC/RCT Archive, 1934–2007. V&A Museum, London. Print.

—. "Rape is the Operative Word in 'The Knack'." Rev. of *The Knack* by Ann Jellicoe. Royal Court Theatre, London. *Stage* 29 March 1962. ESC/RCT Archive, 1934–2007. V&A Museum, London. Print.

Martini, Clem. Personal interview. 19 April 2010.

Maude-Roxby, Roddy. Personal interview. 2 October 2012.

Mayne, Roger. E-mail interview. 20 September 2012.

McCracken, Rosemary. "Birthday Party's Actors Guilty of Excess." Rev. of *The Birthday Party* by Harold Pinter. Loose Moose Theatre Company, Moose Simplex, Calgary. *Calgary Herald* 7 November 1981. Print.

—. "Hammed-Up Ben-Hur is a Hit." Rev. of *Ben Hur*. Loose Moose Theatre Company, Moose Simplex, Calgary. *Calgary Herald* 9 December 1982. Print.

—. "Sci-fi Fare is Lots of Fun." Rev. of *Mindswop* by Keith Johnstone. University of Calgary. *Calgary Herald* 26 March 1983: C2. Print.

—. "Spooky Spoof Not Biting Fare." Rev. of *They Come By Night* by Keith Johnstone. Loose Moose Theatre Company, Moose Simplex, Calgary. *Calgary Herald* 22 July 1984. Print.

McDermott, Phelim. Message to author. 27 February 2013. E-mail.

McNinch, Michael. "University of Calgary Drama Group in Exciting Show." Rev. of *Waiting for Godot* by Samuel Beckett. University of Calgary. *Albertan* 27 November 1972: 11. Microfiche. U of Calgary Library.

Mekler, Eva. *Masters of the Stage: British Acting Teachers Talk About Their Craft*. New York: Grove Weidenfeld, 1989. Print.

Milton, Joyce. *Tramp: The Life of Charlie Chaplin*. New York: Harper Collins, 1996. Print.

Moorhouse, Geoffrey. Rev. of *Clowning*. Royal Court Theatre, London. *Guardian* 22 December 1965. ESC/RCT Archive, 1934–2007. V&A Museum, London. Print.

Morrow, Martin. "Loose Moose Founder Keeping Busy." *Calgary Herald* 17 October 1989. Print.

—. "Loose Moose Offers a Lively, Warm-Blooded Godot." Rev. of *Waiting for Godot* by Samuel Beckett. Loose Moose Theatre Company, Garry Theatre, Calgary. *Calgary Herald* 24 October 1998. Print.

—. "Socialist Folk Tale Hits as Often as It Misses." Rev. of *Caucasian Chalk Circle* by Bertolt Brecht. University of Calgary. *Calgary Herald* 20 October 1989: C12. Print.

Moscheto, Andrei. Personal interview. 17 July 2011.

Musselwhite, Bill. "University of Calgary Succeeds with Beckett Play." Rev. of *Waiting for Godot* by Samuel Beckett. University of Calgary. *Calgary Herald* 25 November 1972: 63. Microfiche. University of Calgary Library.

Nascimento, Daniel. Personal interview. 17 July 2011.

Nicolaïdes, Kimon. *The Natural Way to Draw: A Working Plan for Art Study*. Boston: Houghton Mifflin, 1969. Print.

Northan, Rebecca. Personal interview. 17 August 2012.

Odin Teatret. *Report on Second ISTA Session Volterra, 1981*. October 1981. *Odin Teatret Archives*. Web. 8 September 2011. <http://www.odinteatretarchives.dk/>.

Odin Teatret Archives. *Series Odin*: Binder 11, p. 37. 1–6 April 1971. Web. 17 November 2012. <http://www.odinteatretarchives.com/MEDIA/DOCUMENTS/FONDS_EB_UK.pdf>.

Odsherred Teaterskole: Scenekunstens Udviklingscenter. Web. 8 September 2011. <http://www.otskole.dk/>.

Osten, Suzanne. "Förord." Foreword. *Impro: Improvisation Och Teater*. By Keith Johnstone. Trans. Harriet Ljungkvist Bagdade. Stockholm: Solna Entré/Riksteatern, 1985. Print.

Pertalion, Albert. Rev. of *Impro: Improvisation and the Theatre*, by Keith Johnstone. *Theatre Journal* 36:3 (1984): 441–2. JSTOR. Web. 4 November 2010.

Pink, Daniel H. *To Sell Is Human: The Surprising Truth About Moving Others*. New York: Riverhead Books, 2012. Print.

Pinter, Harold. Letter to Keith Johnstone. 10 March 1966. ESC/RCT Archive, 1934–2007. V&A Museum, London. Print.

Portus, Martin. "Win or Lose, in This Sport it's Irrelevant." Rev. of International Theatresports Tournament, Brisbane's World Expo. *Sydney Morning Herald* 20 July 1988. *LexisNexis Academic*. Web. 29 September 2011.

Pumphousetheatre.ca. 2011. Pumphouse Theatre. 29 September 2011 <http://www.pumphousetheatre.ca/mainstructure/homepage.htm>.

Ravenhill, Mark. "At last, I meet the man who made me a playwright. And we talk about peeling bananas." *The Guardian* [London] 1 March 2009: G2. Web. 21 March 2010. <http://www.guardian.co.uk/stage/2009/mar/02/mark-ravenhill-keith-johnstone-impro/>.

Rebellato, Dan. 1956 *And All That: The Making of Modern British Drama*. London: Routledge, 1999. Print.

"Rehearsal Group." *Bolton Evening News* 12 October 1958. ESC/RCT Archive, 1934–2007. V&A Museum, London. Print.

Rev. of *Brixham Regatta* by Keith Johnstone. Royal Court Theatre, London. *Sunday Times* [London] 29 June 1958. ESC/RCT Archive, 1934–2007. V&A Museum, London. Print.

Rev. of *Caucasian Chalk Circle* by Bertolt Brecht. University of Calgary. *Calgary Tonite* 25 October 1989: 26. Print.

Roberts, Philip. *The Royal Court Theatre and the Modern Stage*. Cambridge, UK: Cambridge University Press, 1999. Print.

—. *The Royal Court Theatre, 1965-1972*. London: Routledge & K. Paul in association with Methuen, 1986. Print.

Royal Court. *Royal Court Announces Return of Theatre Machine at "Come Together" Festival*. London: RCT, 2 November 1970. ESC/RCT Archive, 1934–2007. V&A Museum, London. Print.

—. Copy of Lord Chamberlain's letter. London: RCT, 1965. Keith Johnstone's personal collection. Print.

Rueda, Jorge. Personal interview. 17 July 2011.

Schickel, Richard, ed. *The Essential Chaplin: Perspectives on the Life and Art of the Great Comedian*. Chicago: Ivan R. Dee, 2006. Print.

Schjelbred, Caspar. Message to author. 25 September 2011. E-mail.

Schneider, Rebecca, and Gabrielle H. Cody, eds. *Re:direction: A Theoretical and Practical Guide*. London: Routledge, 2002. Print.

Semple, Gavin. E-mail interview. 12 February 2011.

Seymour, Anthony. "Psychiatry Needed to Explain This Dream." Rev. of *The Performing Giant* by Keith Johnstone. Royal Court Theatre, London. *Yorkshire Post* 4 March 1966. ESC/RCT Archive, 1934–2007. V&A Museum, London. Print.

Shaw, Gillian. Memo to *Day of the Prince* cast and crew. 10 June 1963. ESC/RCT Archive, 1934–2007. V&A Museum, London. Print.

Sheppy, Nikki. "Still Waiting After All These Years: Loose Moose Director Keith Johnstone Remembers Beckett and His Work." *Fast Forward Weekly* [Calgary] 22–28 October 1998: 18. Print.

Shewchuck, Ron. "Loose Moose Recluse: Keith Johnstone is 'An Aardvark among the Camels'." *Calgary Magazine* April 1987: 37. Print.

Shurtleff, Michael. *Audition: Everything an Actor Needs to Know to Get the Part*. New York: Bantam Books, 1980. Print.

Simpson, Lee. Message to author. 25 September 2011. E-mail.

—. Personal interview. 3 October 2011.

Sisi. "Godt gensyn med Godot: Absurd klassiker pa Odense Teater." Trans. Steen Haakon Hansen. Rev. of *Waiting for Godot* by Samuel Beckett. Odense Teater, Denmark. *Jydske Tidende* September 1986. Print.

Skoog, Helge. Personal interview. 11 September 2010.

—. Message to author. 1 February 2011. E-mail.

Slade, Peter. *Child Drama*. London: University of London Press, 1954. Print.

—. *Experience of Spontaneity*. Harlow: Longmans, 1968. Print.

Spolin, Viola. *Improvisation for the Theater: A Handbook of Teaching and Directing Techniques*. 3rd edn. Evanston: Northwestern University Press, 1999. Print.

Stiles, Patti. Messages to author. 5–10 October 2011. E-mails.

Stockley, Rebecca. Personal interview. 8 September 2012.

Taylor, Mark. Rev. of *The Knack* by Ann Jellicoe. Royal Court Theatre, London. *Plays and Players* May 1962: 17. Print.

Thirkell, Arthur. "Nuts!" Rev. of *Day of the Prince* by Frank Hilton. Royal Court Theatre, London. *Daily Mirror* 15 May 1963. ESC/RCT Archive, 1934–2007. V&A Museum, London. Print.

"Three Lessons in Comedy." Rev. of *First Results*. Royal Court Theatre, London. *Times* [London] 29 April 1963. ESC/RCT Archive, 1934–2007. V&A Museum, London. Print.

Tonken, Mel. Personal interview. 16 October 2012.

Totino, Frank. Messages to author. 11 December 2009–20 April 2011. E-mails.

—. Personal interview. 21 April 2010.

Totino, Tony. Personal interview. 5 September 2010.

The Totnesian. The Totnes Grammar School magazine. Vol. XX, Summer 1950, No. 65. Keith Johnstone's personal collection. Print.

Wardle, Irving. "Introduction." *Impro: Improvisation and the Theatre*. 1979. By Keith Johnstone. New York: Routledge, 1992. Print.

Way, Brian. *Development Through Drama*. London: Longmans, 1967. Print.

Whitehead, Jaan. "ART WILL OUT." *American Theatre* 19:8 (2002): 30–6, 130–2. *Academic Search Premier*. EBSCO. Web. 14 September 2011.

Wiener, Daniel J. *Rehearsals for Growth: Theater Improvisation for Psychotherapists*. New York: Norton, 1994. Print.

Wilson, Cecil. "No Script but What Passion." Rev. of *Eleven Men Dead at Hola Camp*. Royal Court Theatre, London. *Daily Mail* 20 July 1959. ESC/RCT Archive, 1934–2007. V&A Museum, London. Print.

Wolpe, Joseph, and Arnold A. Lazarus. *Behavior Therapy Techniques: A Guide to the Treatment of Neuroses*. New York: Pergamon Press, 1968. Print.

The World According to Keith. Dir. Arlene Rimer. Prod. Executive Pictures, Inc., and Bravo, 2003. DVD.

Worsley, T. C. Rev. of *Day of the Prince* by Frank Hilton. Royal Court Theatre, London. *Financial Times* [London] 15 May 1963. ESC/RCT Archive, 1934–2007. V&A Museum, London. Print.

—. Rev. of *The Knack* by Ann Jellicoe. Royal Court Theatre, London. *Financial Times* [London] 28 March 1962. ESC/RCT Archive, 1934–2007. V&A Museum, London. Print.

Young, B. A. Rev. of *Clowning*. Royal Court Theatre, London. *Financial Times* [London] 21 December 1965. ESC/RCT Archive, 1934–2007. V&A Museum, London. Print.

Young, Elizabeth. "Gallant Attempt." Rev. of *Eleven Men Dead at Hola Camp*. Royal Court Theatre, London. *Tribune* [London] 24 July 1959. ESC/RCT Archive, 1934–2007. V&A Museum, London. Print.

Zimbardo, Phillip G. Letter to Dean, Faculty of Arts and Sciences, University of Calgary, in support of Johnstone's tenure promotion. 2 December 1982. Keith Johnstone's personal collection. Print.

Zimmerman, Kate. "Big Apple Bites Local Acting Group." *Calgary Herald* 3 May 1984: D5. Print.

—. "Loose Moose's Mock Beauty Bout Kicks Off Season." *Calgary Herald* 4 September 1986. Print.

—. "Fuzzy Script Mars Mutiny." Rev. of *Mutiny on the Bounty* by Keith Johnstone. Loose Moose Theatre Company, Moose Simplex, Calgary. *Calgary Herald* 29 March 1985. Print.

Zinger, David. E-mail interview. 27 September 2011.

INDEX